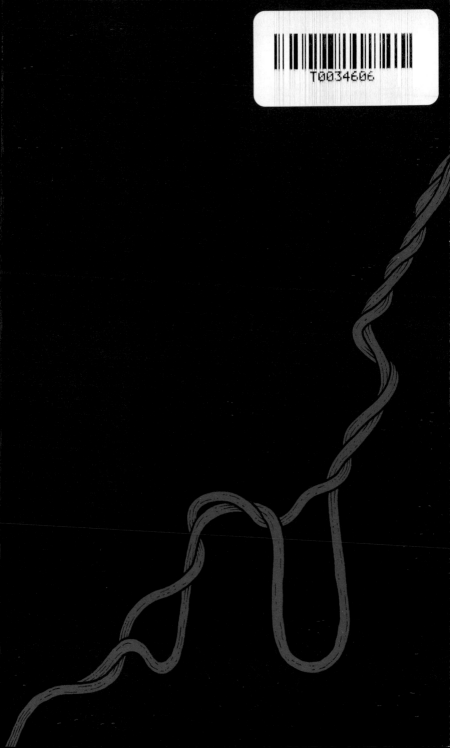

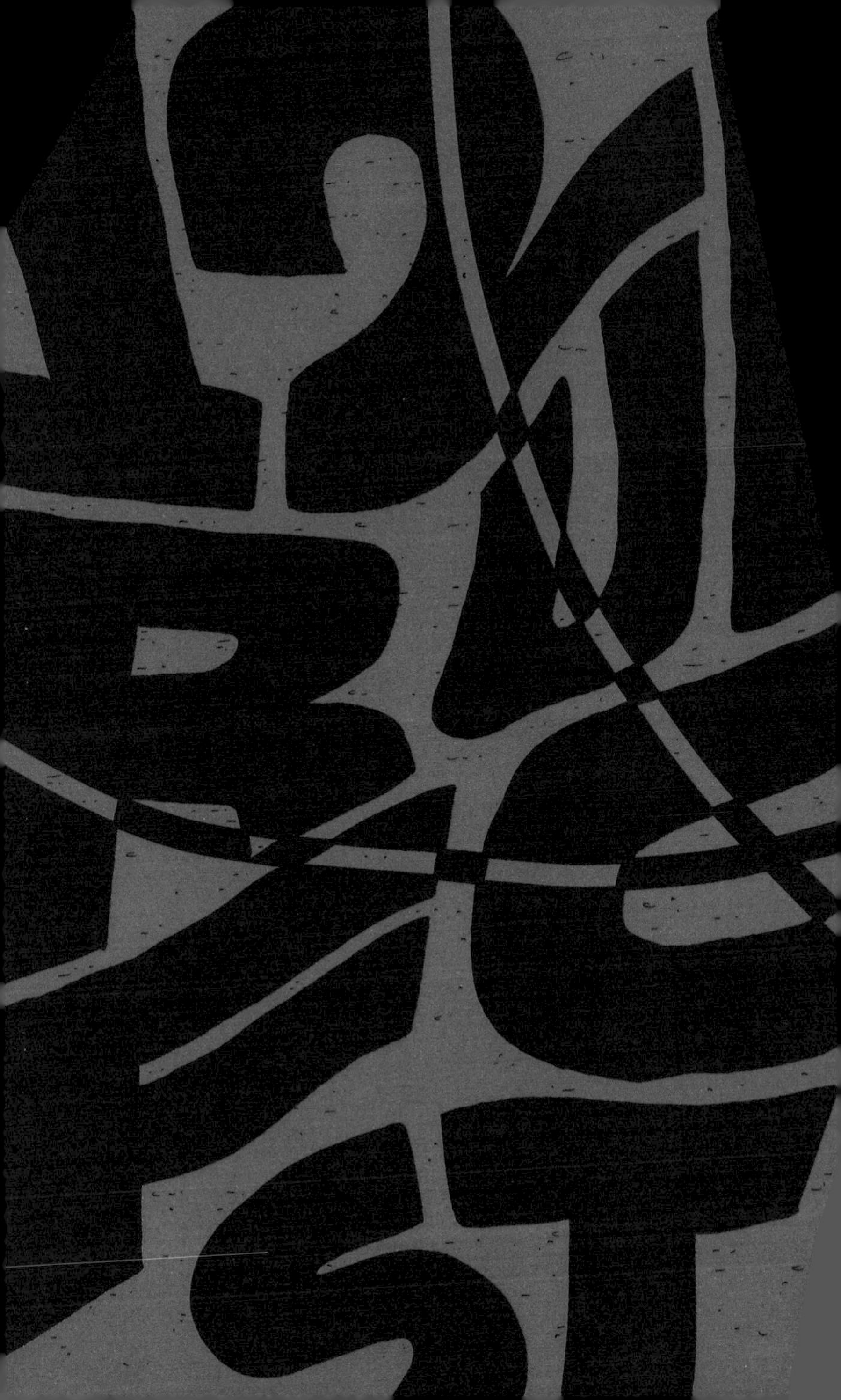

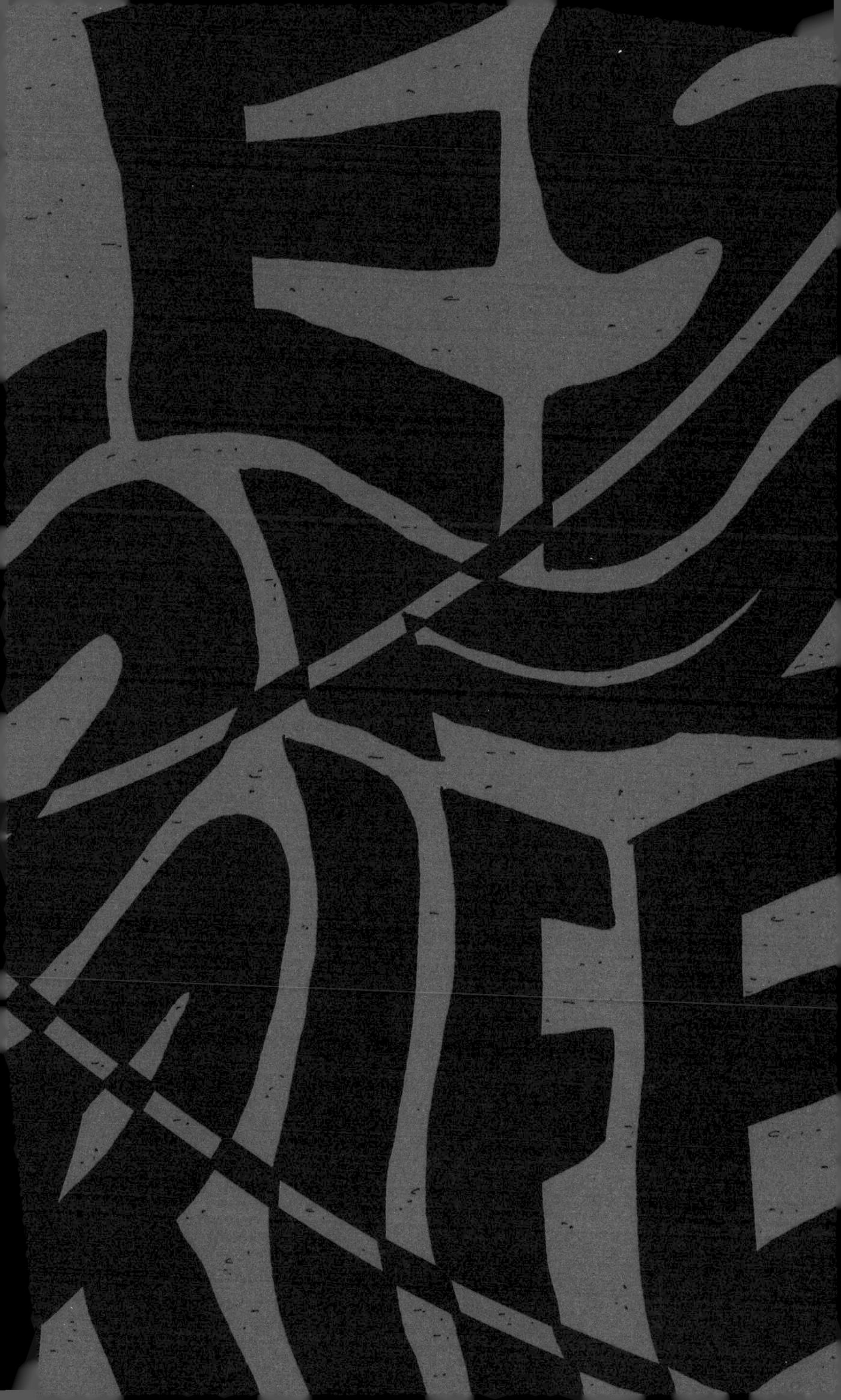

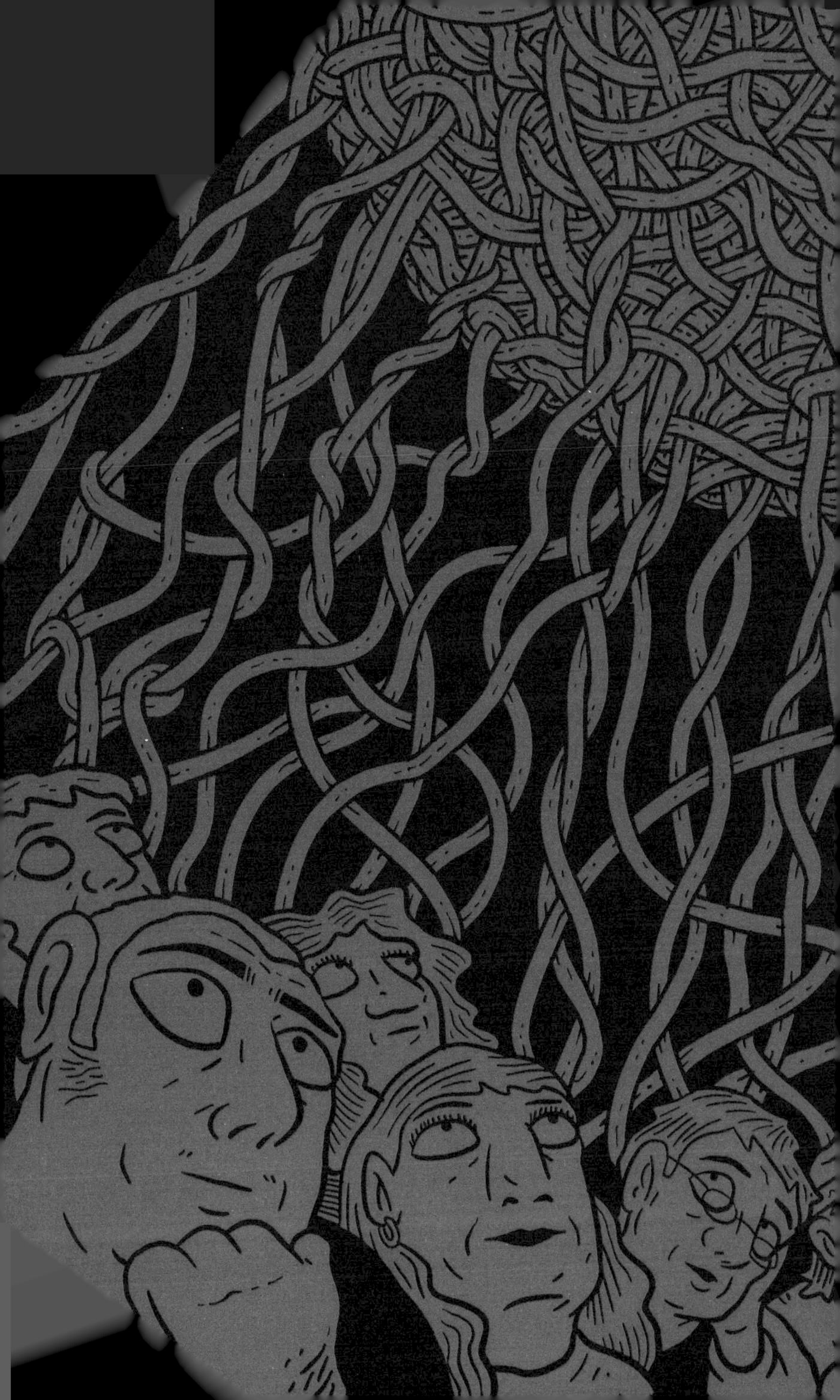

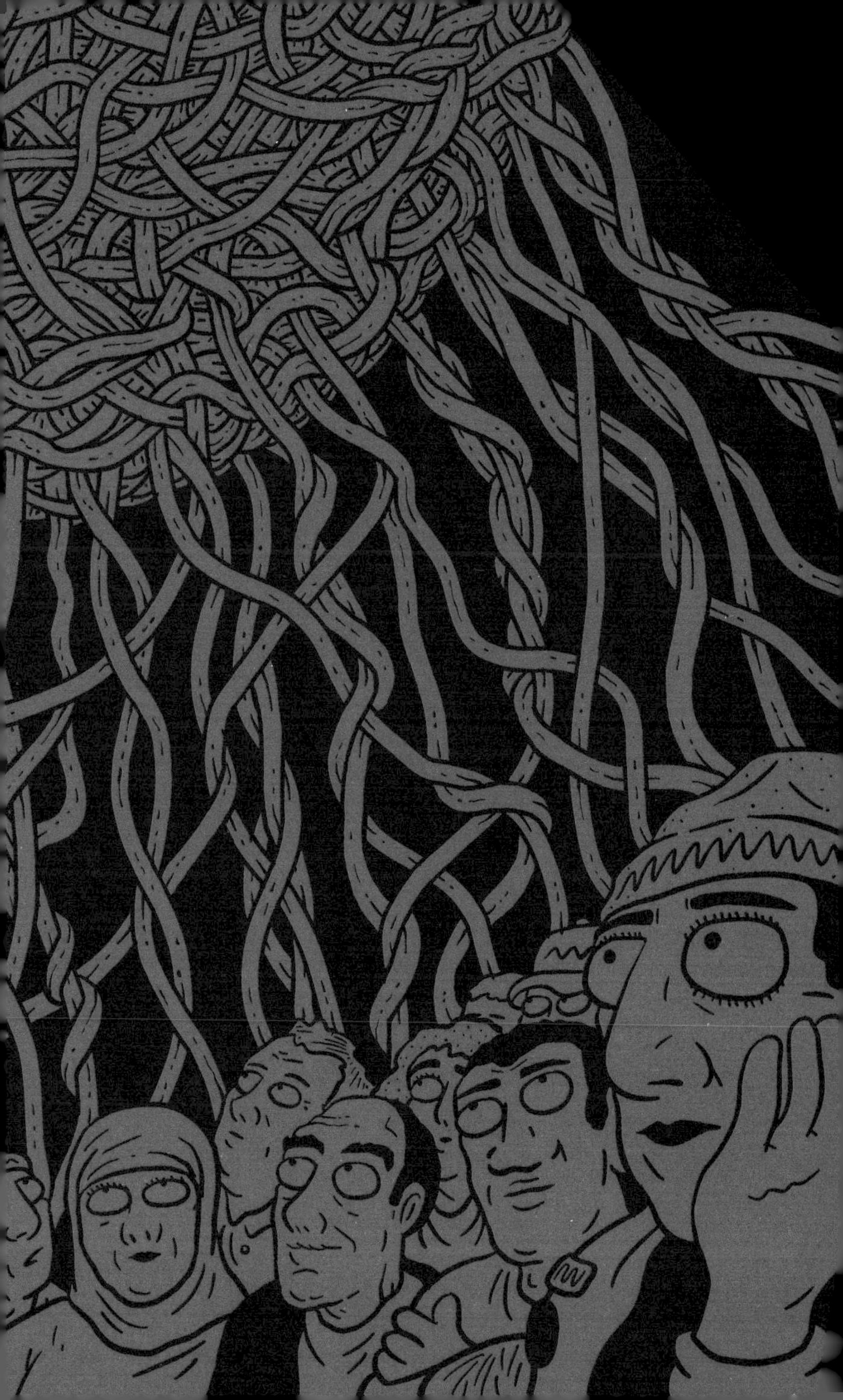

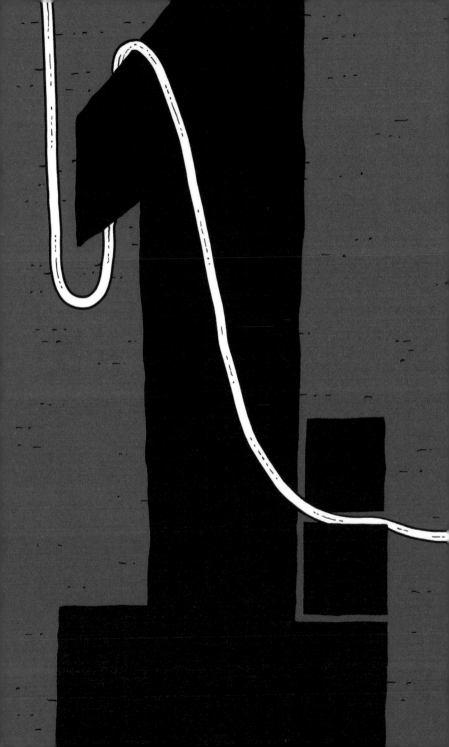

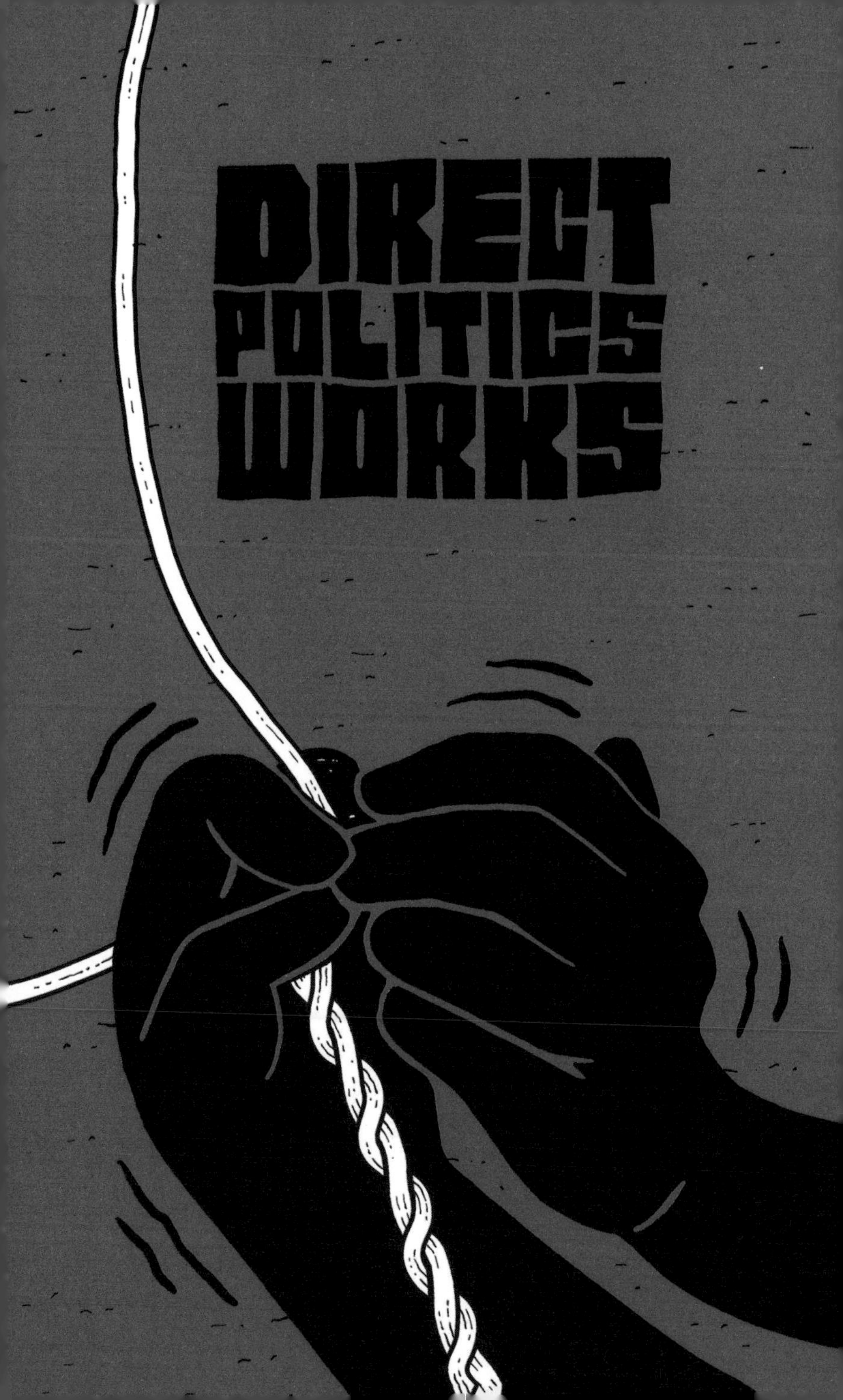
DIRECT
POLITICS
WORKS

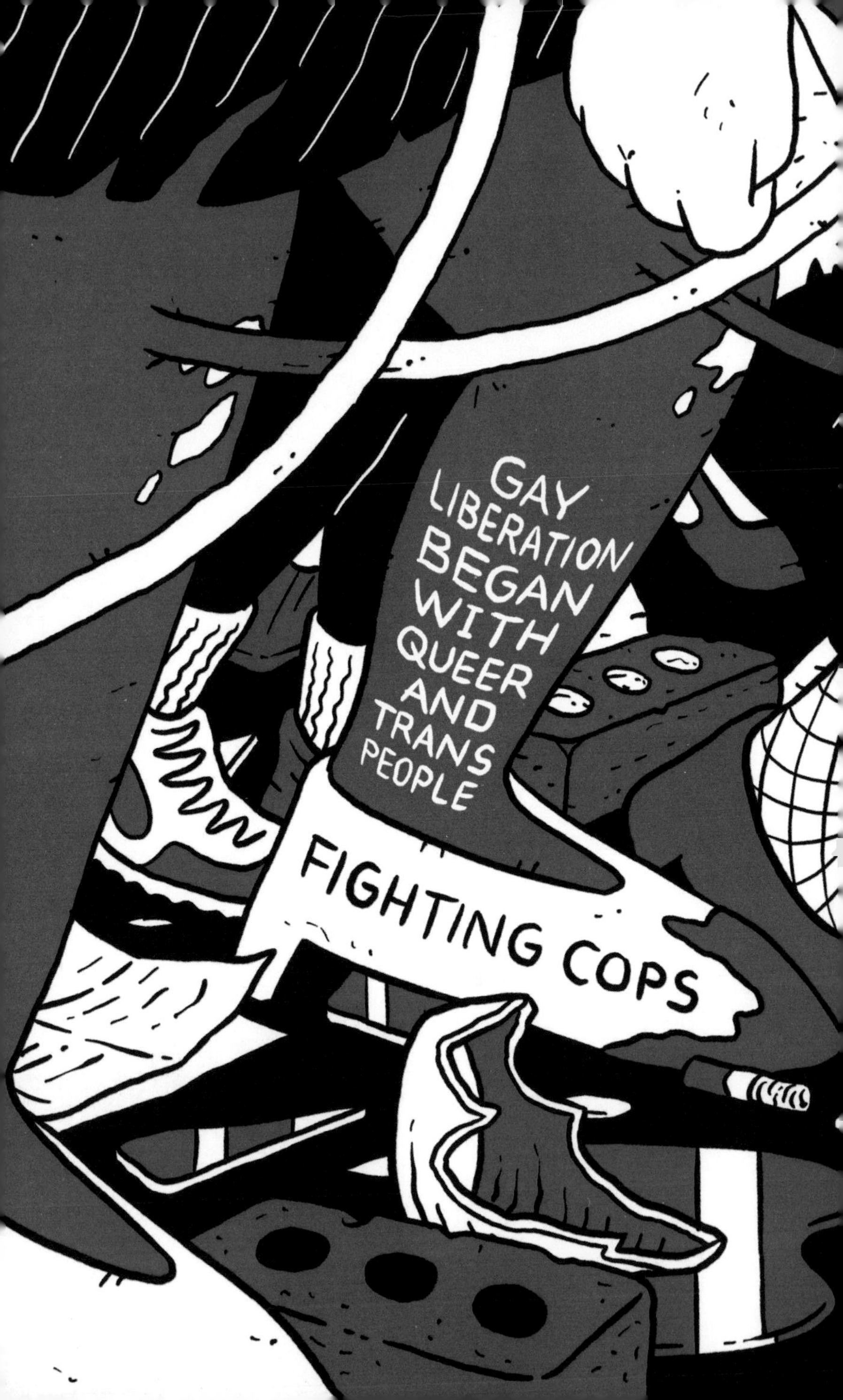
GAY LIBERATION BEGAN WITH QUEER AND TRANS PEOPLE
FIGHTING COPS

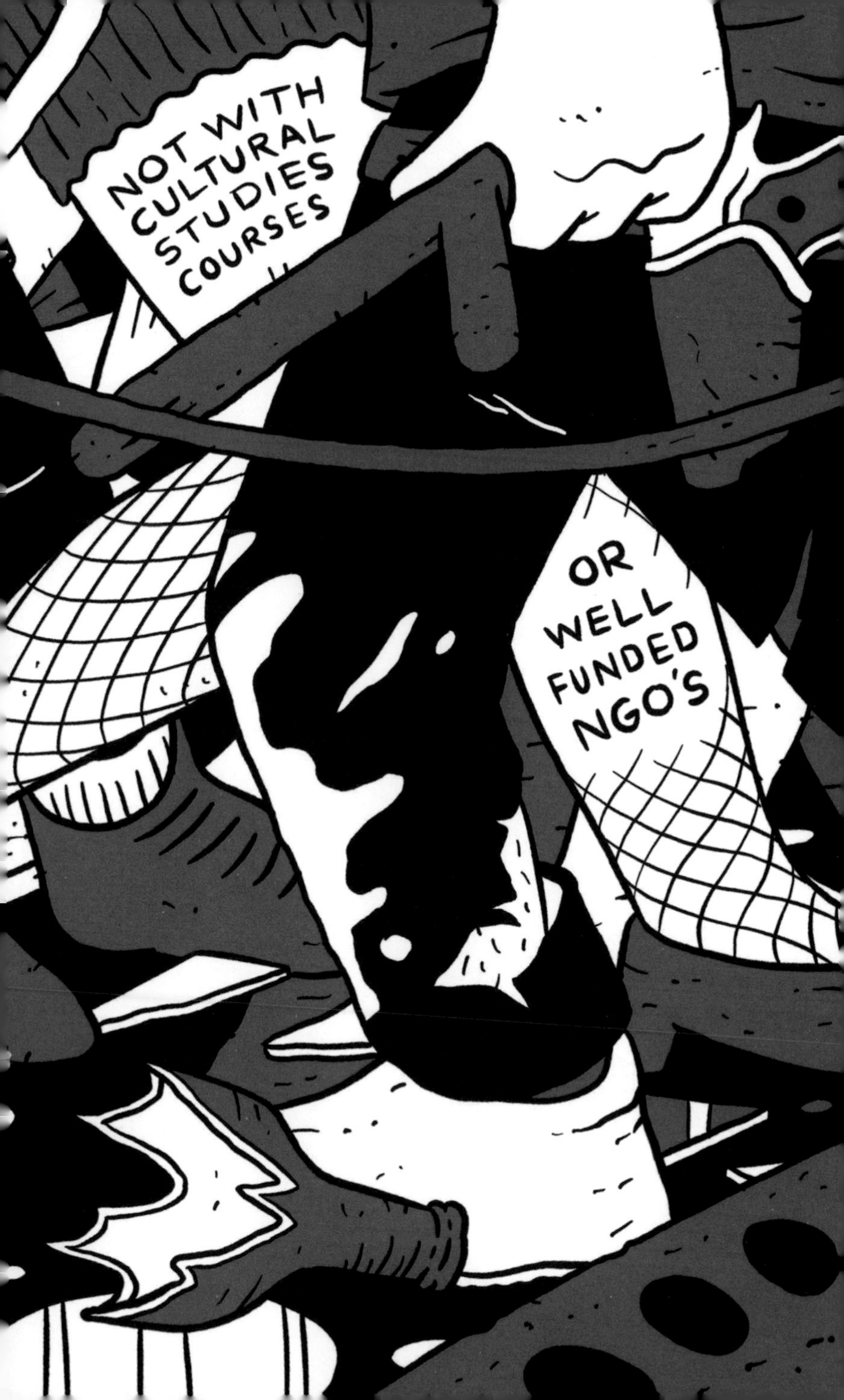
NOT WITH CULTURAL STUDIES COURSES
OR WELL FUNDED NGO'S

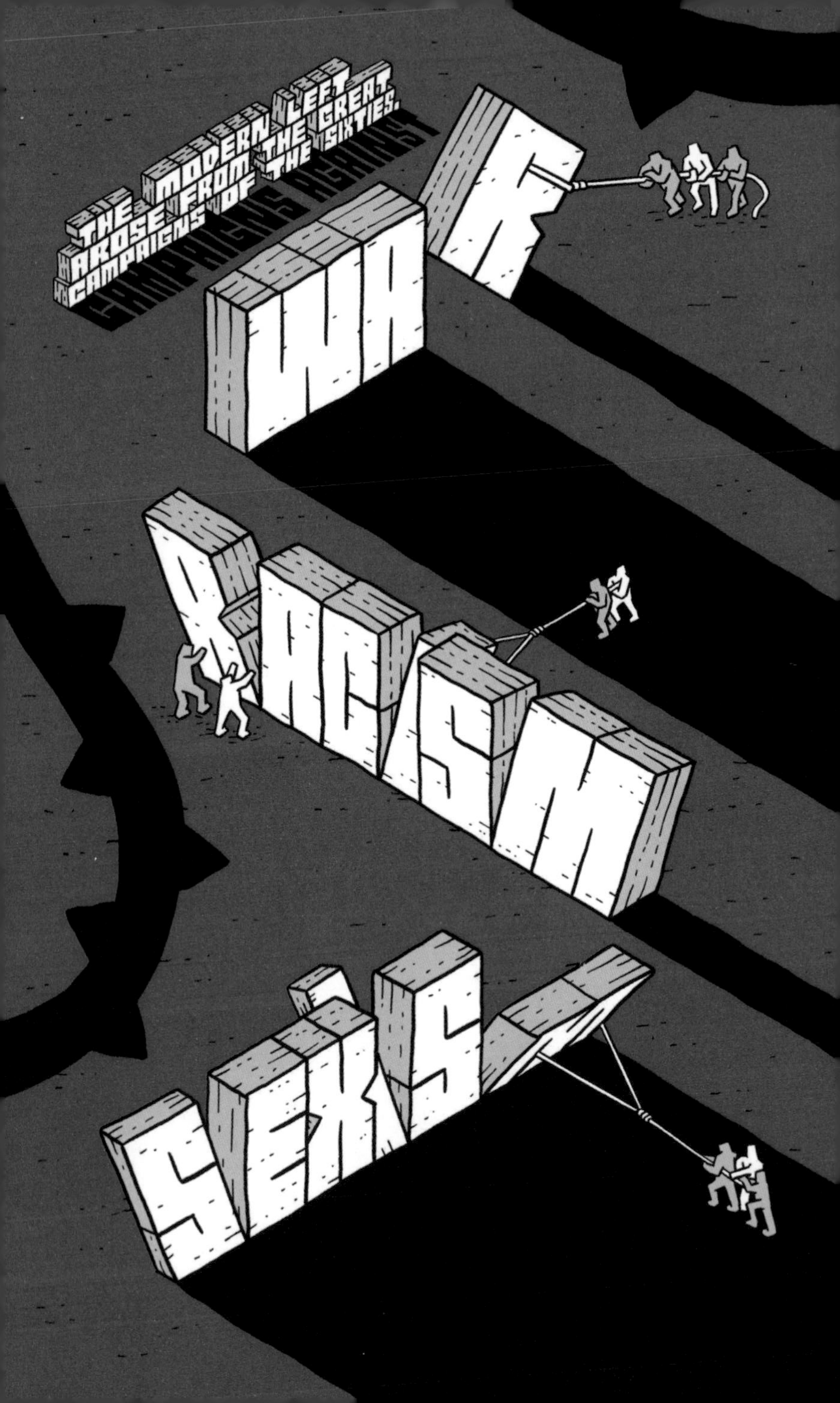
THE MODERN LEFT AROSE FROM THE GREAT CAMPAIGNS OF THE SIXTIES. CAMPAIGNS AGAINST
WAR
RACISM
SEXISM

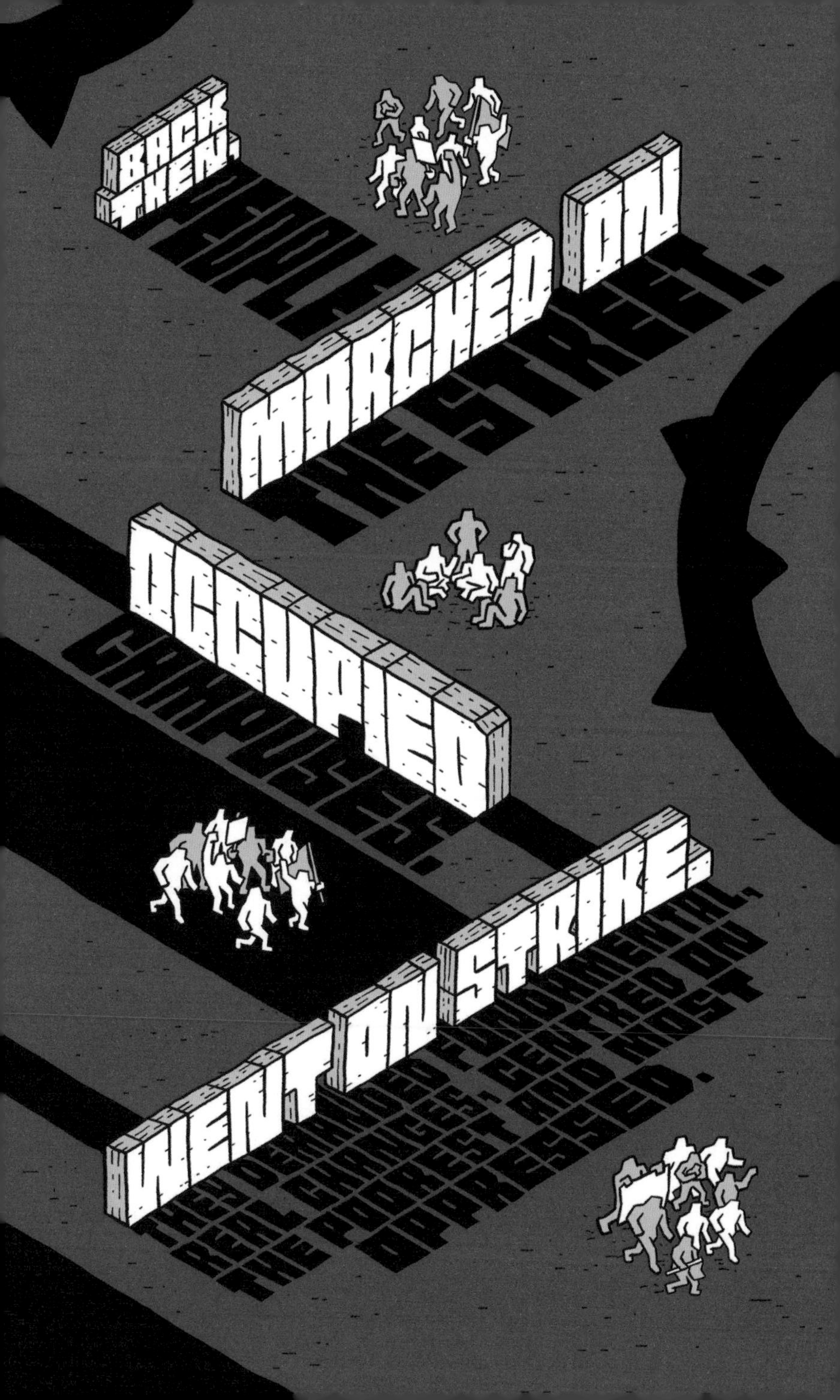
BACK THEN,
PEOPLE
MARCHED ON
THE STREET.
OCCUPIED
CAMPUSES.
WENT ON STRIKE.
THEY DEMANDED FUNDAMENTAL,
REAL CHANGES, CENTRED ON
THE POOREST AND MOST
OPPRESSED.

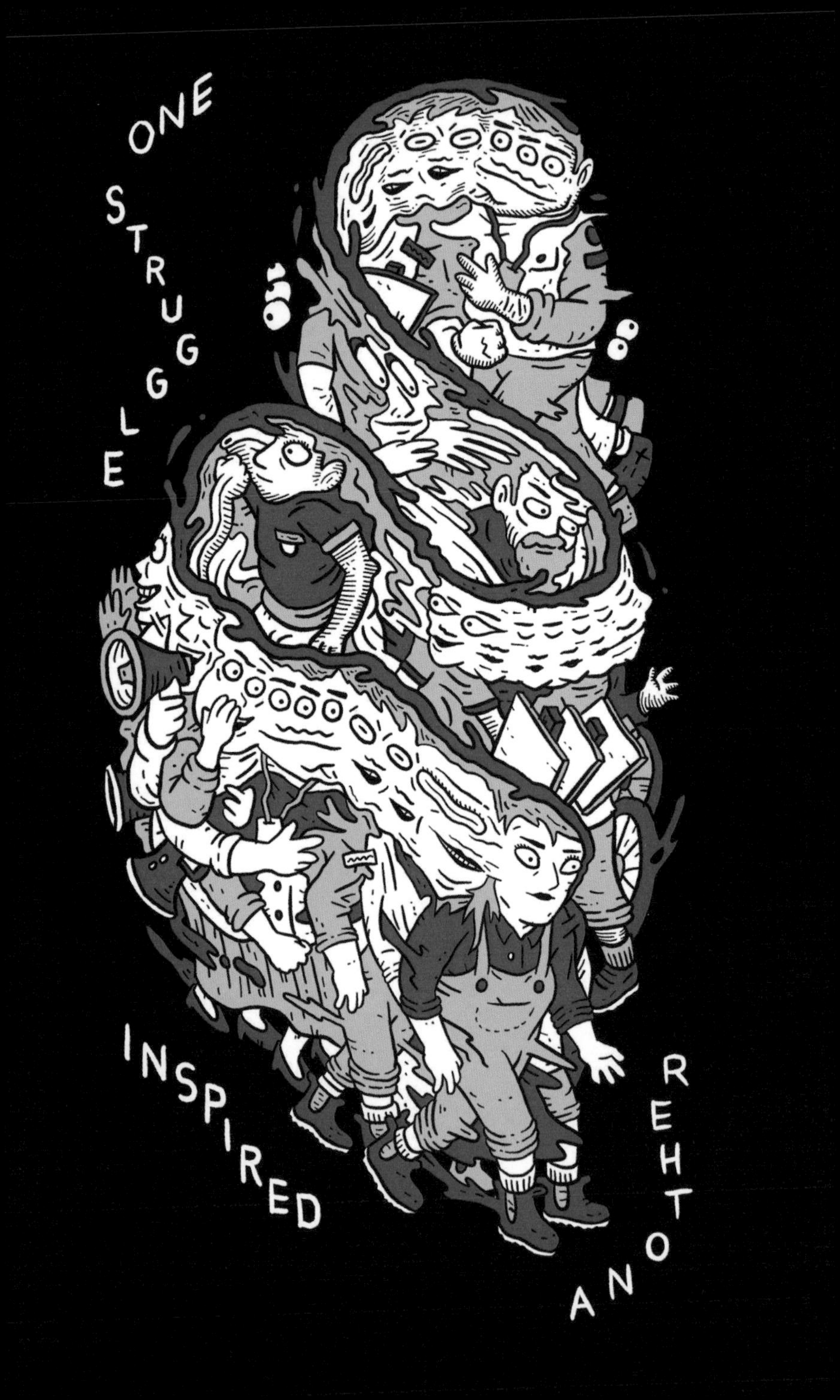
ONE
STRUGGLE
INSPIRED
ANOTHER

NATIONAL
LIBERATION
SPURRED
BLACK
LIBERATION
BLACK
LIBERATION
INSPIRED
WOMEN'S
LIBERATION
WOMEN'S
LIBERATION
LED TO GAY
LIBERATION

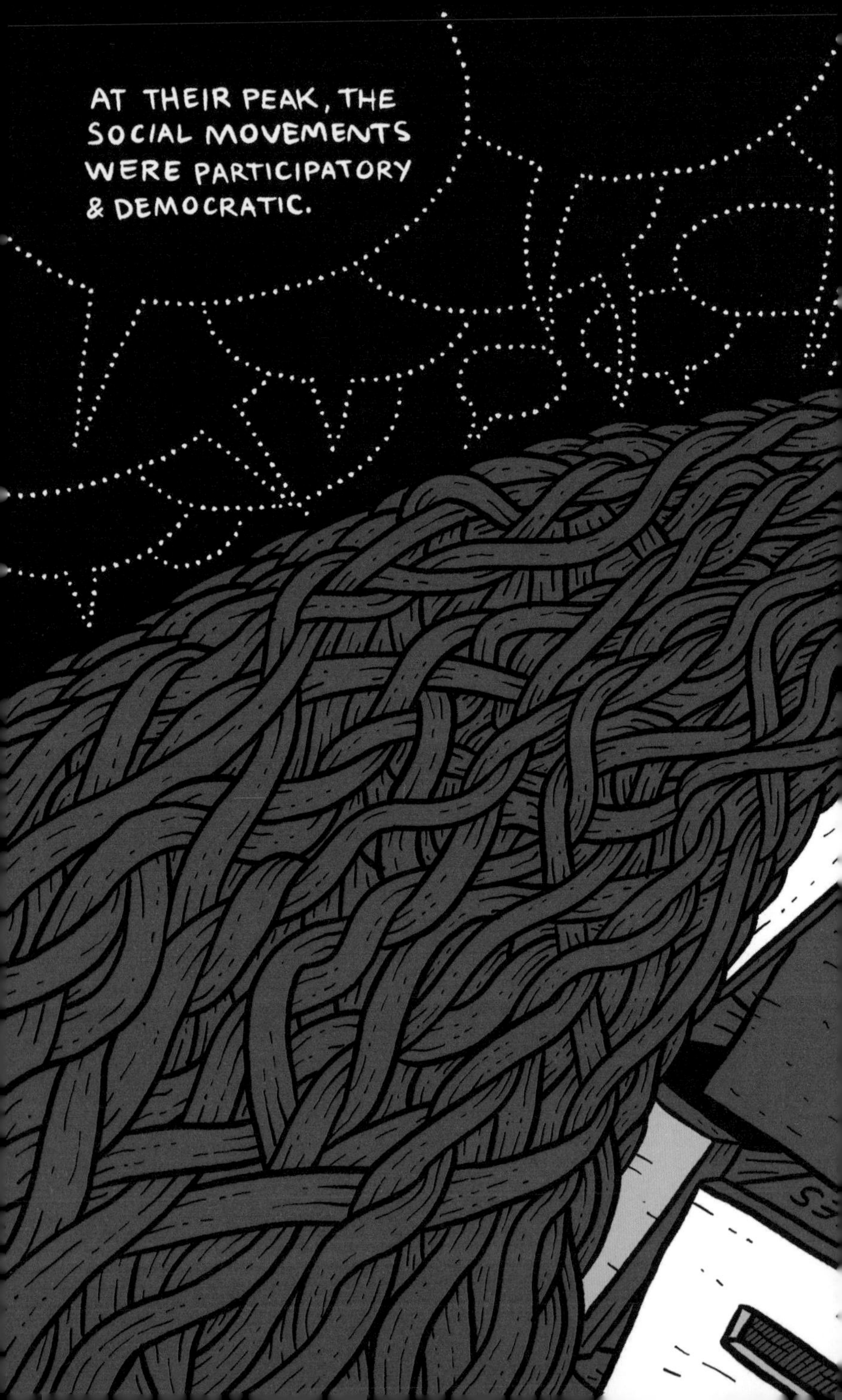
AT THEIR PEAK, THE SOCIAL MOVEMENTS WERE PARTICIPATORY & DEMOCRATIC.

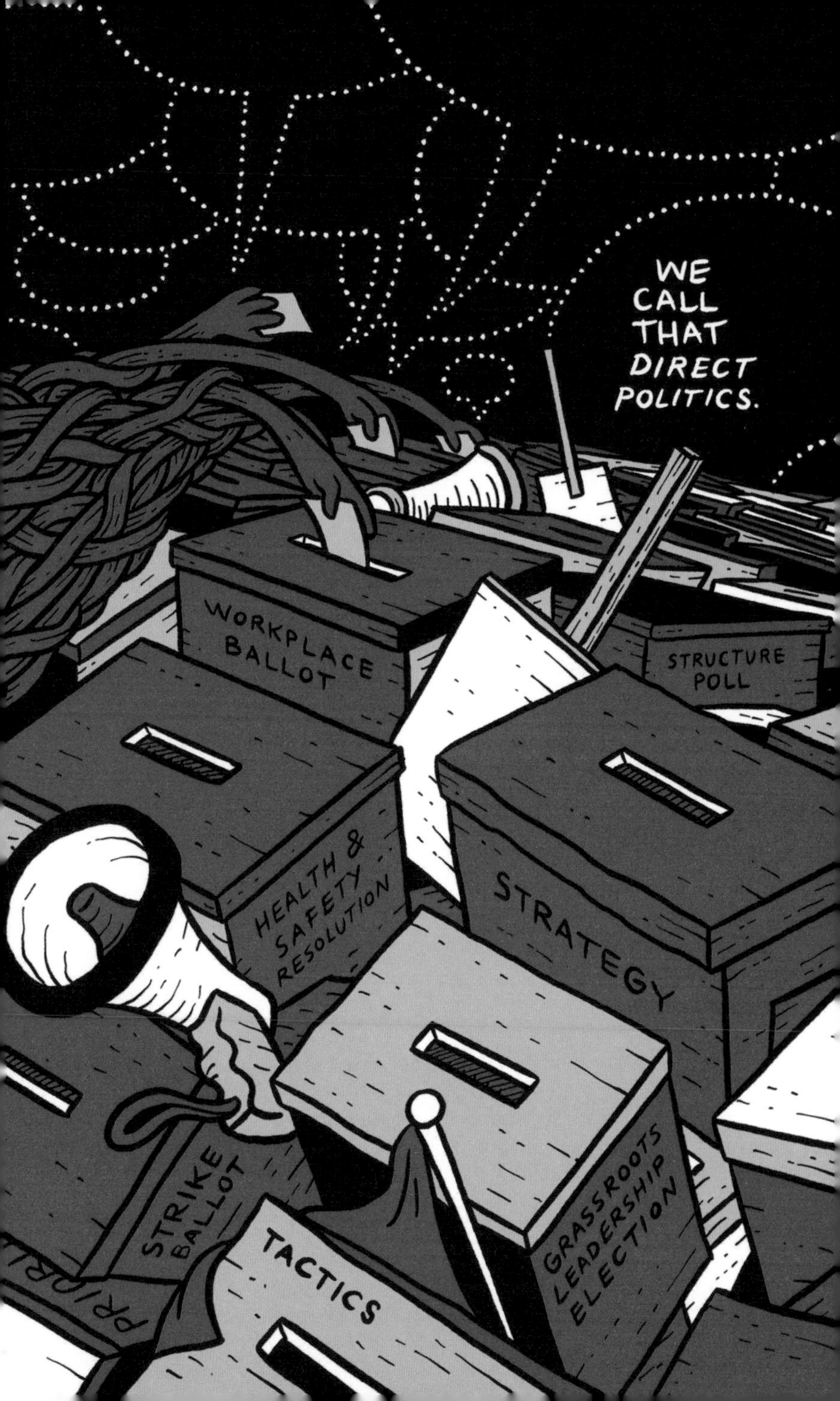
WE CALL THAT *DIRECT* POLITICS.
WORKPLACE BALLOT
STRUCTURE POLL
HEALTH & SAFETY RESOLUTION
STRATEGY
STRIKE BALLOT
TACTICS
GRASSROOTS LEADERSHIP ELECTION

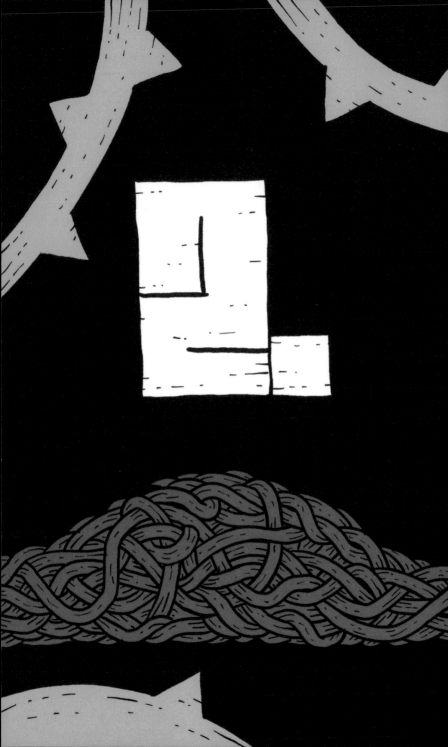

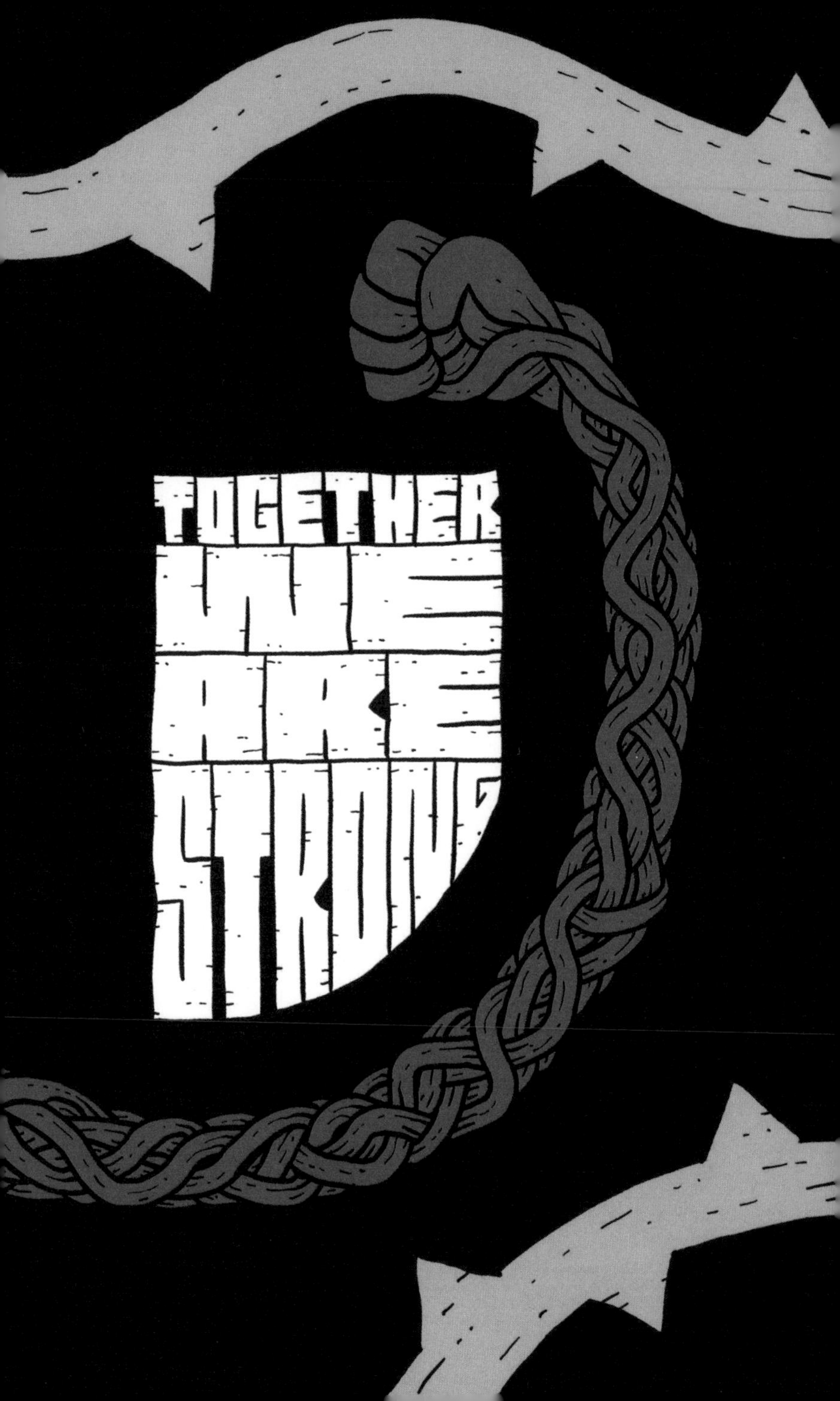
TOGETHER
WE
ARE
STRONG

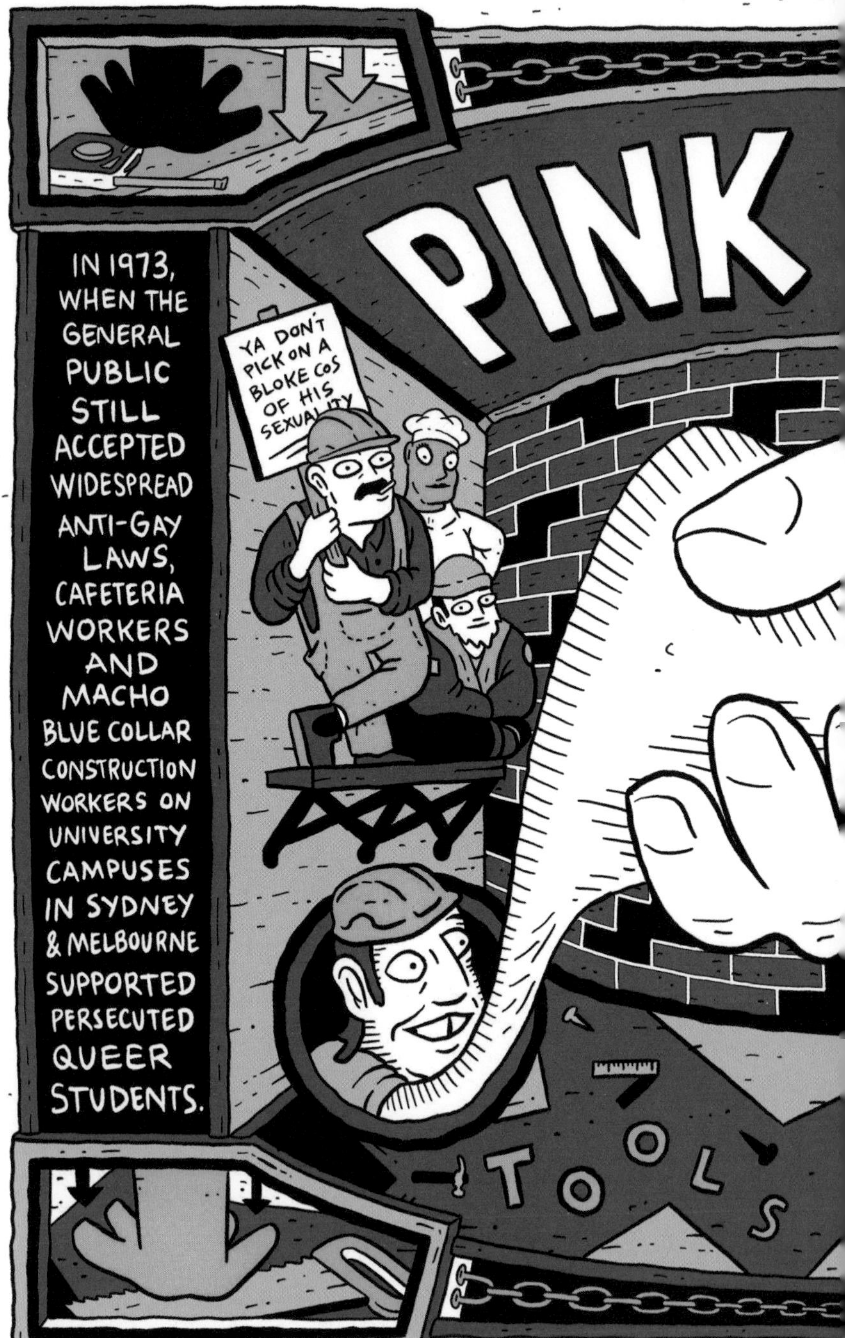
IN 1973, WHEN THE GENERAL PUBLIC STILL ACCEPTED WIDESPREAD ANTI-GAY LAWS, CAFETERIA WORKERS AND MACHO BLUE COLLAR CONSTRUCTION WORKERS ON UNIVERSITY CAMPUSES IN SYDNEY & MELBOURNE SUPPORTED PERSECUTED QUEER STUDENTS.
YA DON'T PICK ON A BLOKE COS OF HIS SEXUALITY
PINK
TOOLS

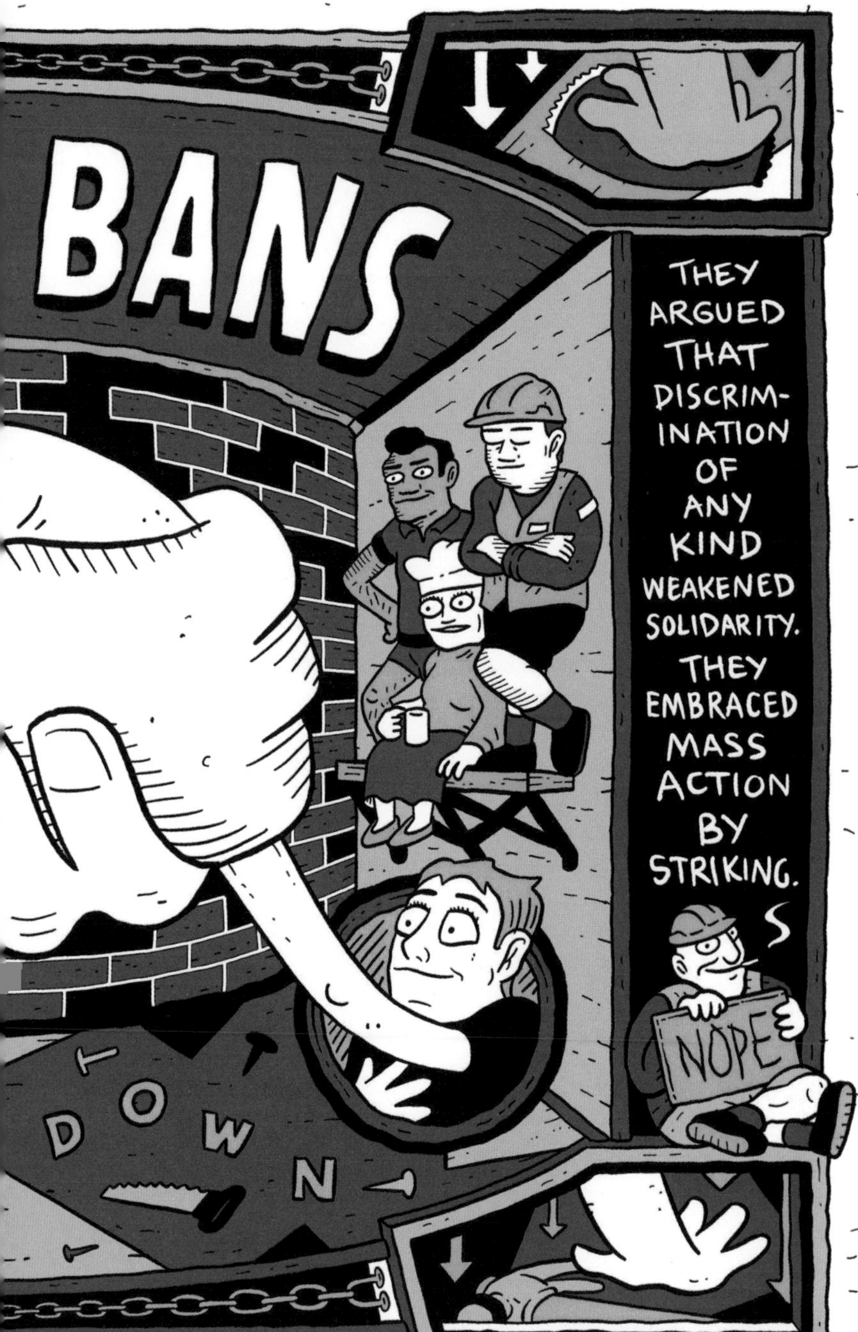
BANS
THEY ARGUED THAT DISCRIMINATION OF ANY KIND WEAKENED SOLIDARITY. THEY EMBRACED MASS ACTION BY STRIKING.
NOPE
DOWN

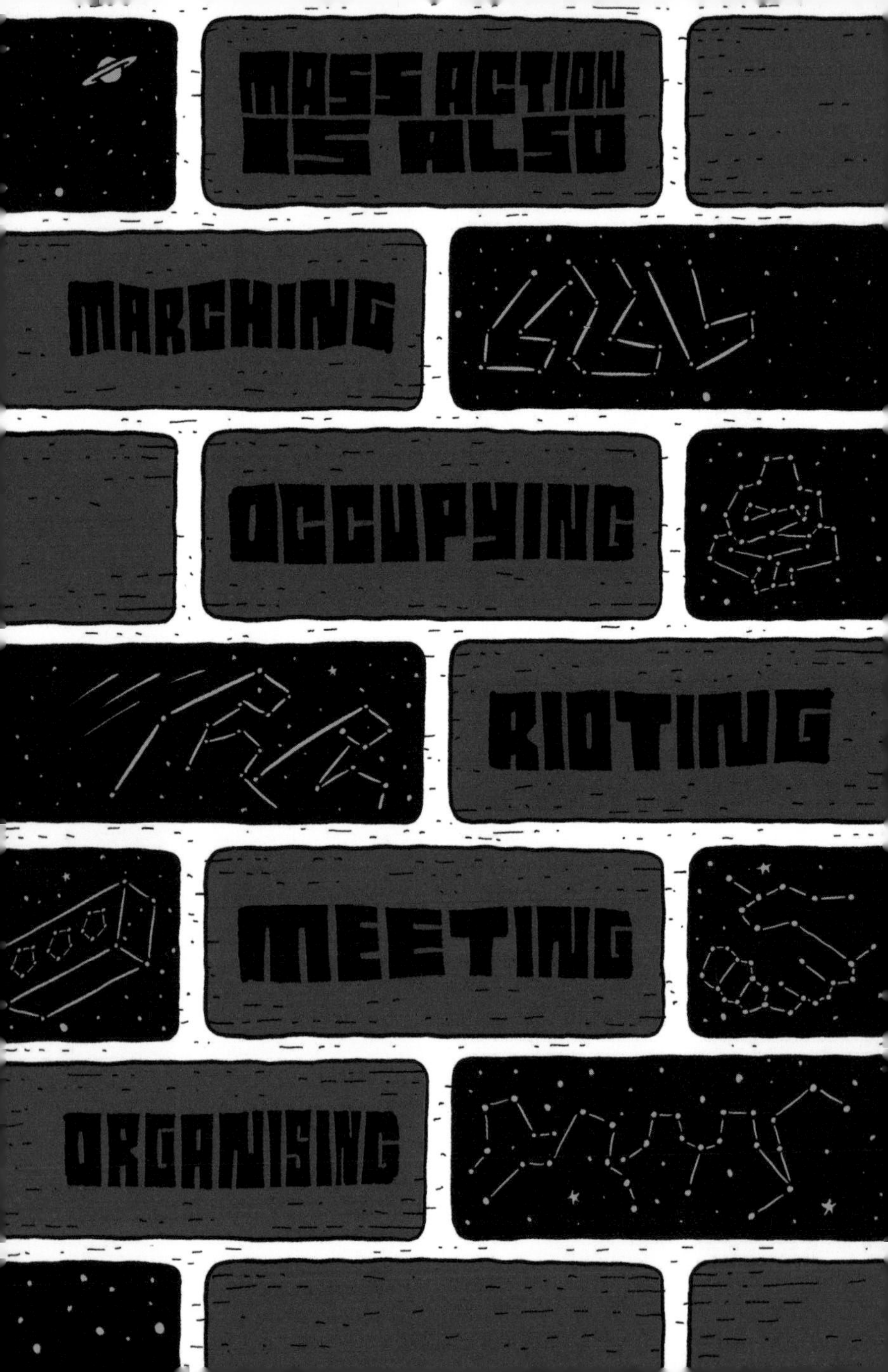
MASS ACTION IS ALSO
MARCHING
OCCUPYING
RIOTING
MEETING
ORGANISING

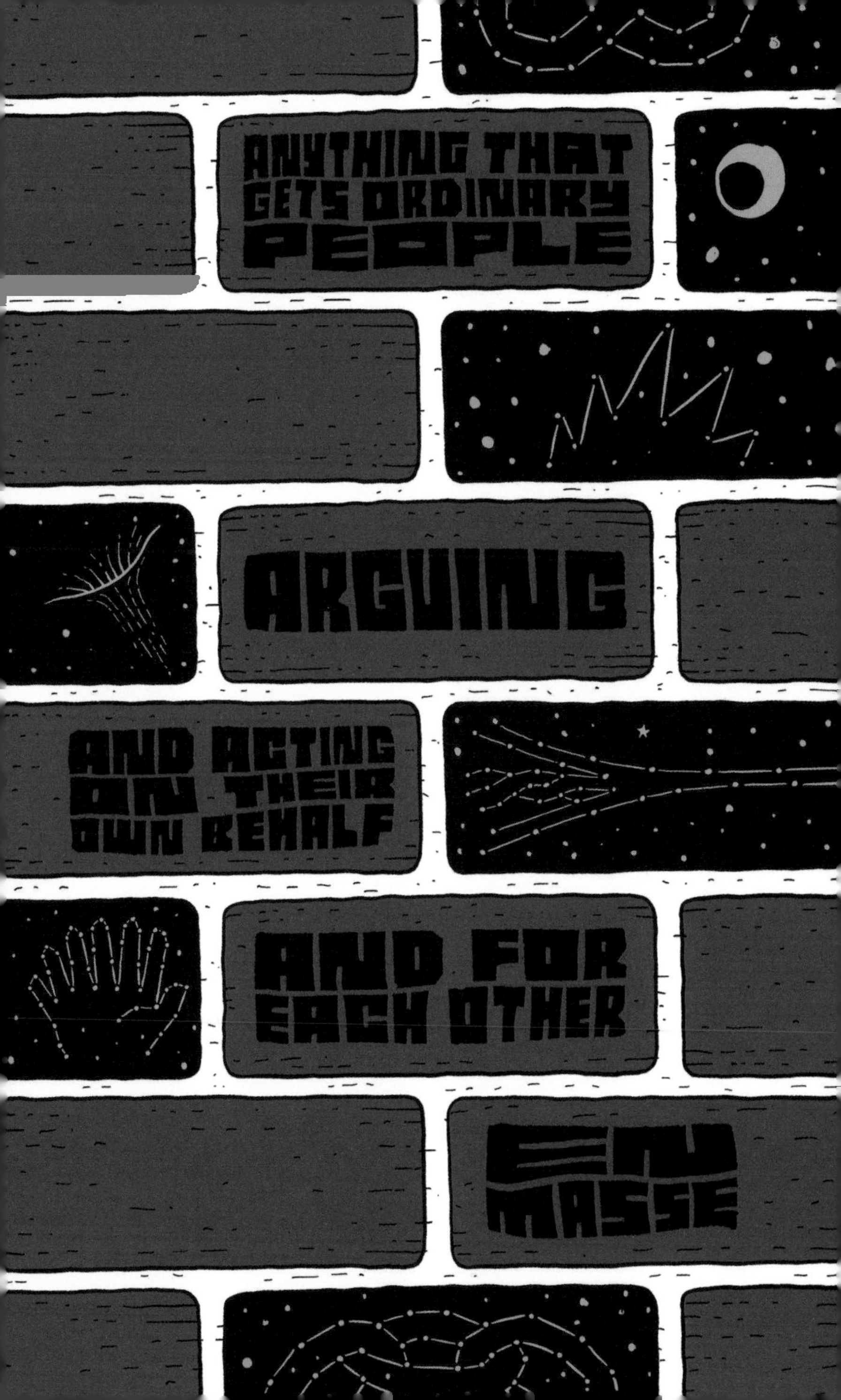
ANYTHING THAT GETS ORDINARY PEOPLE
ARGUING
AND ACTING ON THEIR OWN BEHALF
AND FOR EACH OTHER
EN MASSE

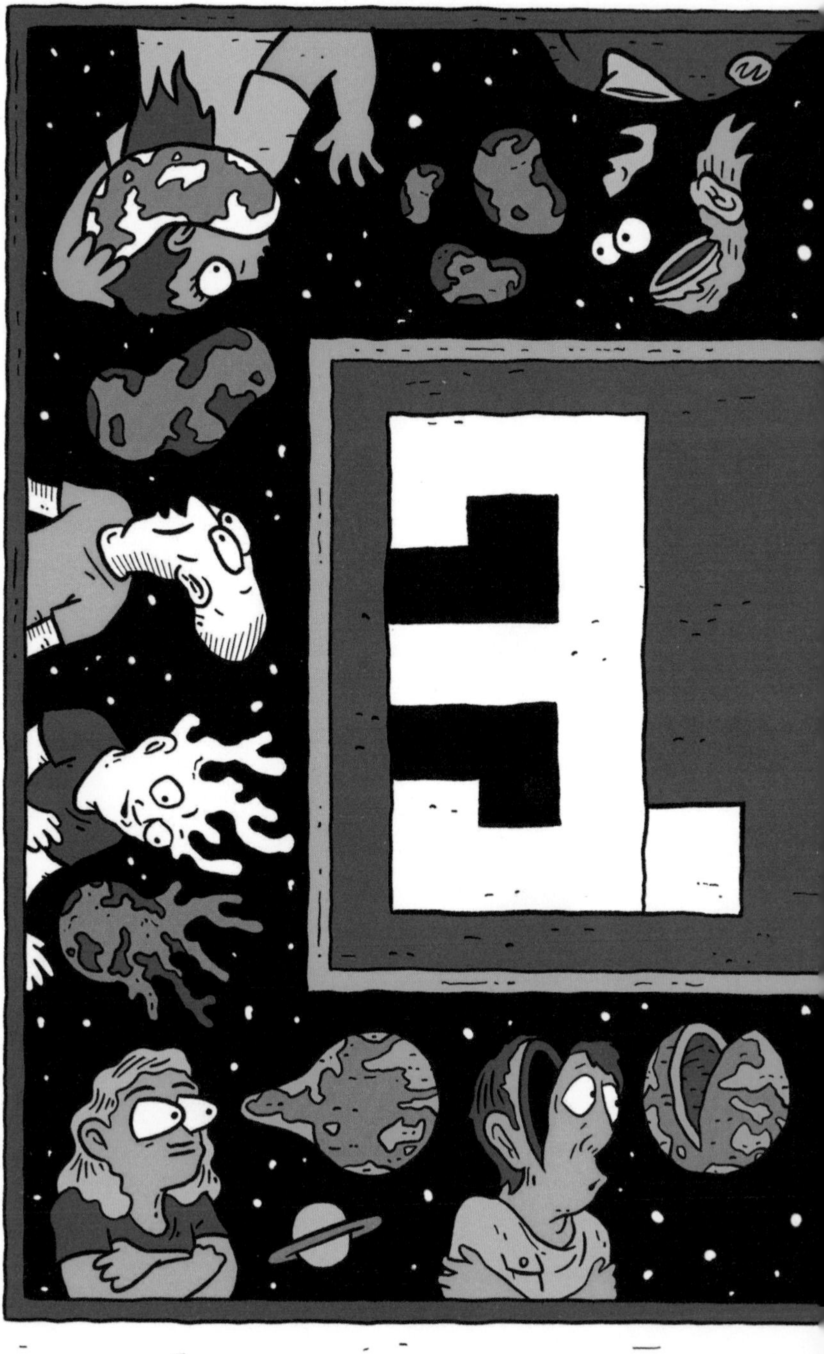
3

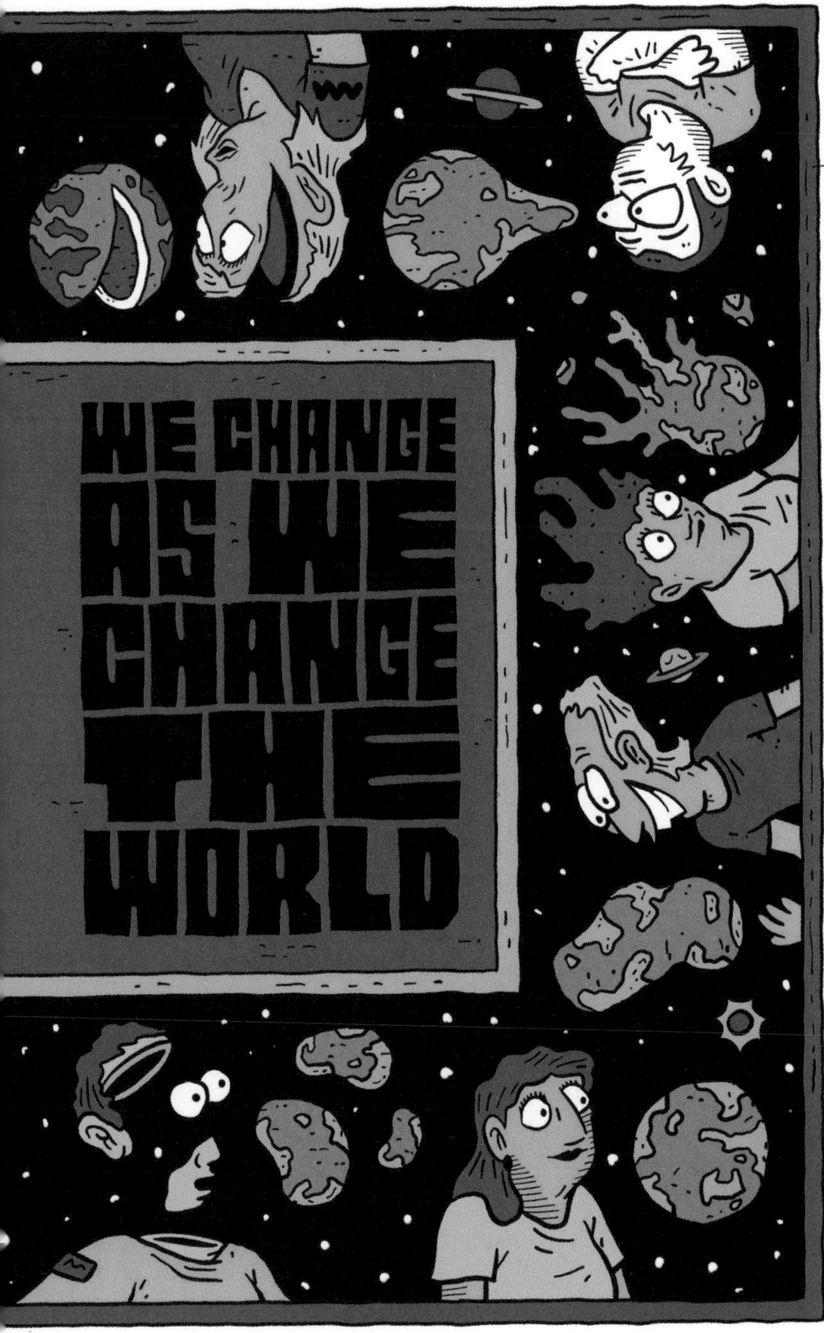
WE CHANGE
AS WE
CHANGE
THE
WORLD

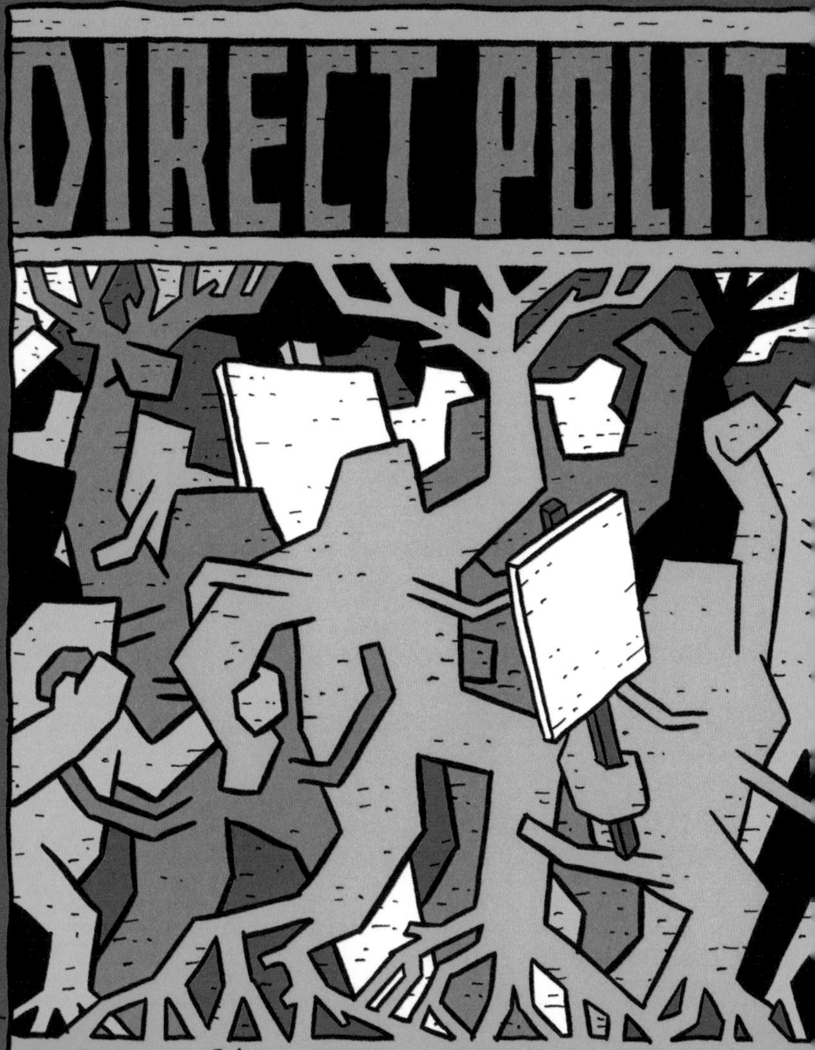
DIRECT POLIT
ITS PART

ICS CHANGES
ICIPANTS

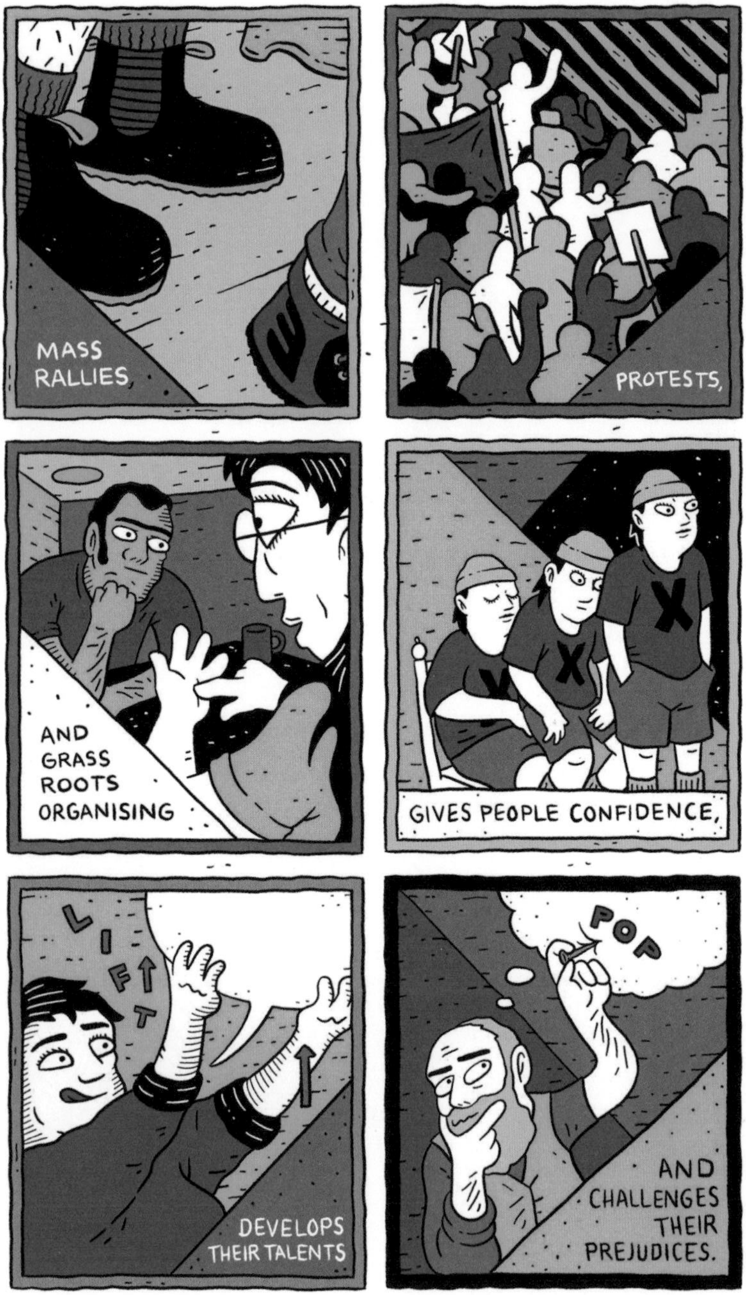
MASS RALLIES,
PROTESTS,
AND GRASS ROOTS ORGANISING
GIVES PEOPLE CONFIDENCE,
LIFT
DEVELOPS THEIR TALENTS
POP
AND CHALLENGES THEIR PREJUDICES.

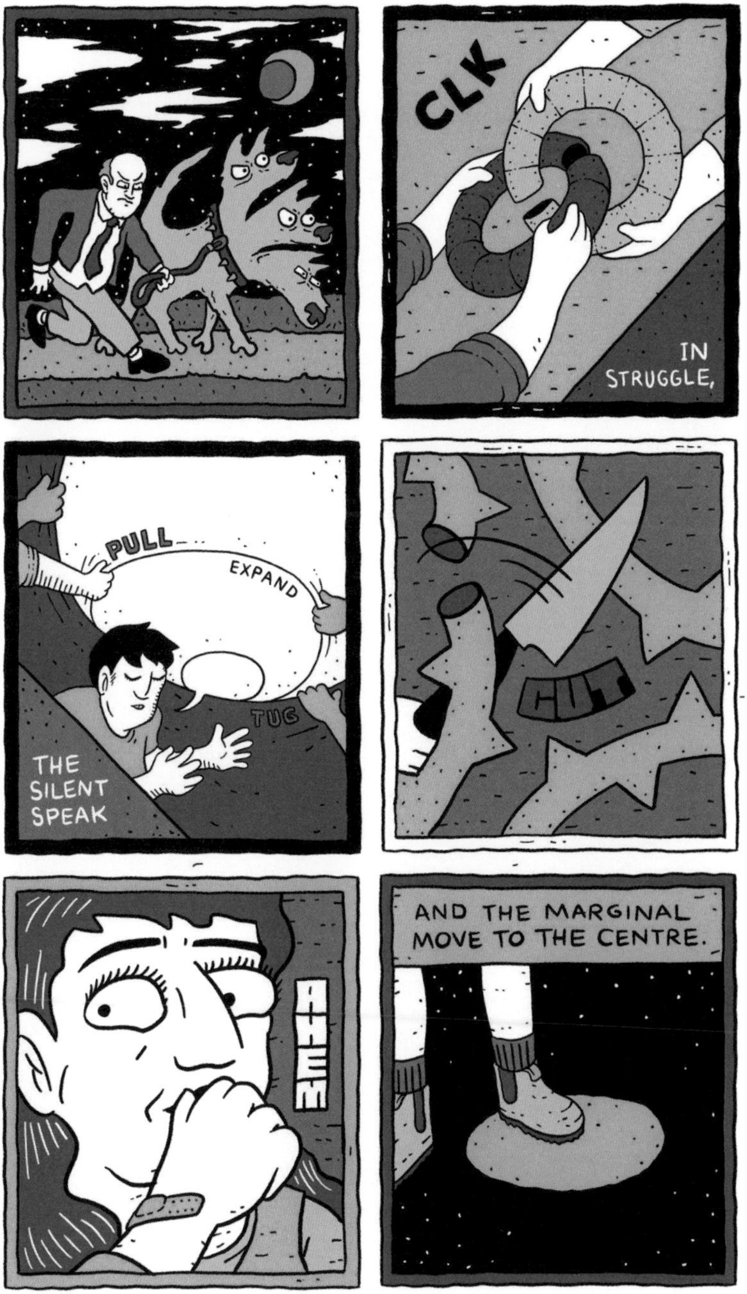
CLK
IN STRUGGLE,
PULL
EXPAND
TUG
THE SILENT SPEAK
CUT
AHEM
AND THE MARGINAL MOVE TO THE CENTRE.

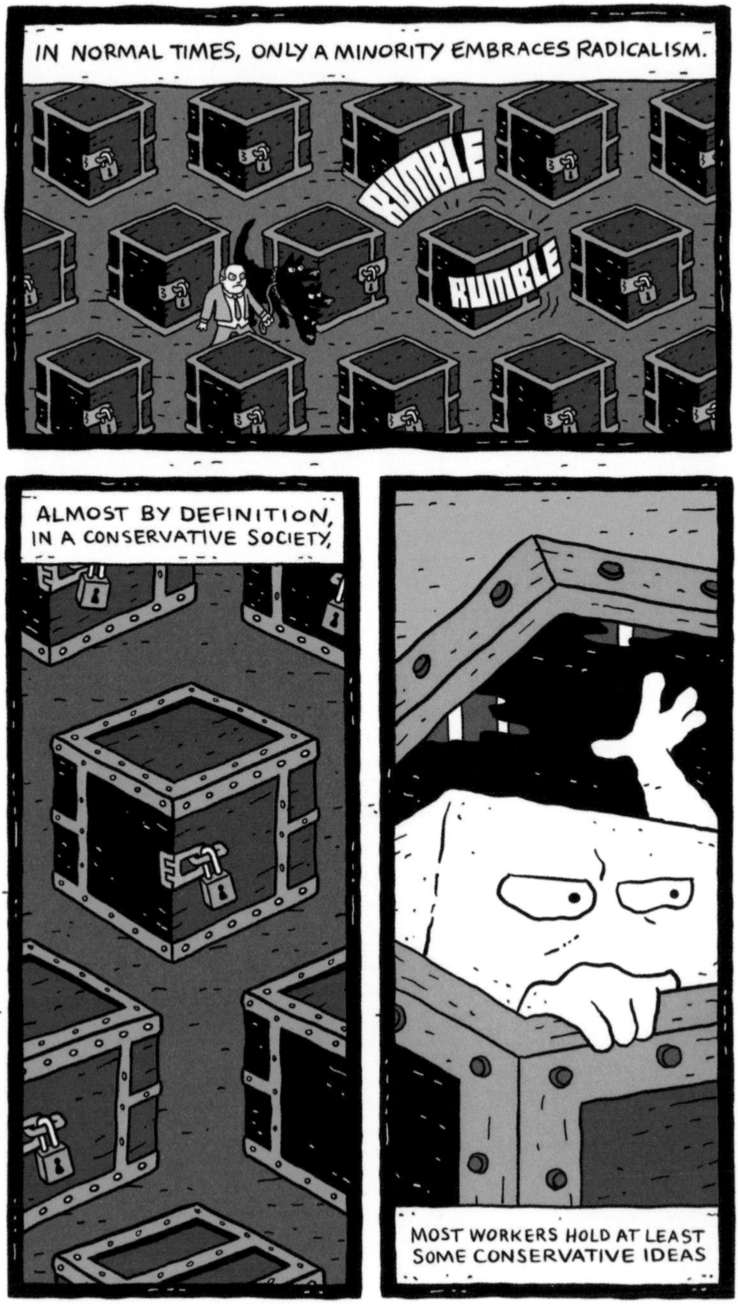
IN NORMAL TIMES, ONLY A MINORITY EMBRACES RADICALISM.
RUMBLE
RUMBLE
ALMOST BY DEFINITION, IN A CONSERVATIVE SOCIETY,
MOST WORKERS HOLD AT LEAST SOME CONSERVATIVE IDEAS

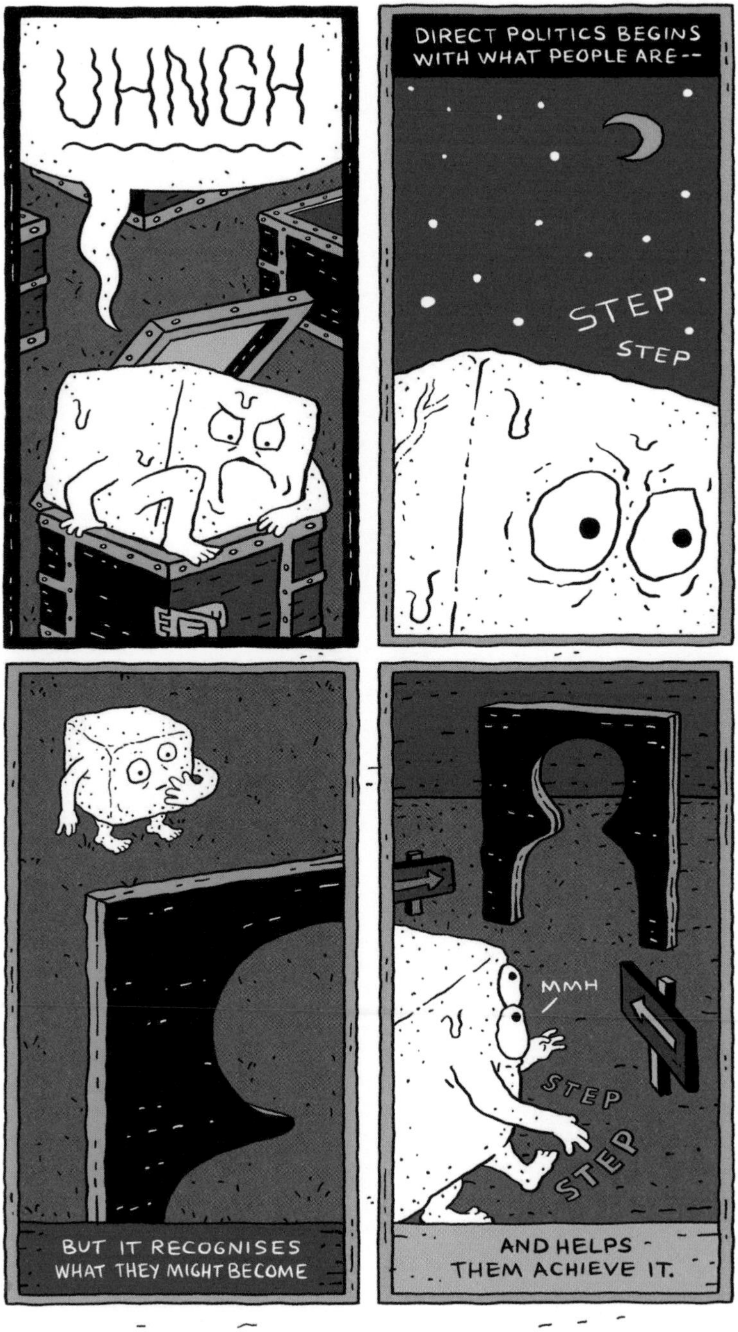
UHNGH
DIRECT POLITICS BEGINS WITH WHAT PEOPLE ARE--
STEP
STEP
BUT IT RECOGNISES WHAT THEY MIGHT BECOME
MMH
STEP
STEP
AND HELPS THEM ACHIEVE IT.

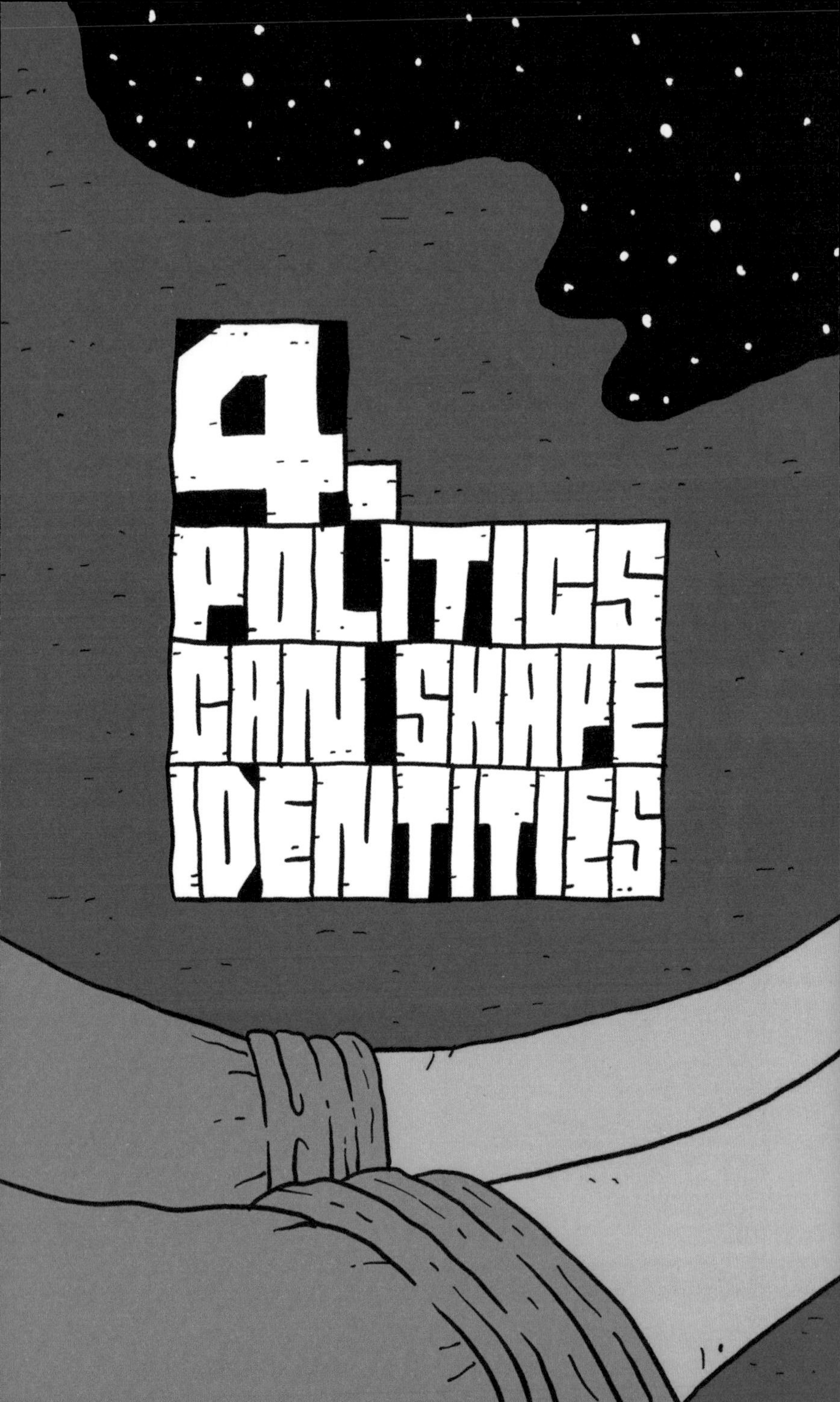
4.
POLITICS CAN SHAPE IDENTITIES

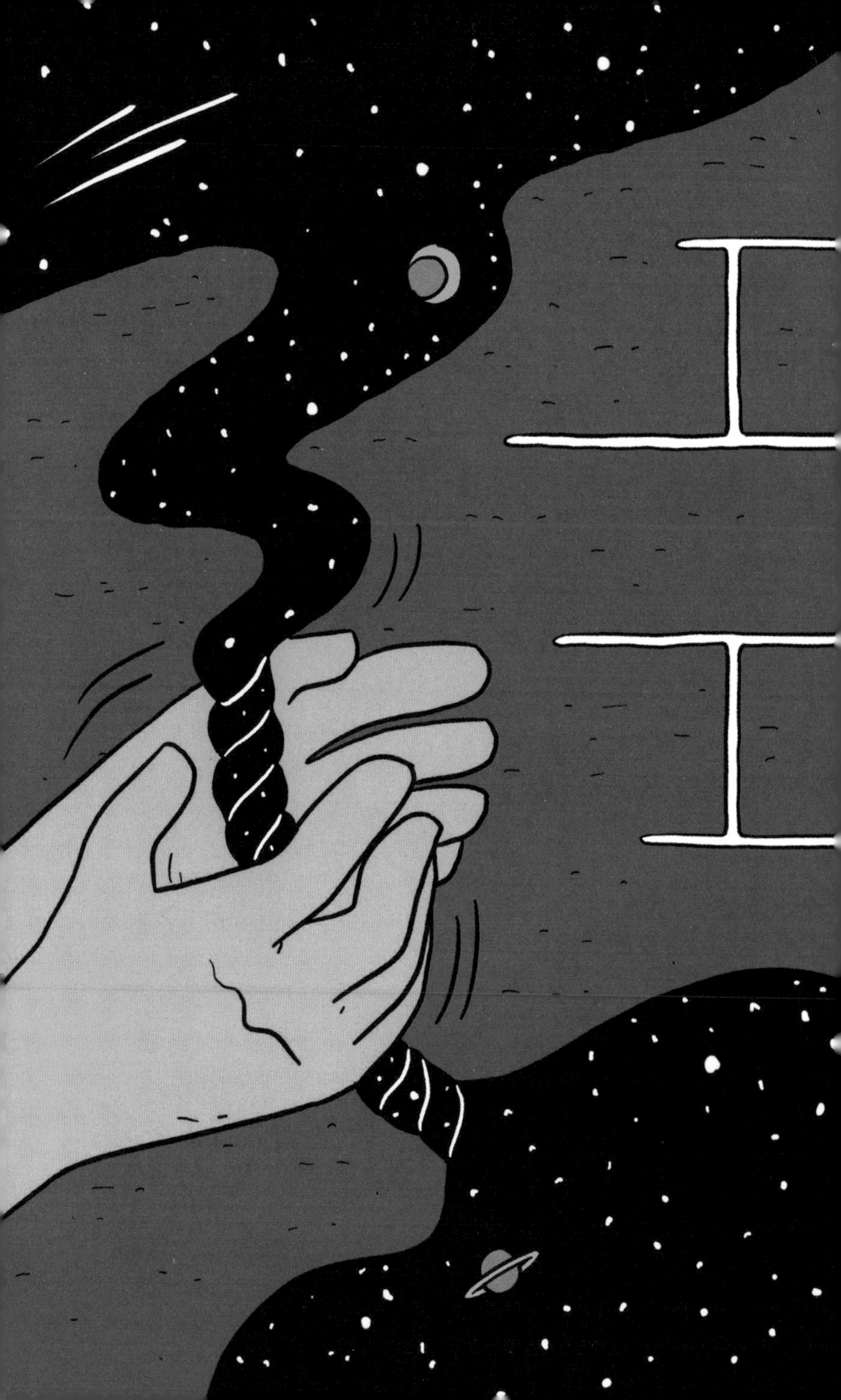
II

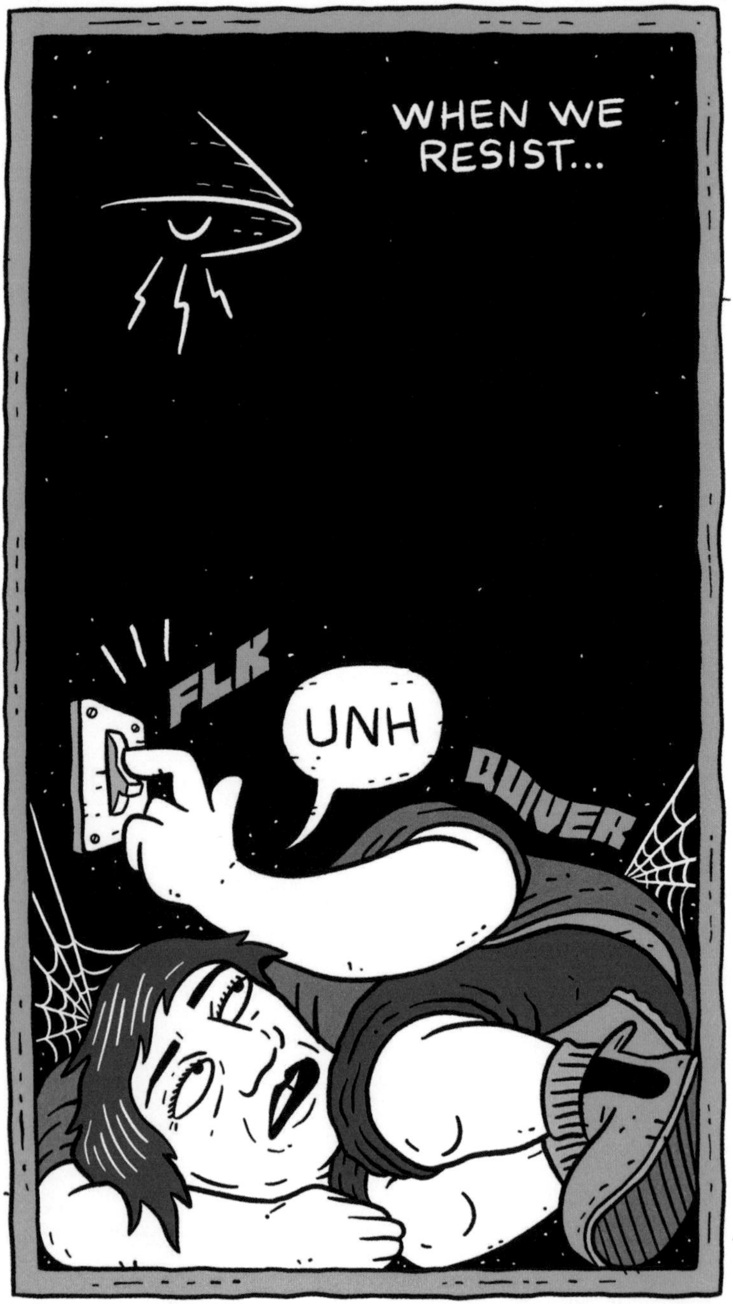
WHEN WE RESIST...
FLK
UNH
QUIVER

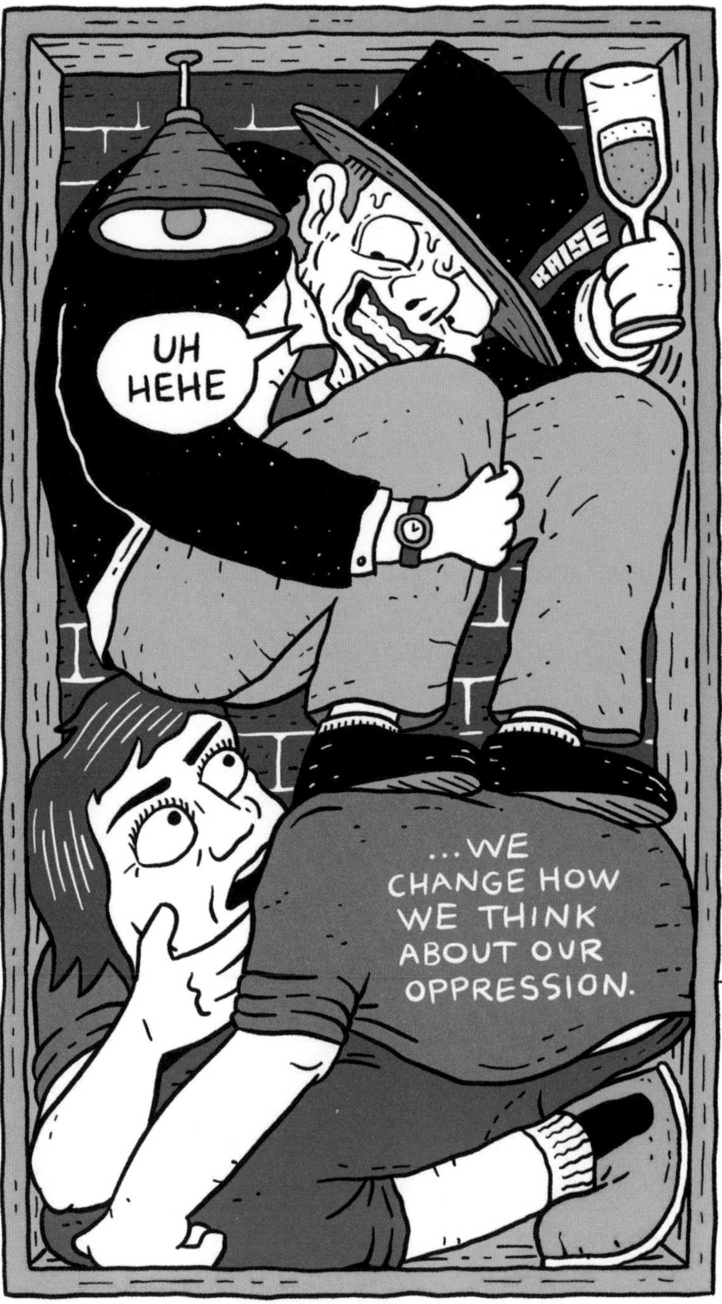
RAISE
UH HEHE
...WE CHANGE HOW WE THINK ABOUT OUR OPPRESSION.

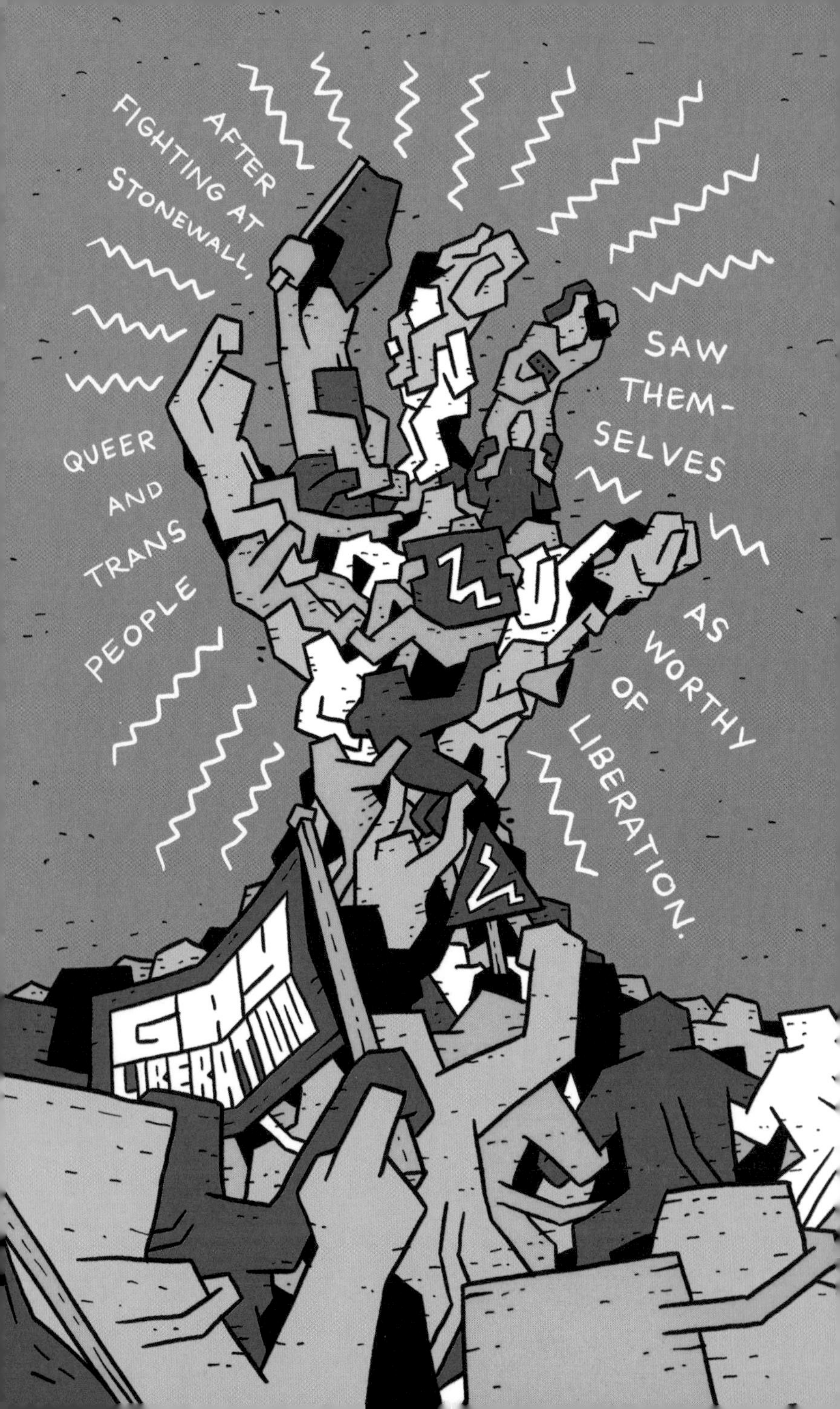

AFTER FIGHTING AT STONEWALL,
QUEER AND TRANS PEOPLE
SAW THEM-SELVES AS WORTHY OF LIBERATION.
GAY LIBERATION

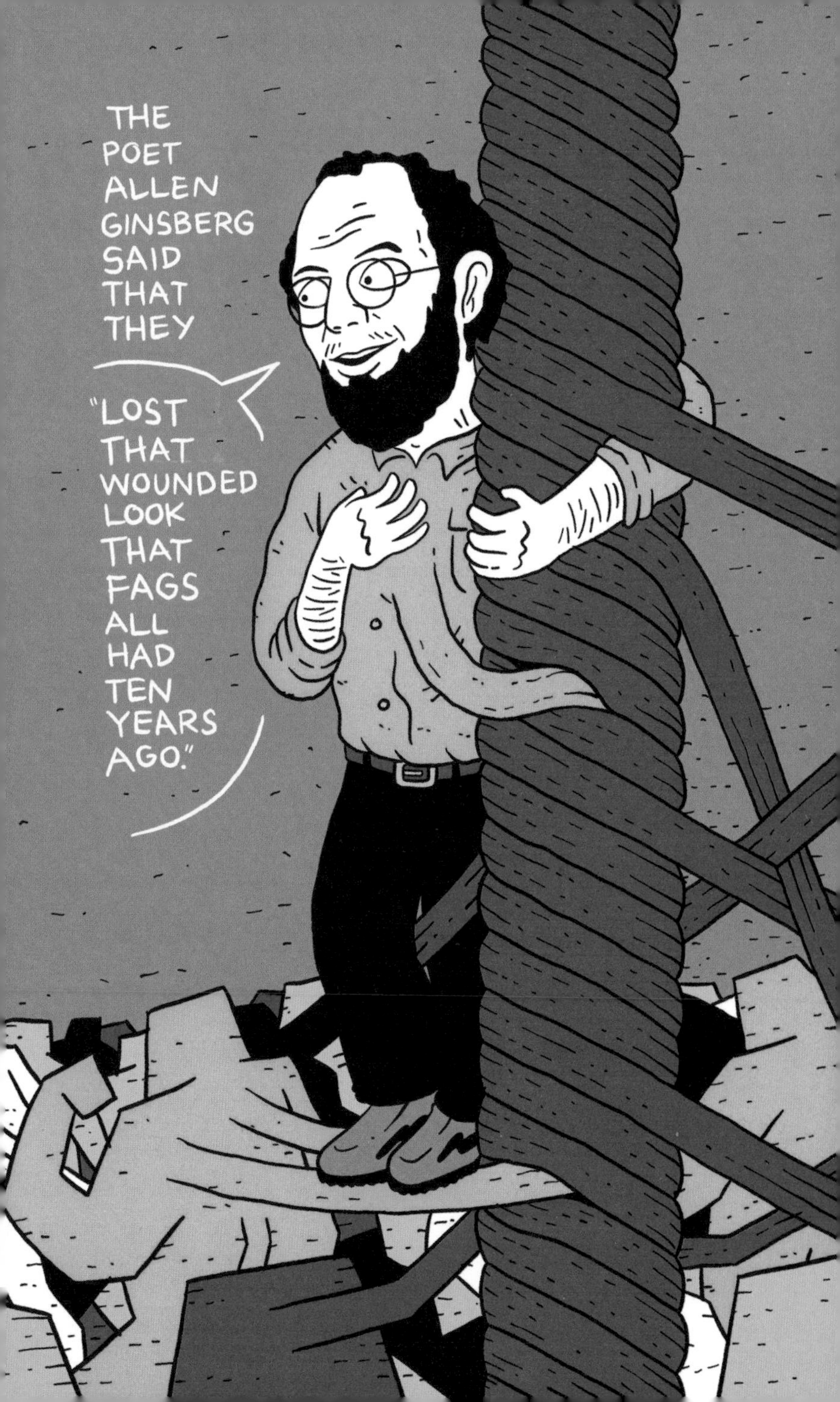
THE POET ALLEN GINSBERG SAID THAT THEY
"LOST THAT WOUNDED LOOK THAT FAGS ALL HAD TEN YEARS AGO."

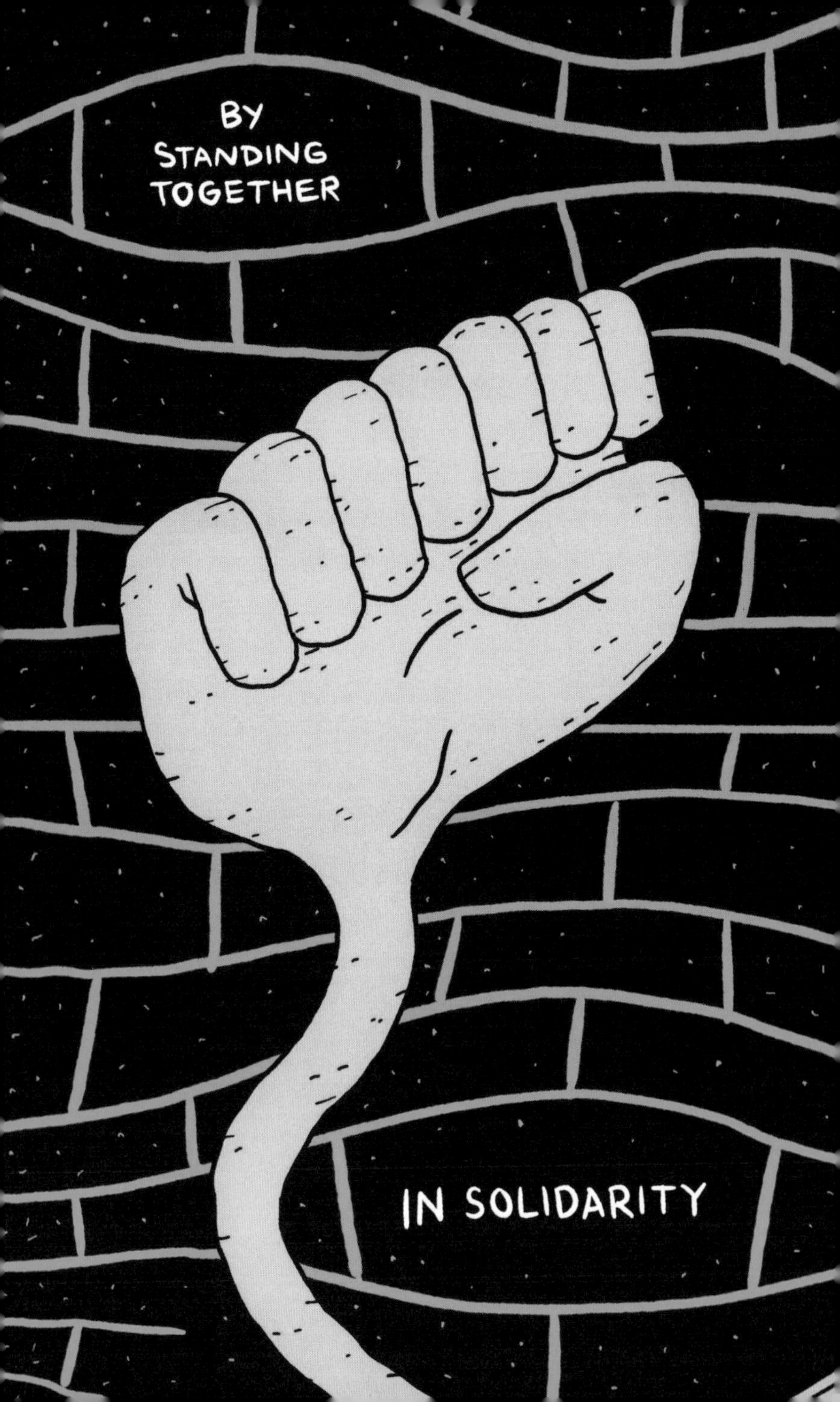
BY STANDING TOGETHER
IN SOLIDARITY

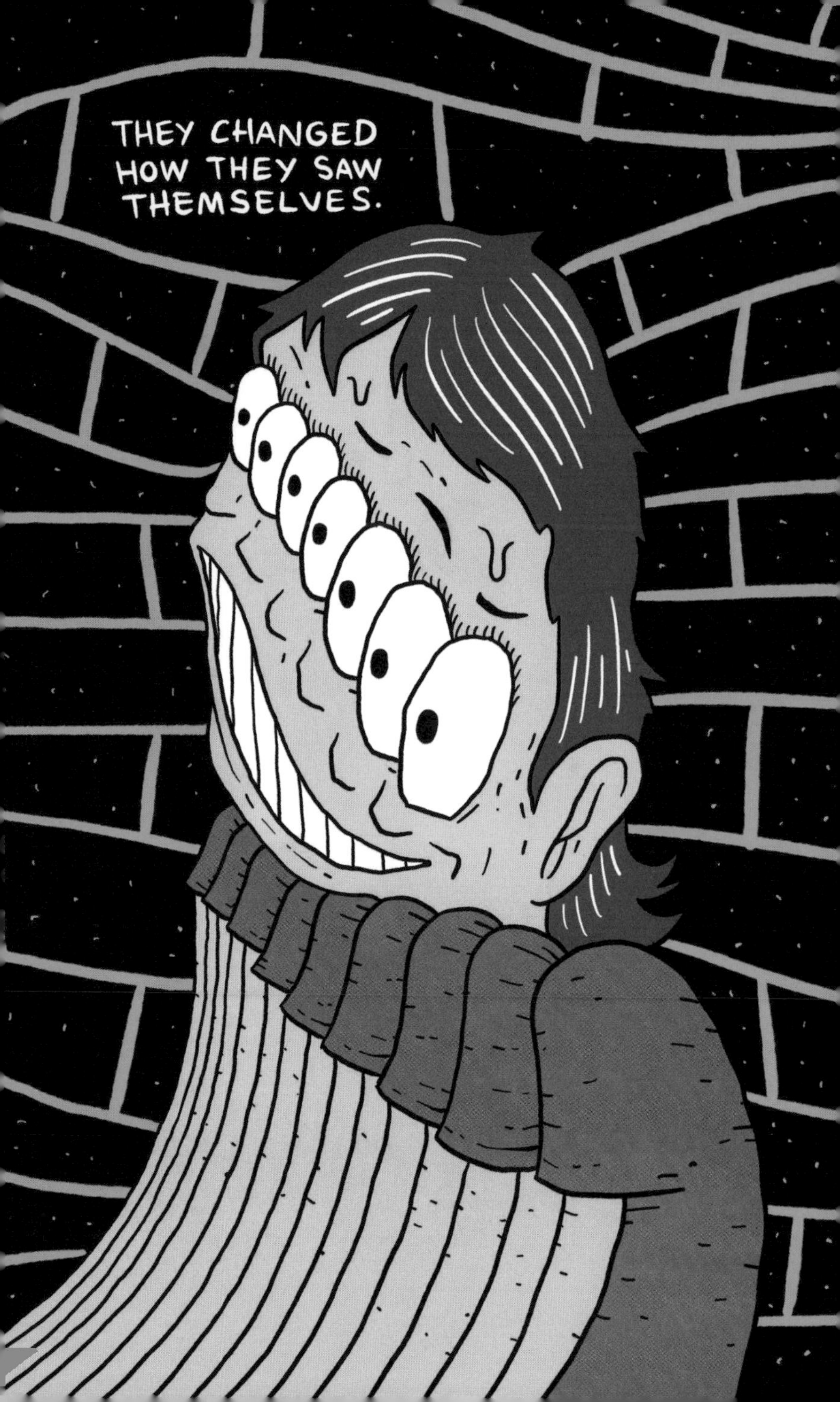
THEY CHANGED HOW THEY SAW THEMSELVES.

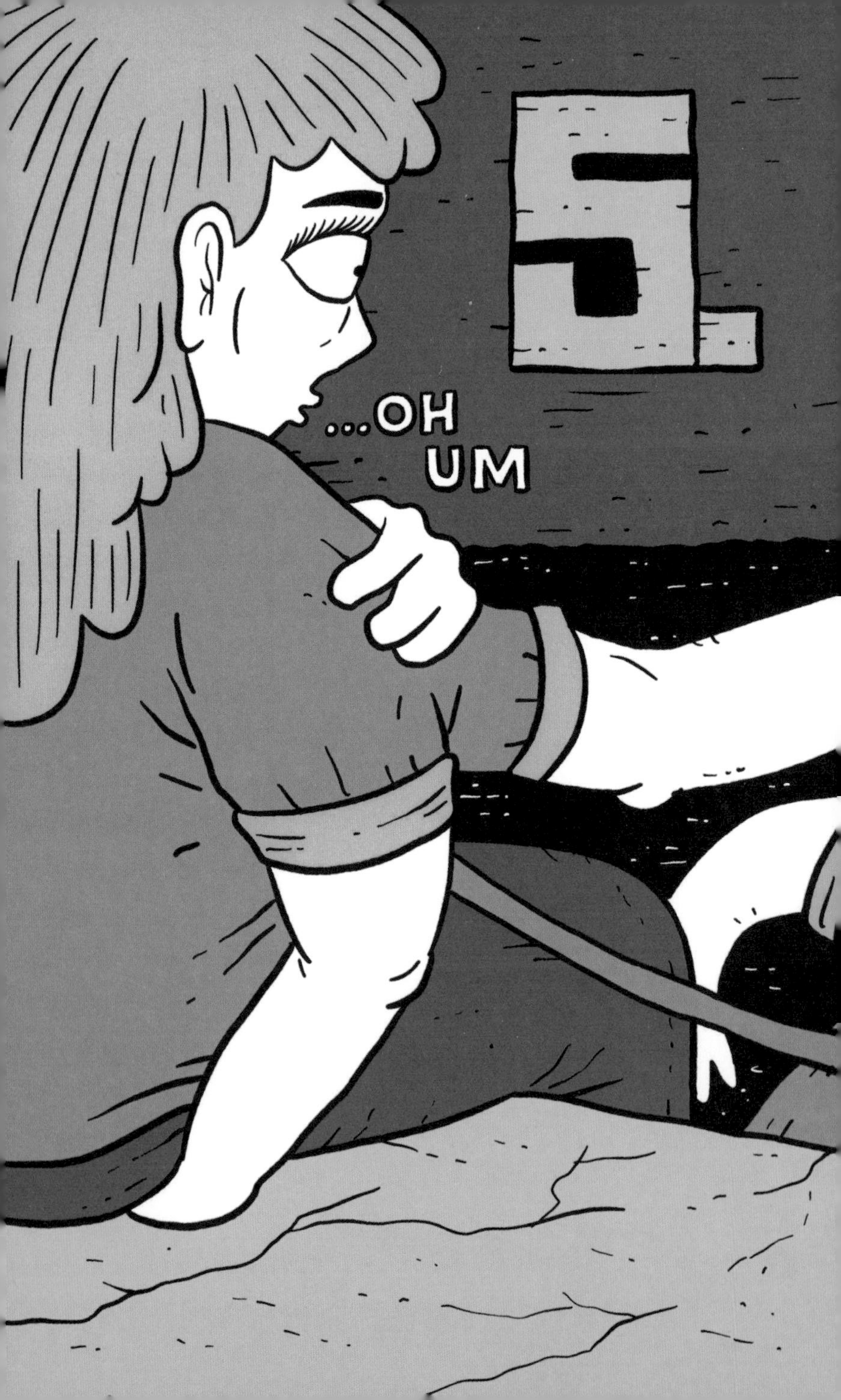

...OH
UM

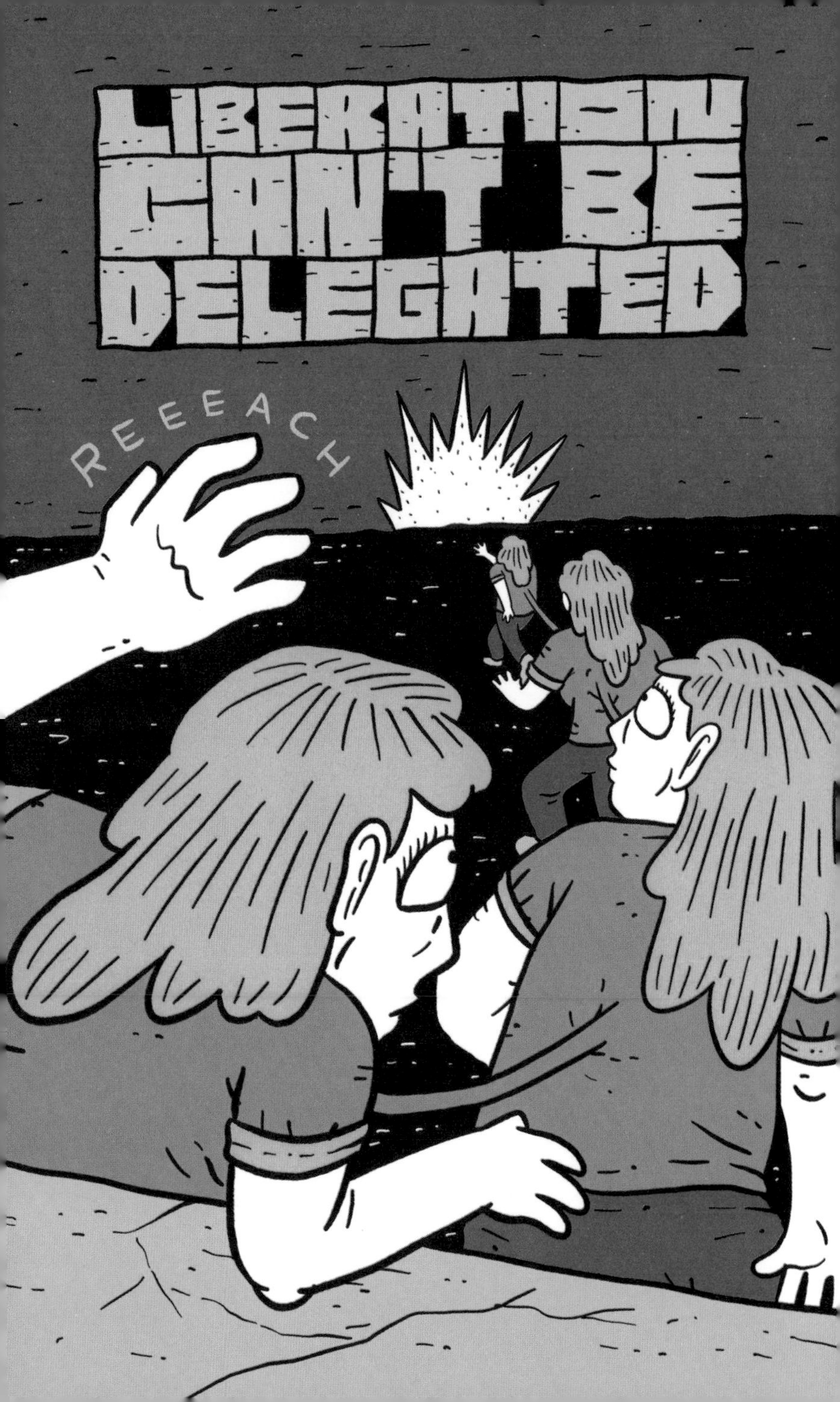

LIBERATION CAN'T BE DELEGATED
REEEACH

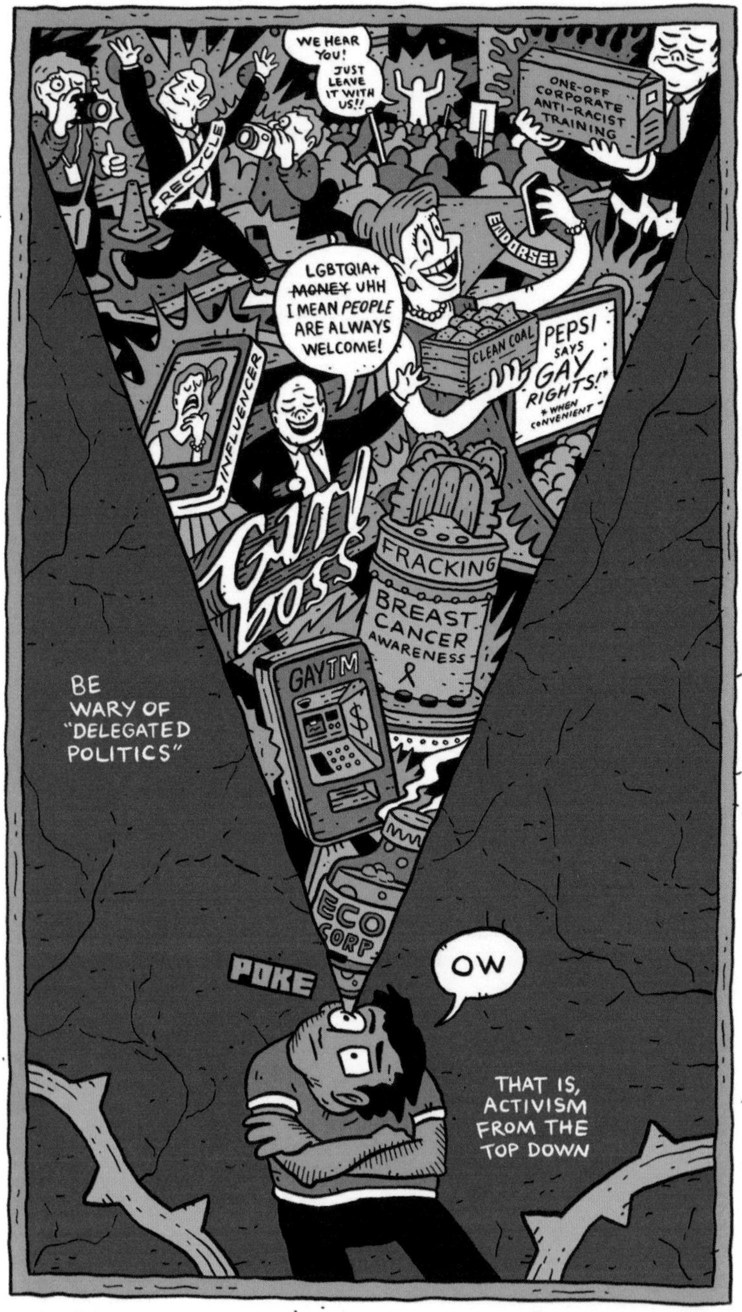

WE HEAR YOU! JUST LEAVE IT WITH US!!
ONE-OFF CORPORATE ANTI-RACIST TRAINING
RECYCLE
ENDORSE!
LGBTQIA+ ~~MONEY~~ UHH I MEAN *PEOPLE* ARE ALWAYS WELCOME!
CLEAN COAL
PEPSI SAYS GAY RIGHTS!* *WHEN CONVENIENT
INFLUENCER
GIRL BOSS
FRACKING
BREAST CANCER AWARENESS
GAYTM
$
ECO CORP
POKE
OW
BE WARY OF "DELEGATED POLITICS"
THAT IS, ACTIVISM FROM THE TOP DOWN

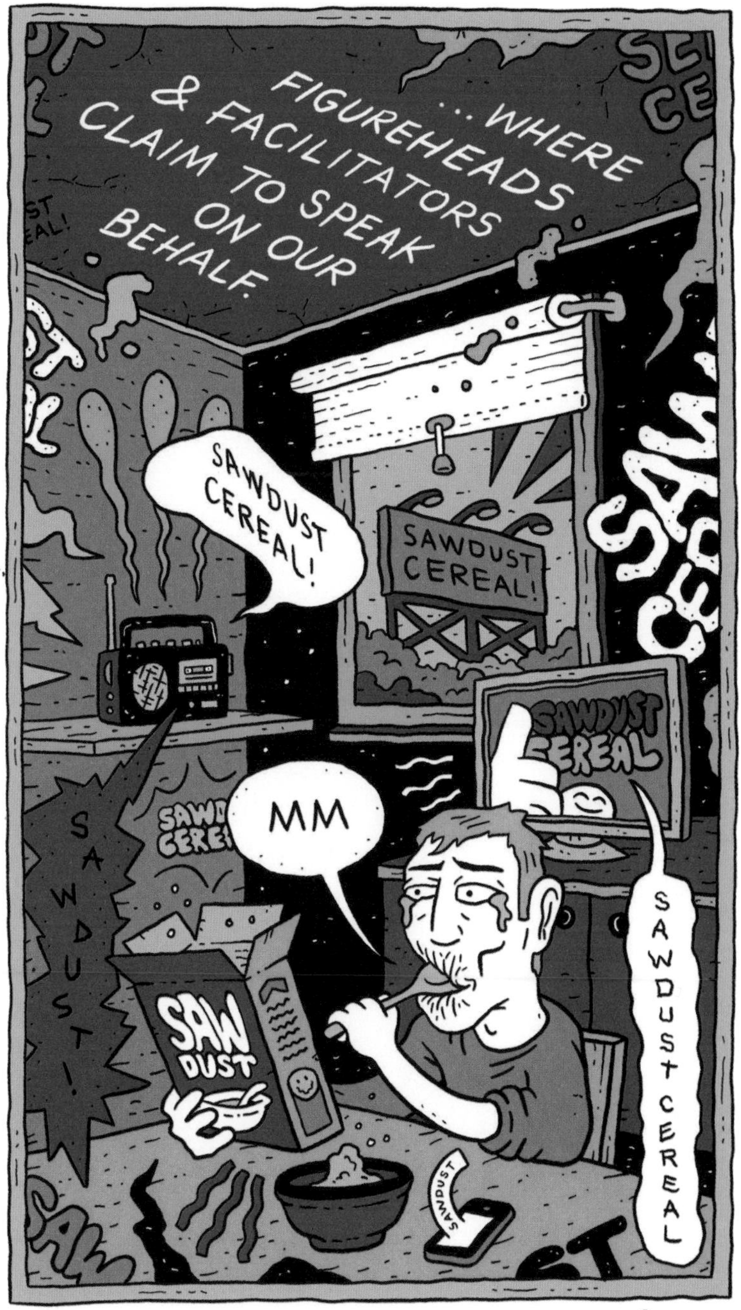

...WHERE FIGUREHEADS & FACILITATORS CLAIM TO SPEAK ON OUR BEHALF.
SAWDUST CEREAL!
SAWDUST CEREAL!
SAWDUST CEREAL
MM
SAWDUST!
SAWDUST CEREAL
SAW DUST
SAWDUST

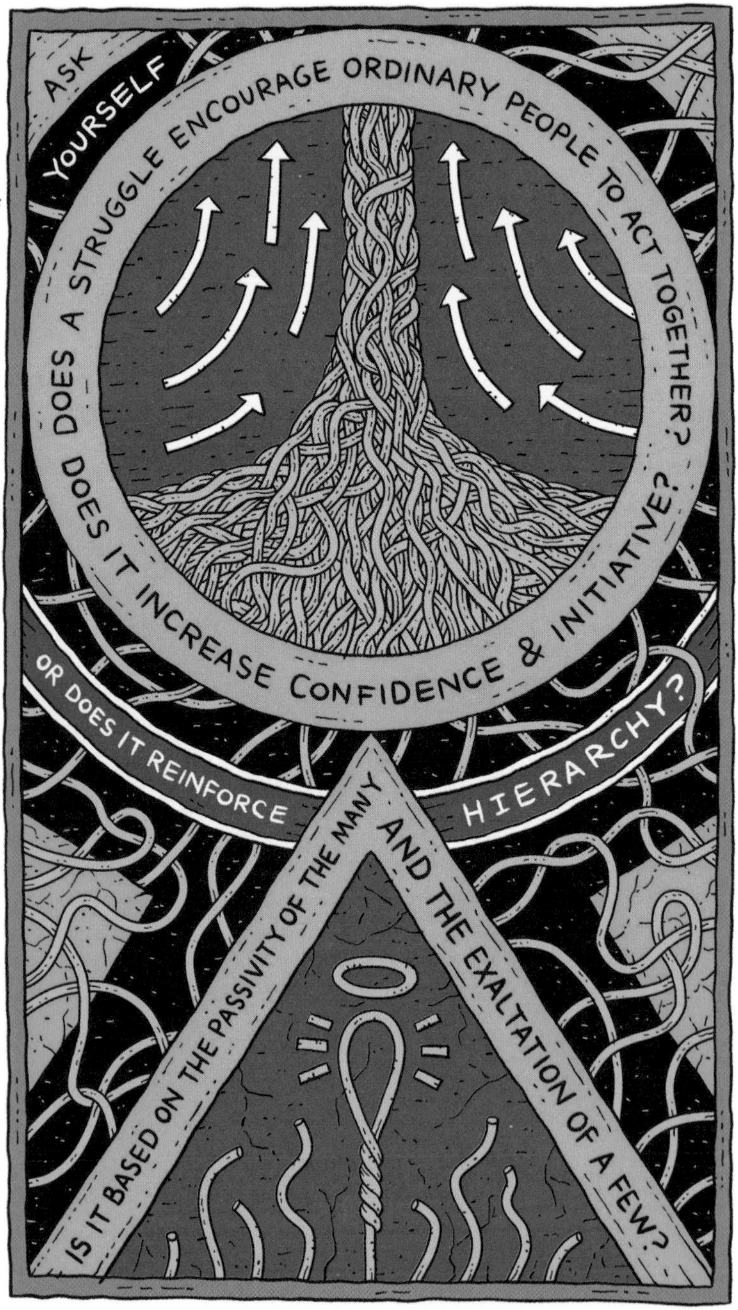
ASK
YOURSELF
DOES A STRUGGLE ENCOURAGE ORDINARY PEOPLE TO ACT TOGETHER?
DOES IT INCREASE CONFIDENCE & INITIATIVE?
OR DOES IT REINFORCE HIERARCHY?
IS IT BASED ON THE PASSIVITY OF THE MANY AND THE EXALTATION OF A FEW?

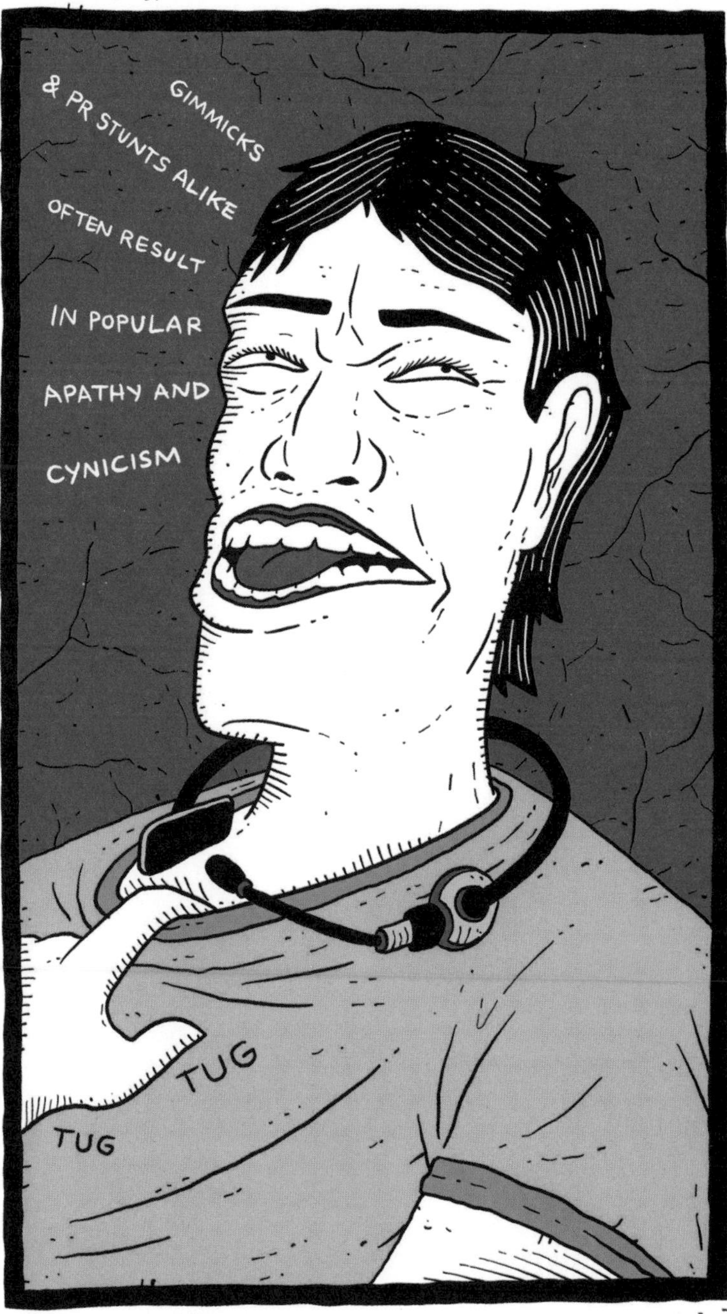
GIMMICKS
& PR STUNTS ALIKE
OFTEN RESULT
IN POPULAR
APATHY AND
CYNICISM
TUG
TUG

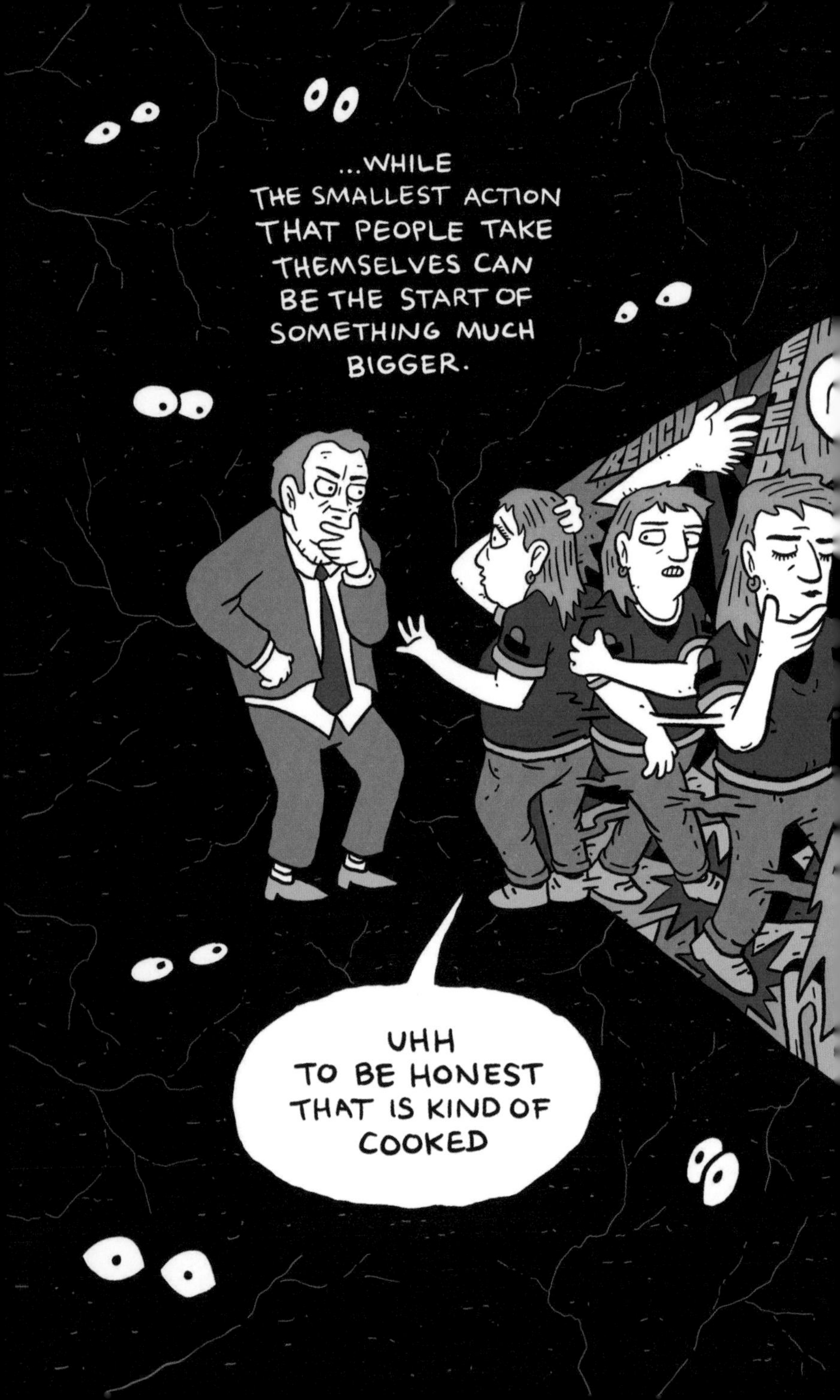
...WHILE THE SMALLEST ACTION THAT PEOPLE TAKE THEMSELVES CAN BE THE START OF SOMETHING MUCH BIGGER.
REACH
UHH TO BE HONEST THAT IS KIND OF COOKED

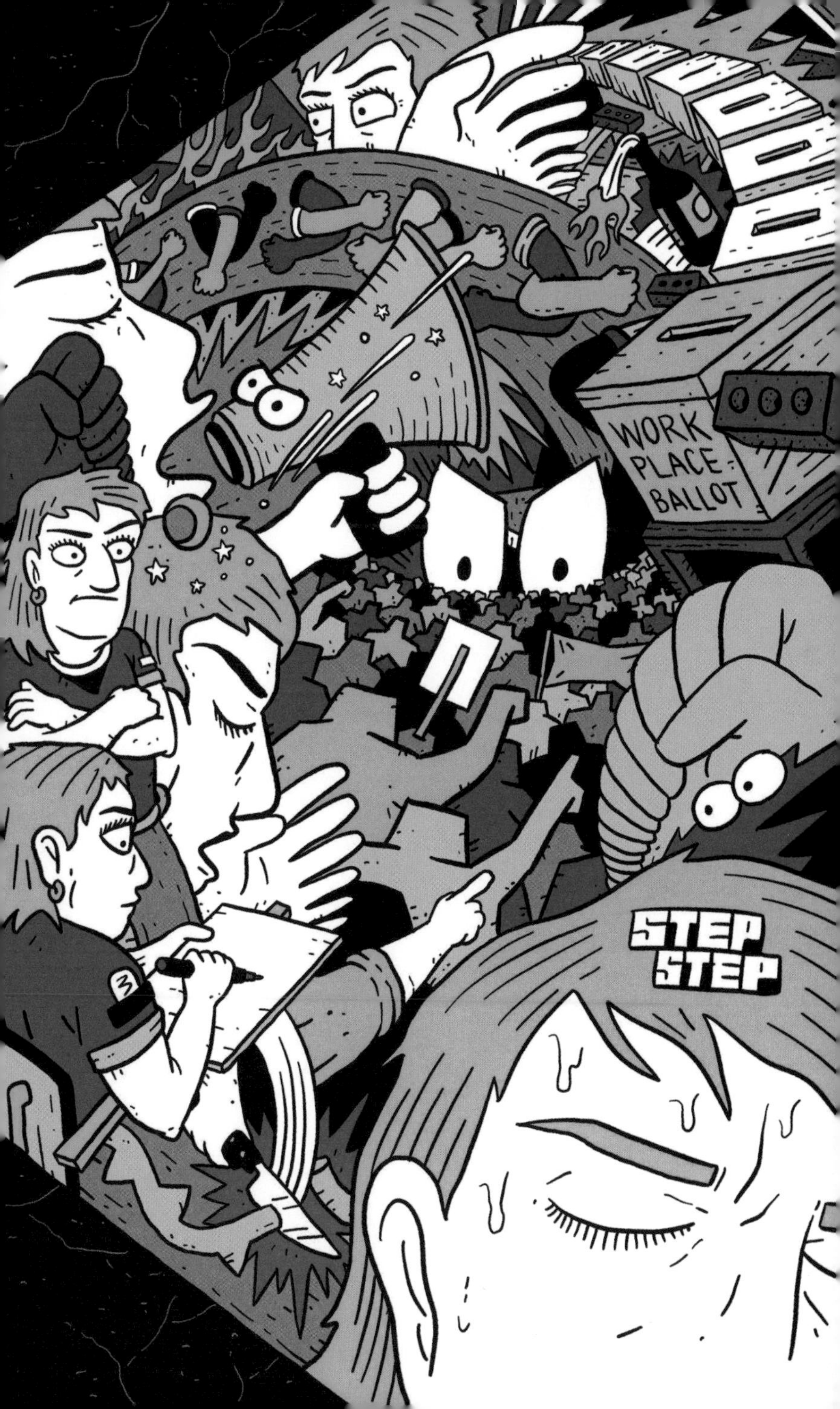
WORK PLACE BALLOT
STEP STEP

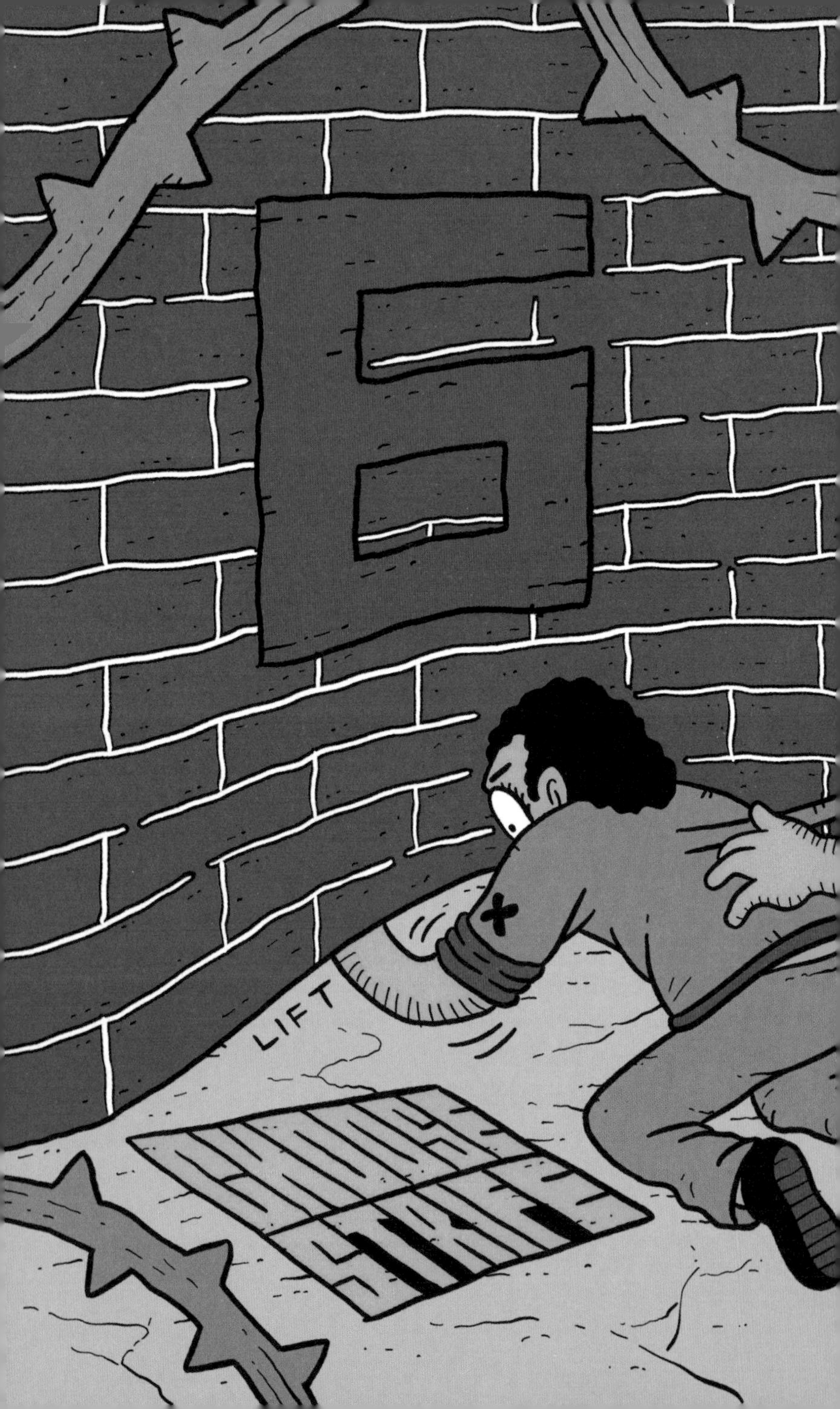
LIFT

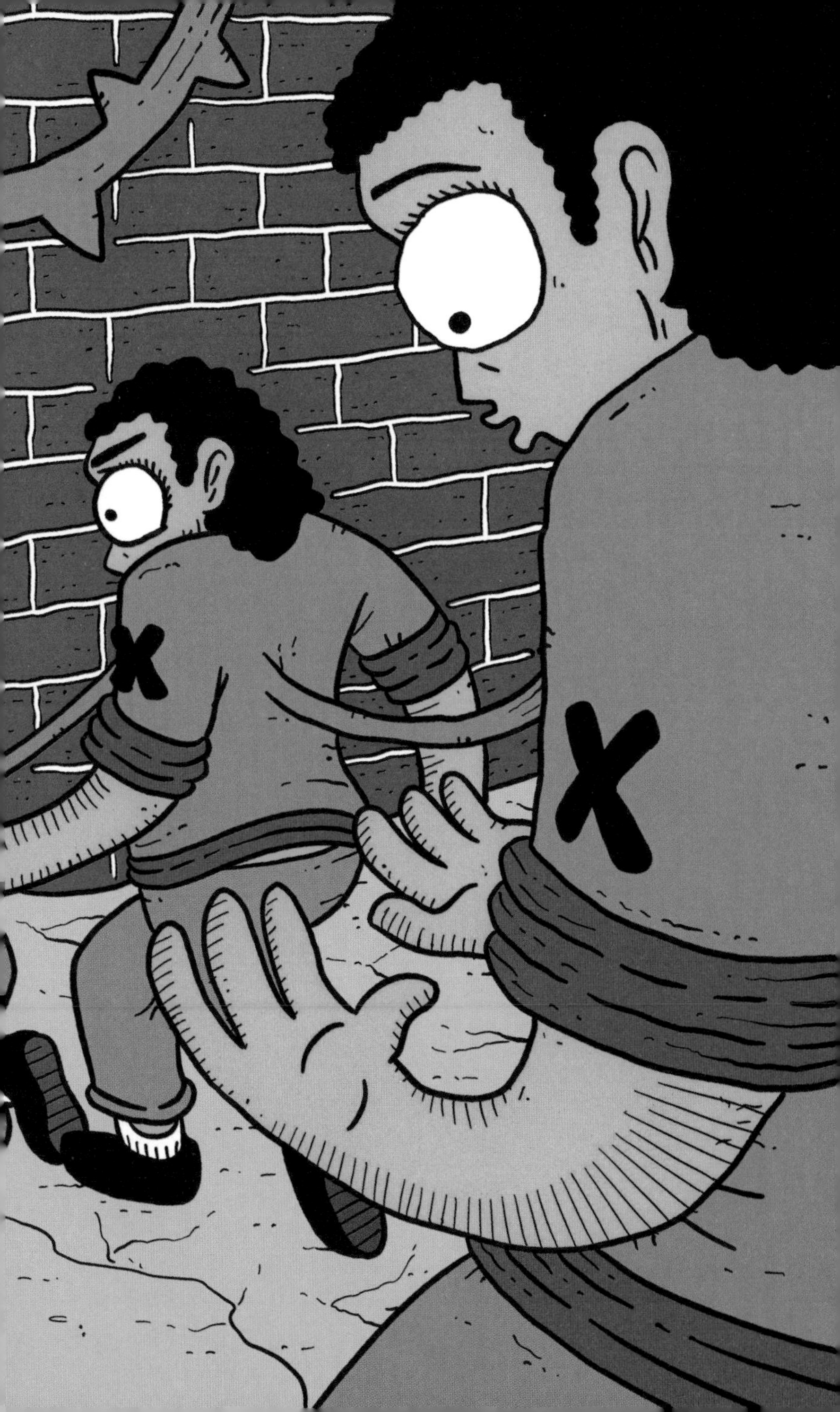

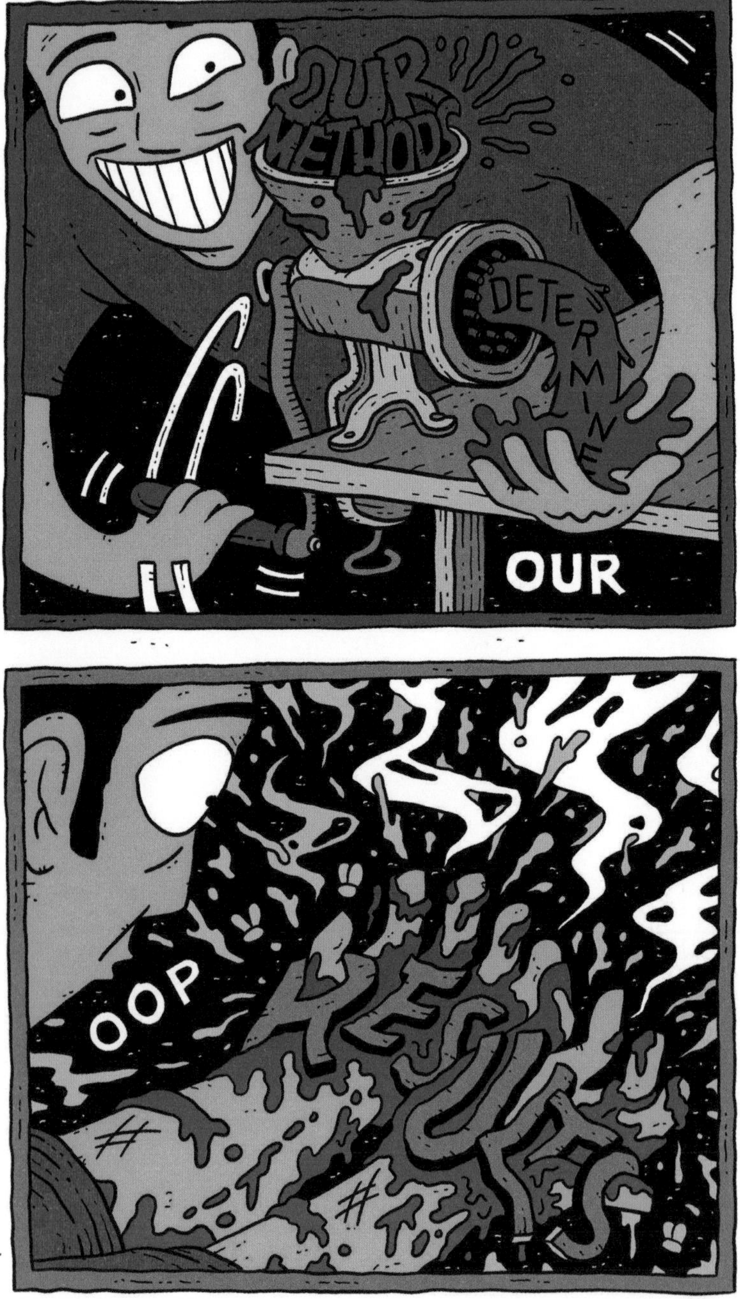
OUR METHODS
DETERMINE
OUR
OOP

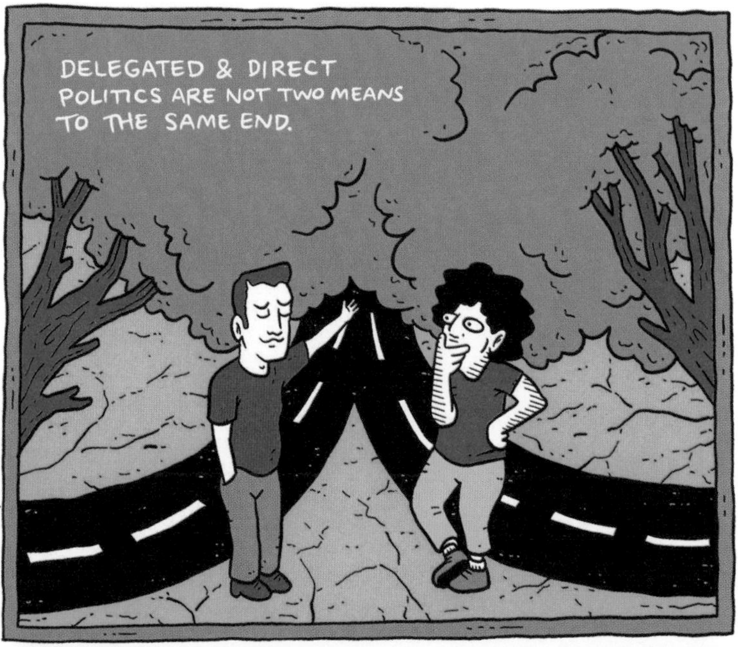
DELEGATED & DIRECT POLITICS ARE NOT TWO MEANS TO THE SAME END.

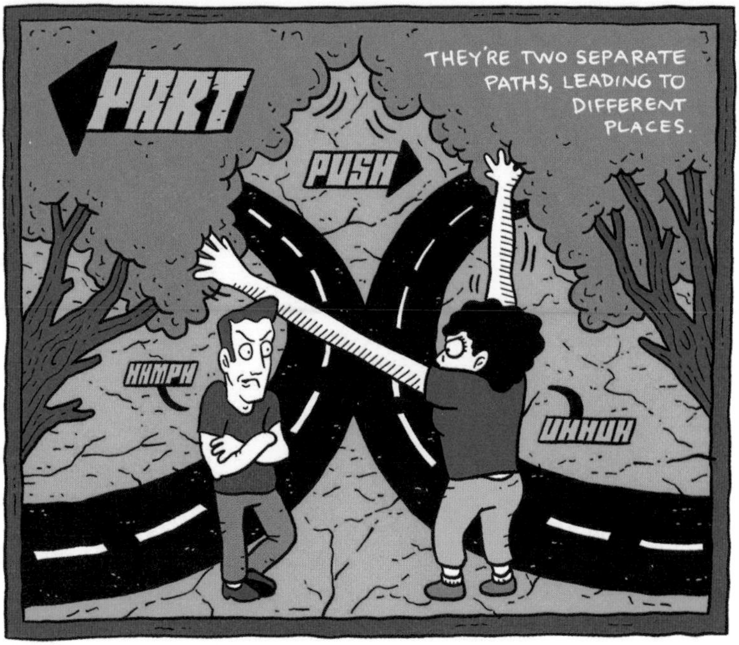
PART
PUSH
THEY'RE TWO SEPARATE PATHS, LEADING TO DIFFERENT PLACES.
HHMPH
UHHUH

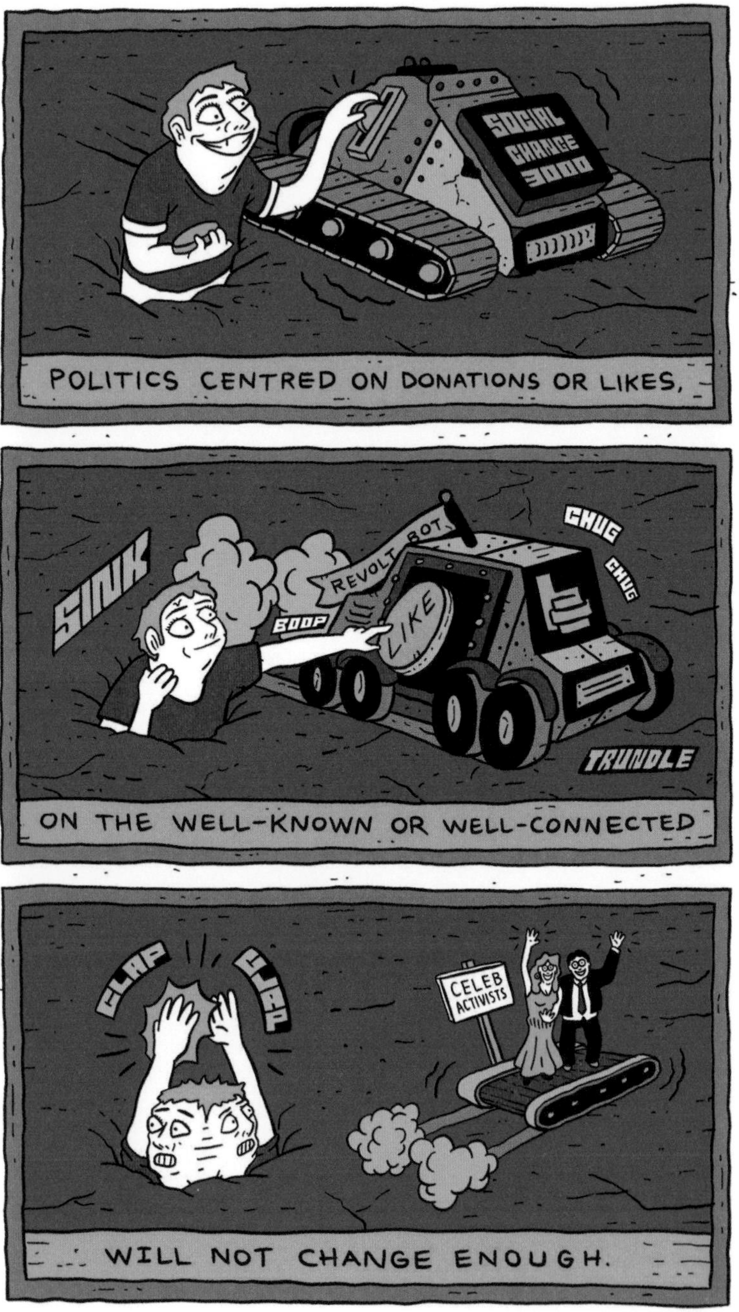
SOCIAL CHANGE 3000
POLITICS CENTRED ON DONATIONS OR LIKES,
SINK
REVOLT BOT
BOOP
LIKE
CHUG
CHUG
TRUNDLE
ON THE WELL-KNOWN OR WELL-CONNECTED
CLAP
CLAP
CELEB ACTIVISTS
WILL NOT CHANGE ENOUGH.

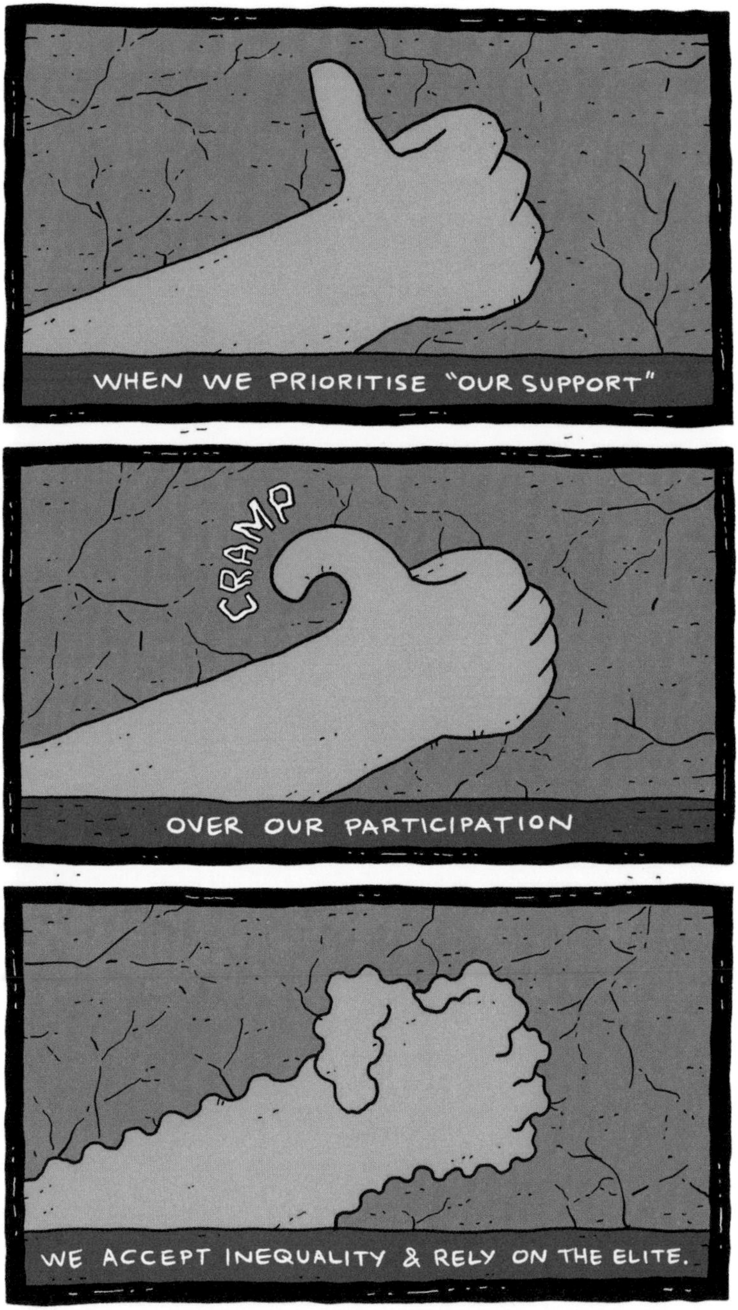
WHEN WE PRIORITISE "OUR SUPPORT"
CRAMP
OVER OUR PARTICIPATION
WE ACCEPT INEQUALITY & RELY ON THE ELITE.

DIRECT POLITICS

WORKERS COLLECTIVELY ORGANISING

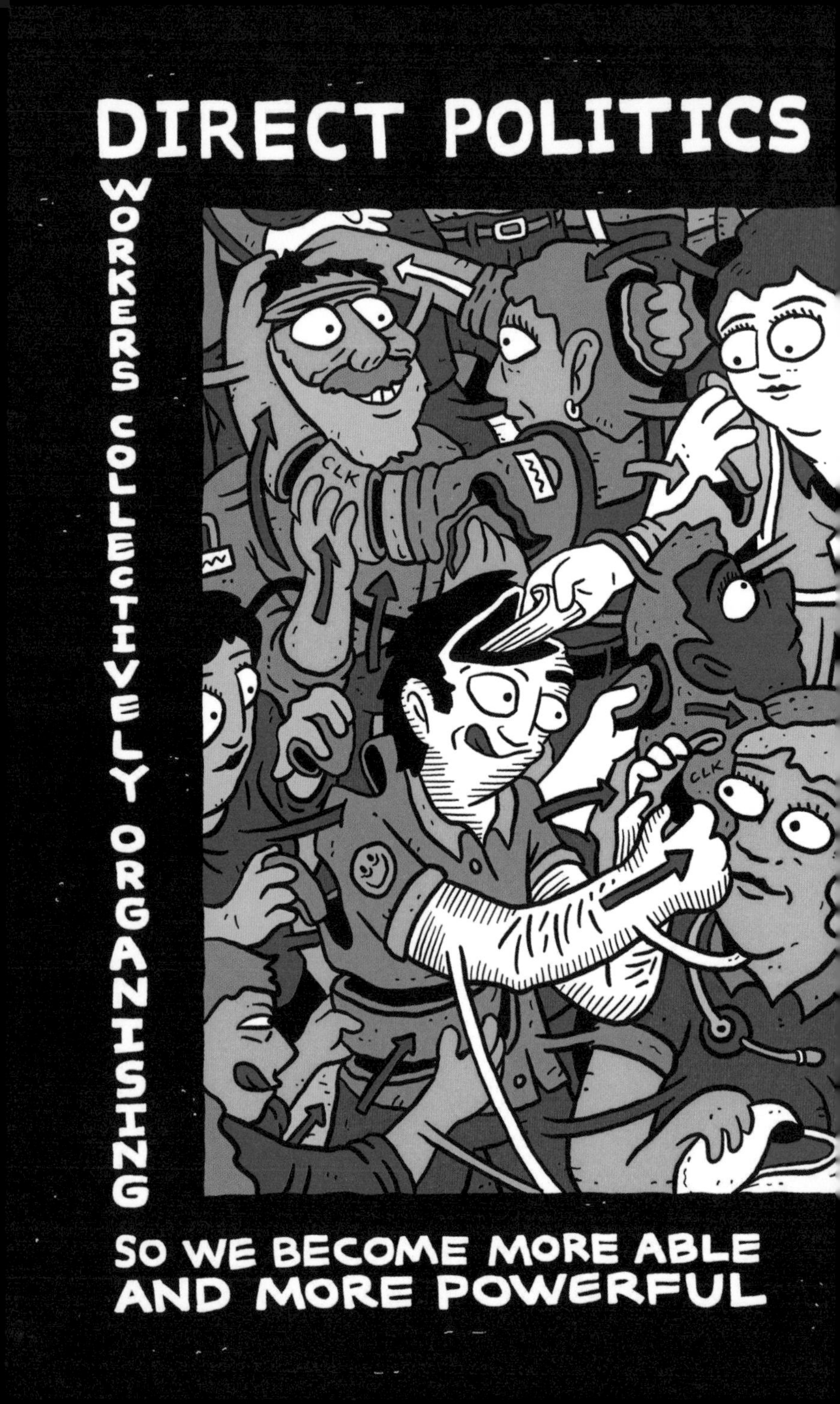
CLK
CLK

SO WE BECOME MORE ABLE
AND MORE POWERFUL

MEANS TAKING PART:

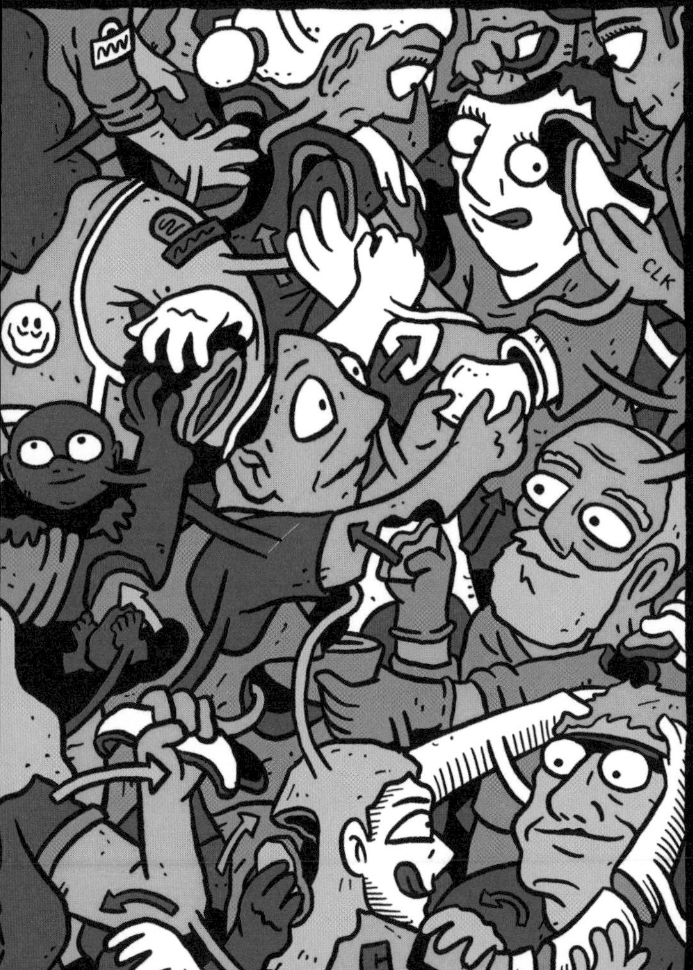

WORKERS COLLECTIVELY ORGANISING

AS WE REMAKE OURSELVES AND THE WORLD.

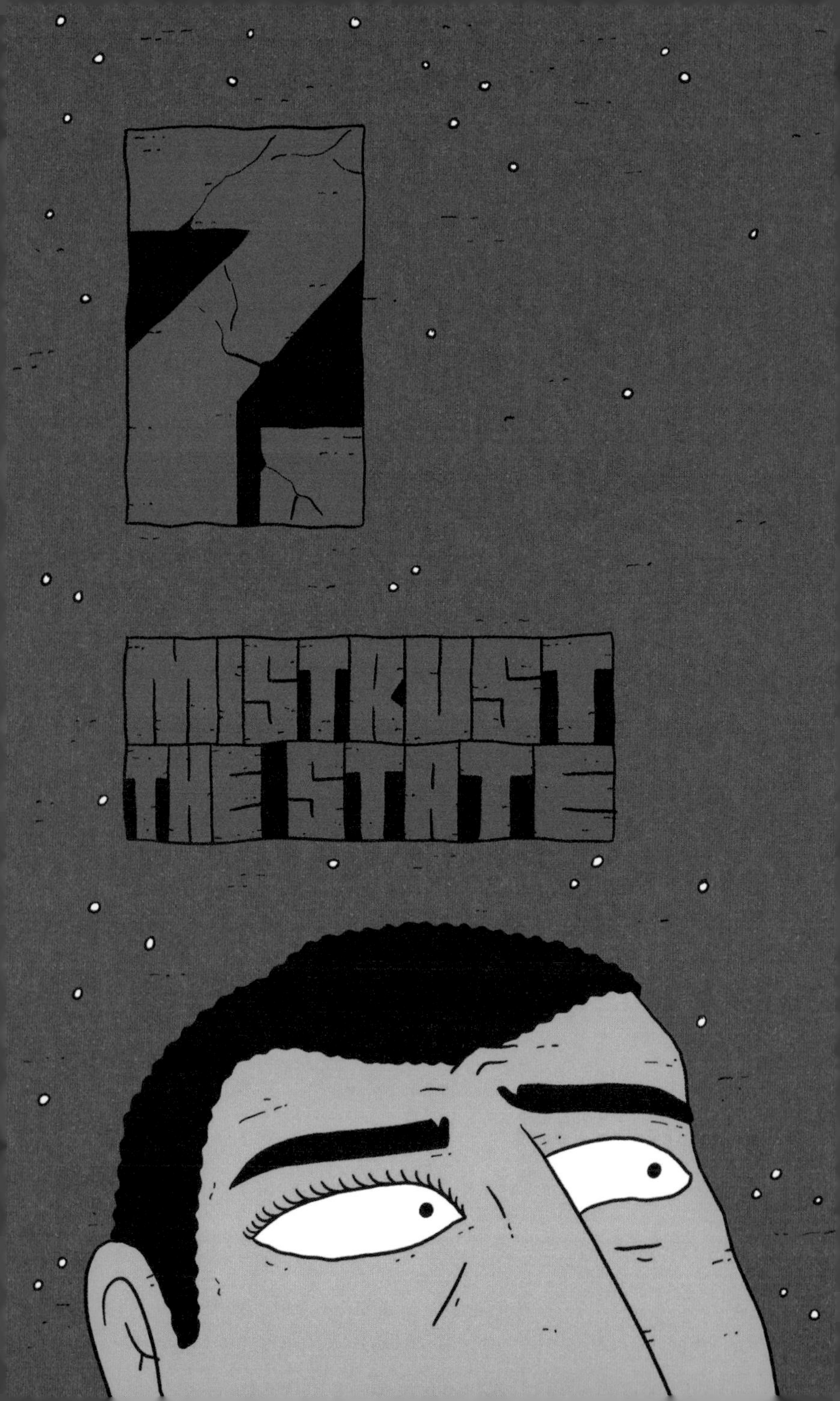
MISTRUST THE STATE

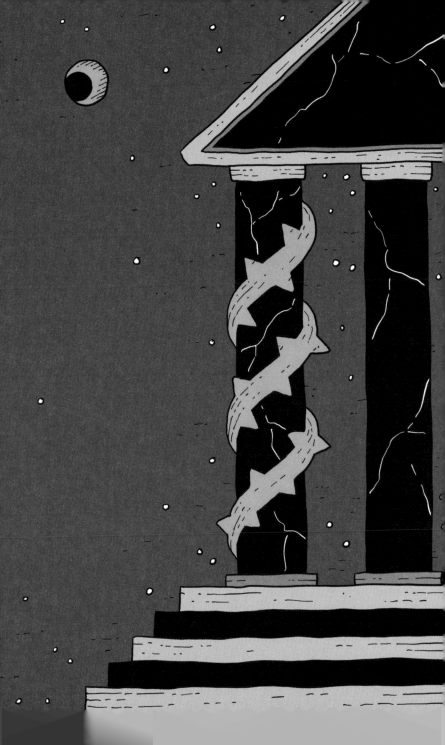

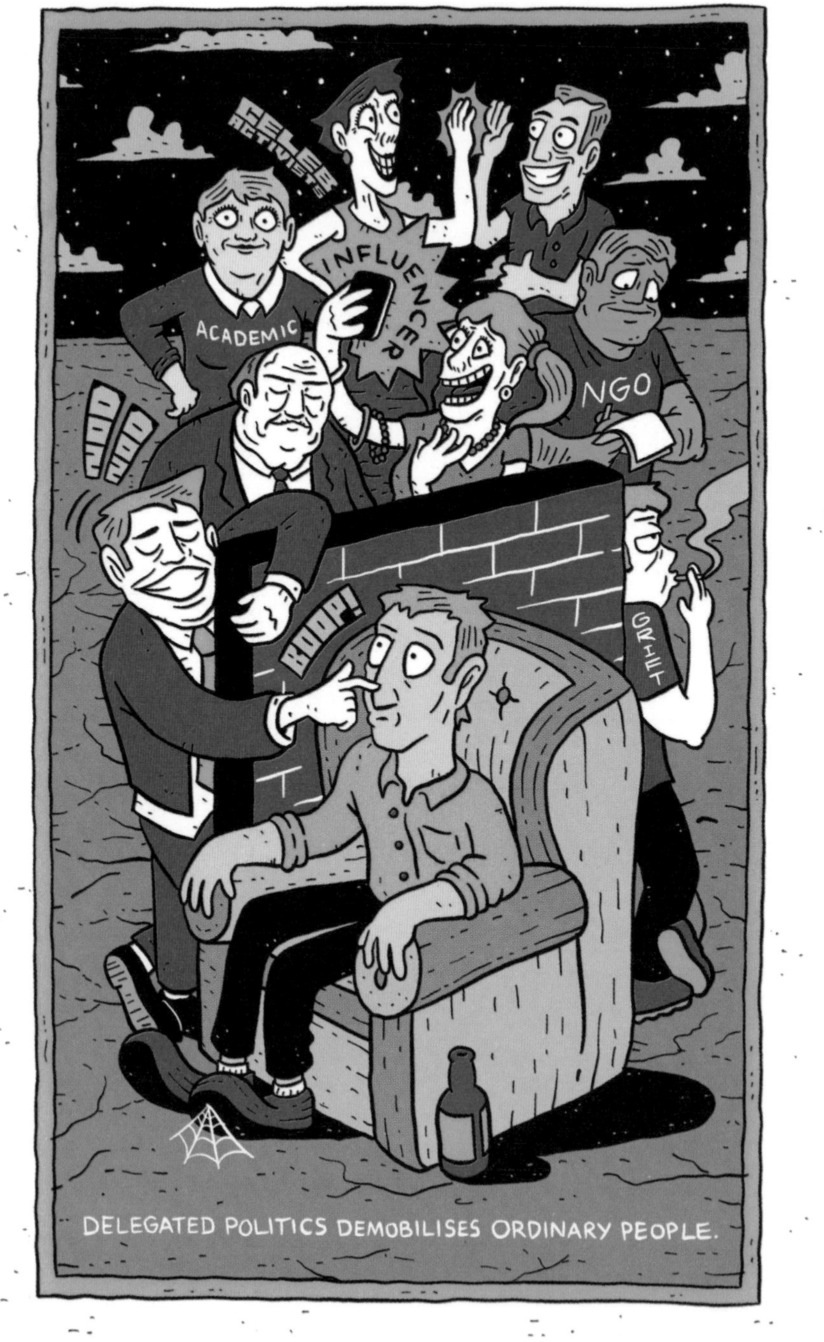
CELEB ACTIVISTS
INFLUENCER
ACADEMIC
NGO
NOD NOD
BOOP!
GRIET
DELEGATED POLITICS DEMOBILISES ORDINARY PEOPLE.

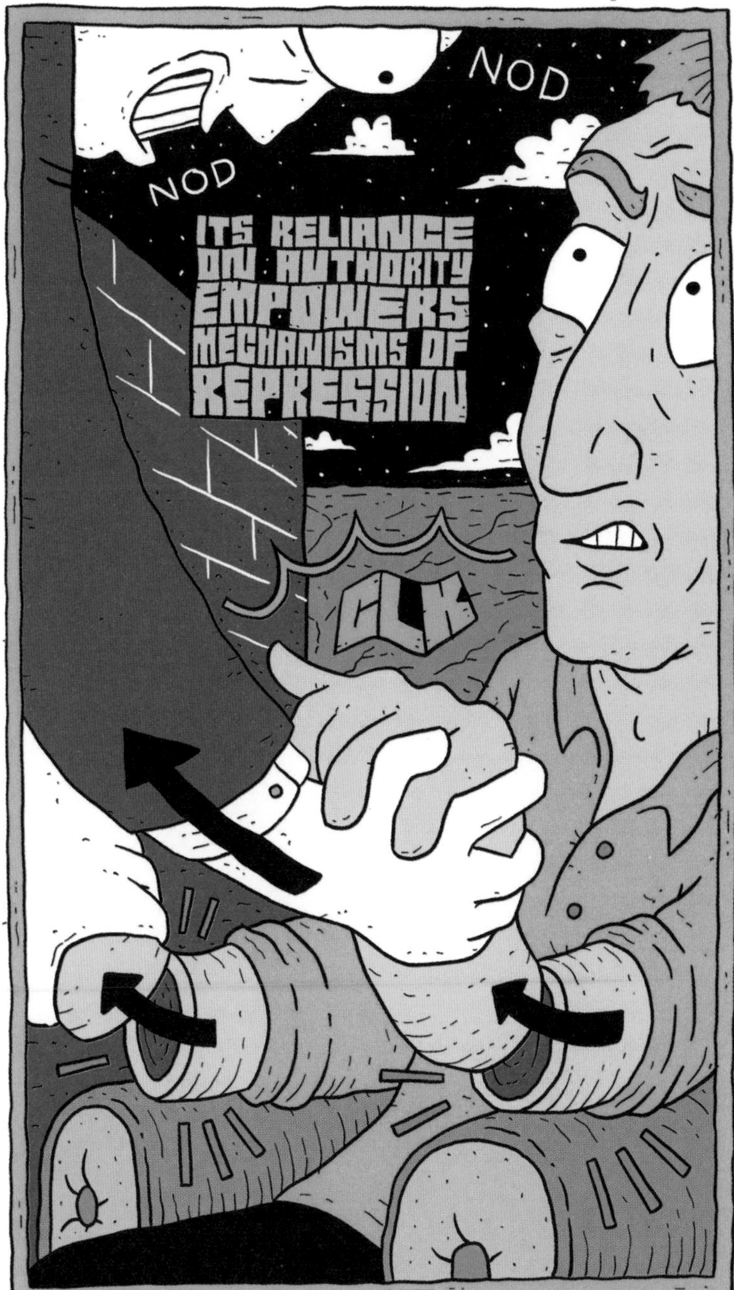

NOD
NOD
ITS RELIANCE ON AUTHORITY EMPOWERS MECHANISMS OF REPRESSION
CLK

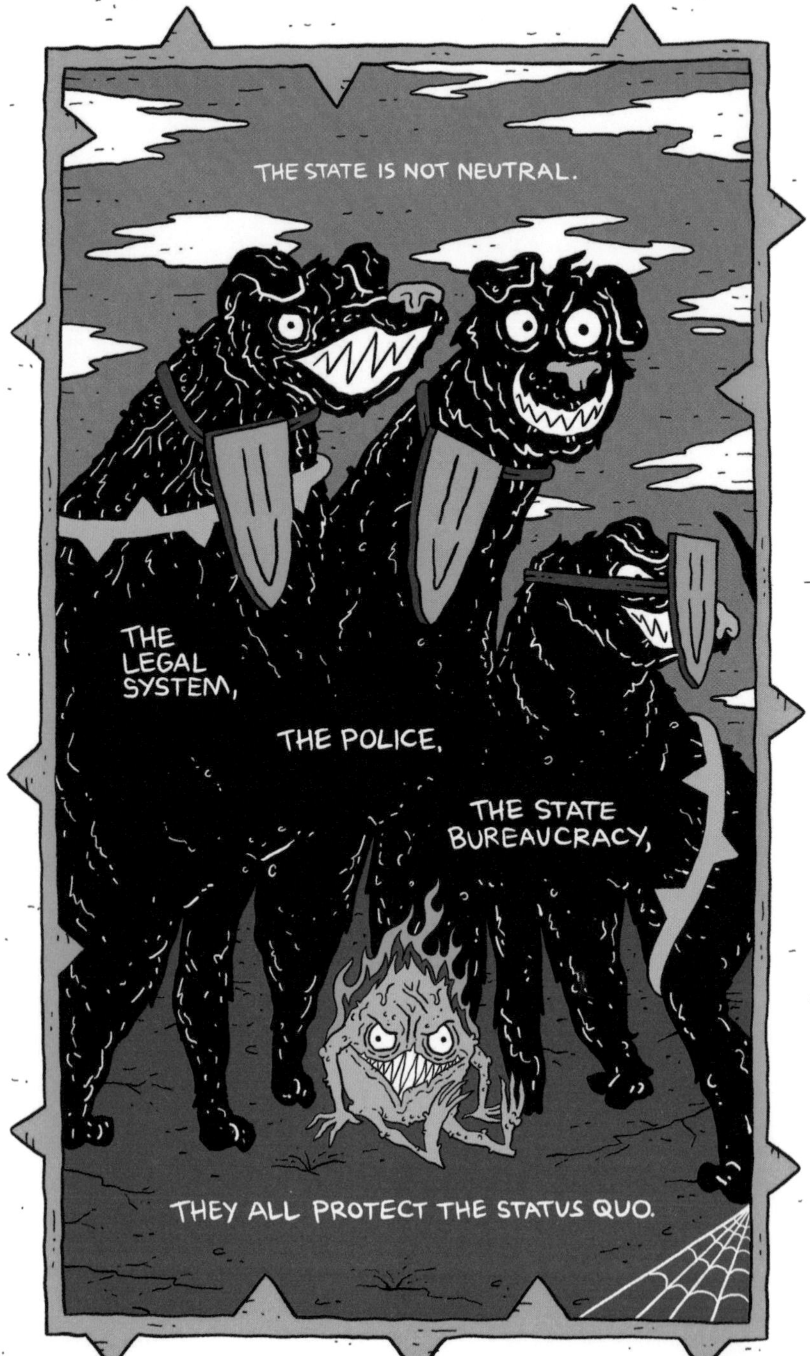
THE STATE IS NOT NEUTRAL.
THE LEGAL SYSTEM,
THE POLICE,
THE STATE BUREAUCRACY,
THEY ALL PROTECT THE STATUS QUO.

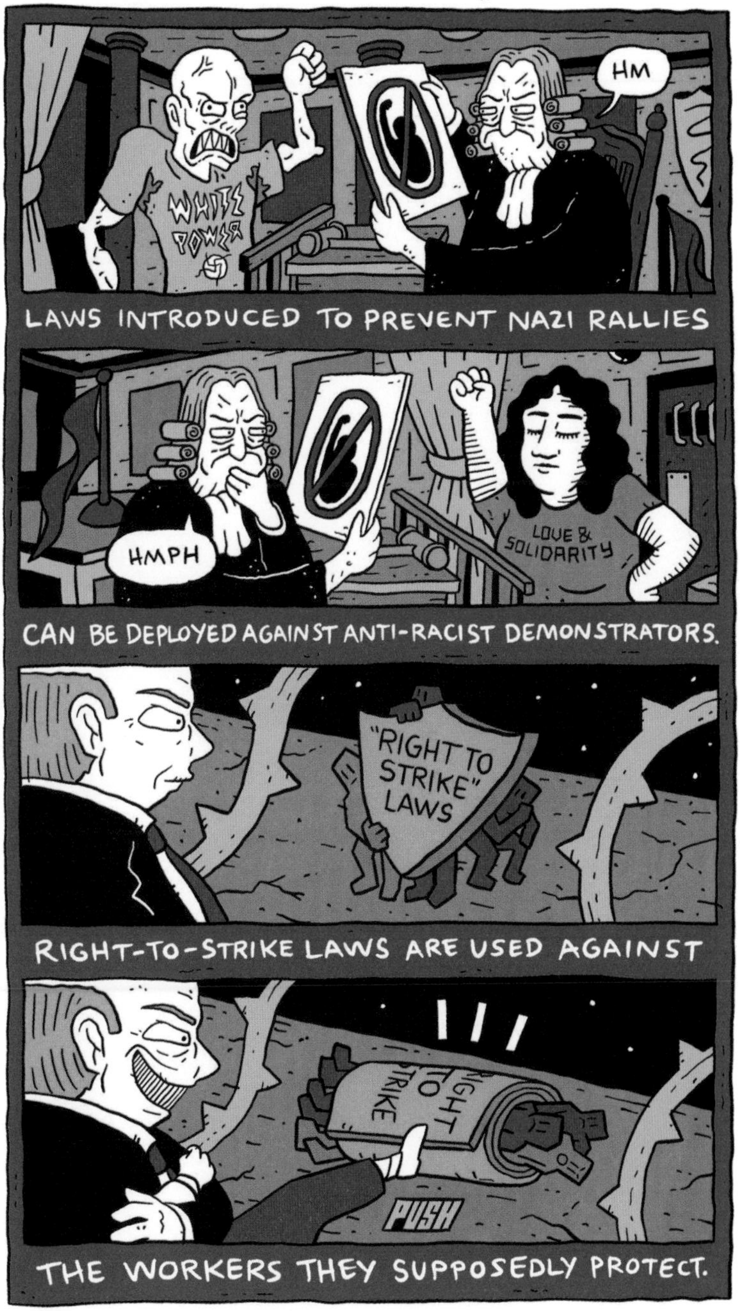
WHITE POWER
HM
LAWS INTRODUCED TO PREVENT NAZI RALLIES
HMPH
LOVE & SOLIDARITY
CAN BE DEPLOYED AGAINST ANTI-RACIST DEMONSTRATORS.
"RIGHT TO STRIKE" LAWS
RIGHT-TO-STRIKE LAWS ARE USED AGAINST
RIGHT TO STRIKE
PUSH
THE WORKERS THEY SUPPOSEDLY PROTECT.

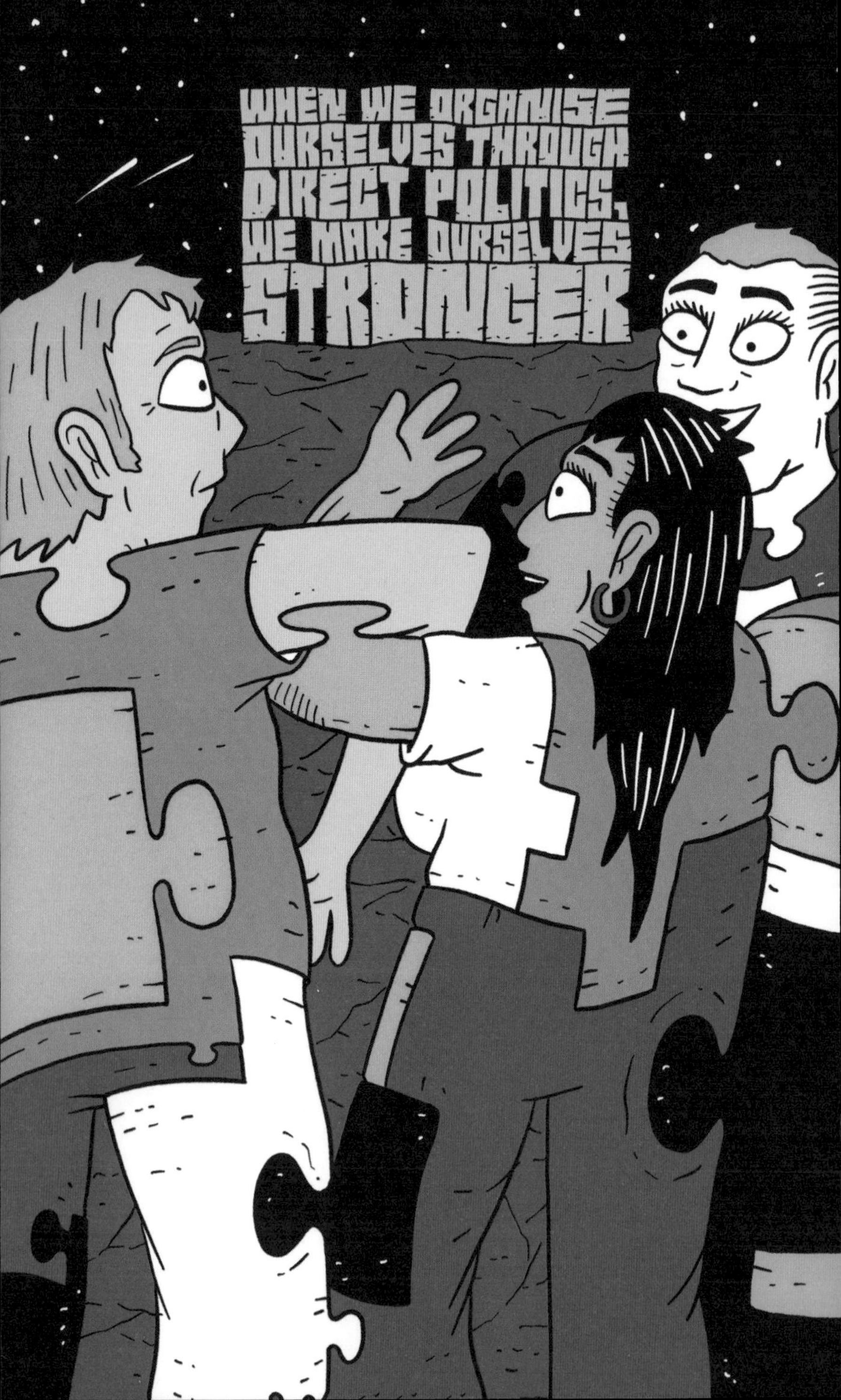
WHEN WE ORGANISE OURSELVES THROUGH DIRECT POLITICS, WE MAKE OURSELVES STRONGER

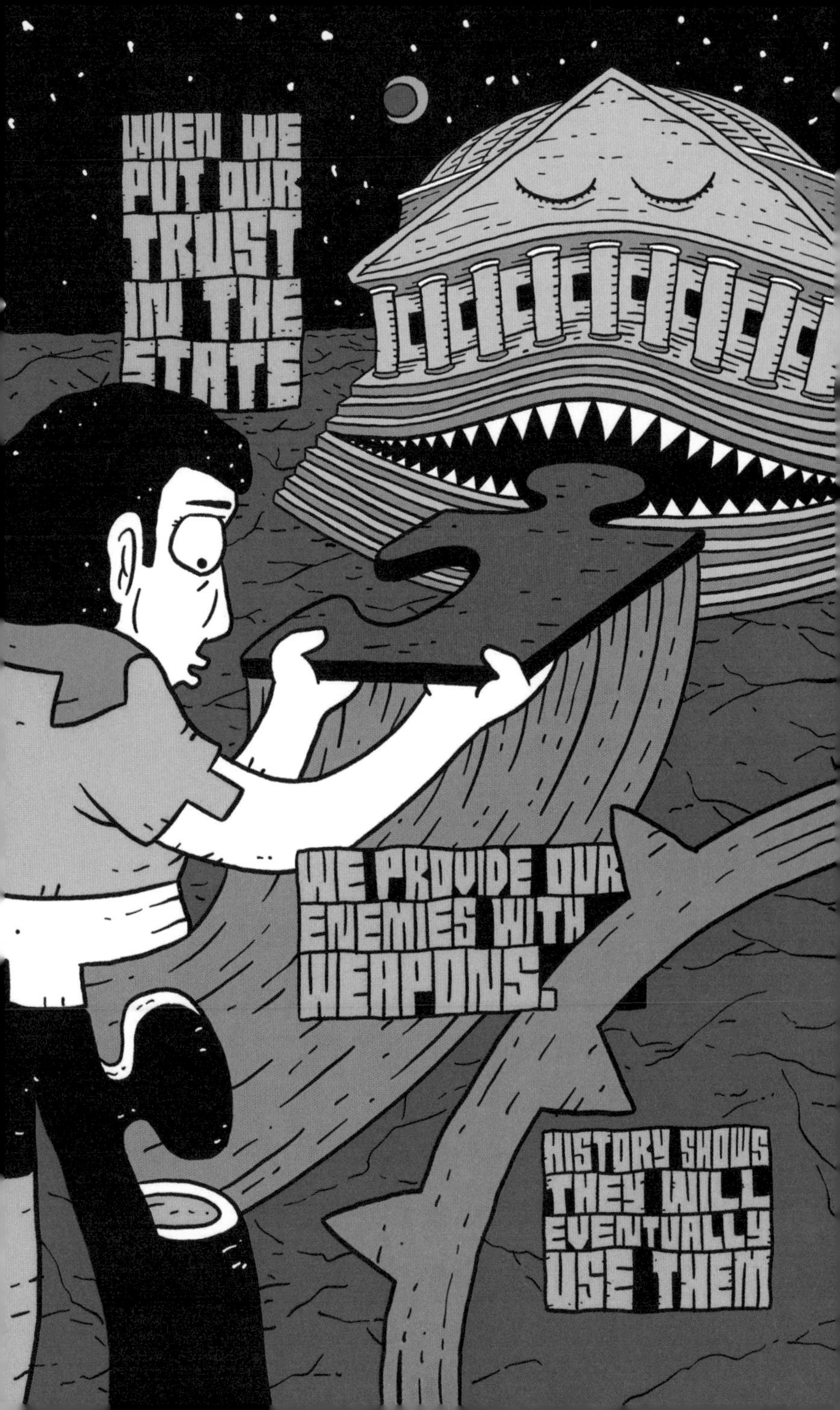
WHEN WE PUT OUR TRUST IN THE STATE
WE PROVIDE OUR ENEMIES WITH WEAPONS.
HISTORY SHOWS THEY WILL EVENTUALLY USE THEM

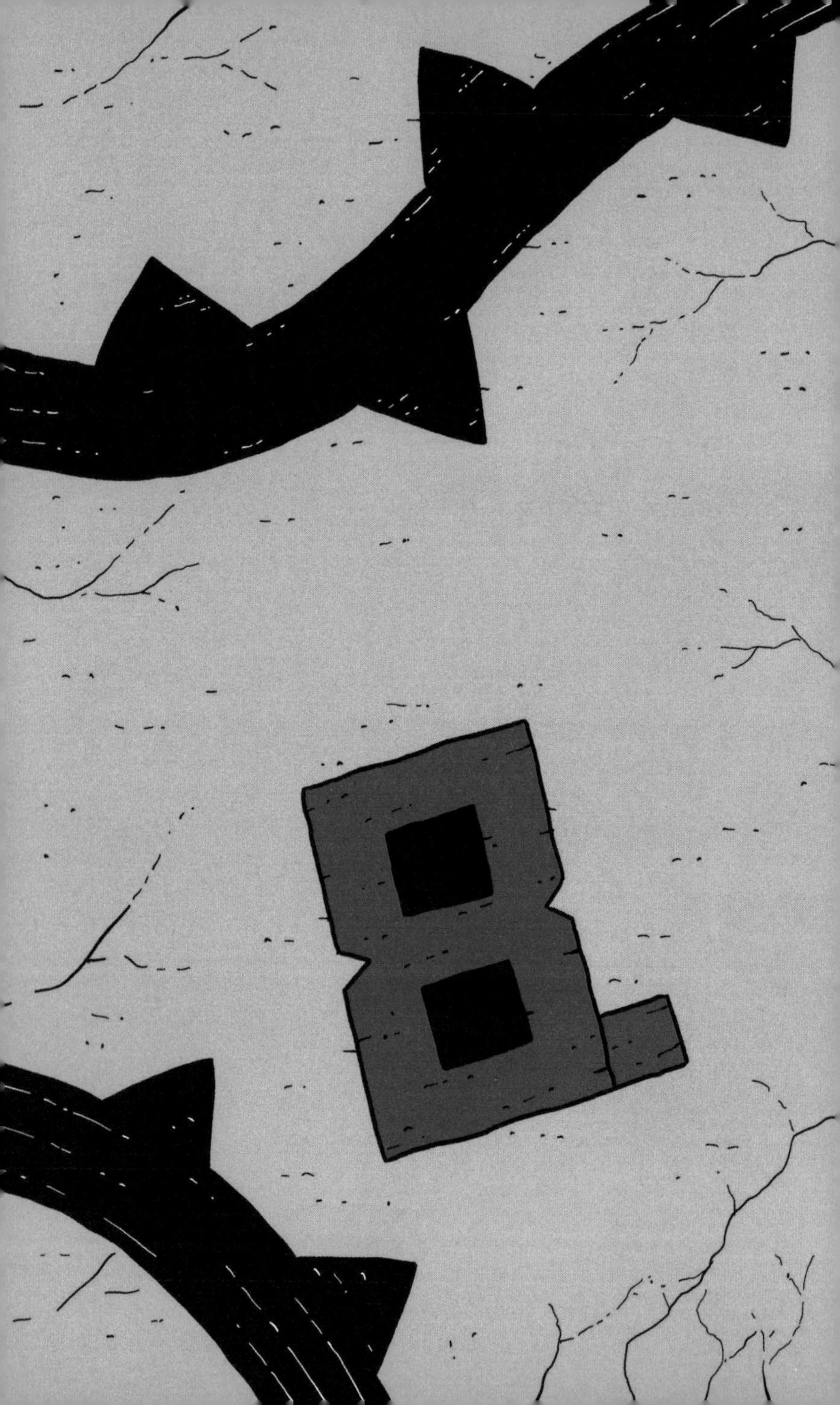
8

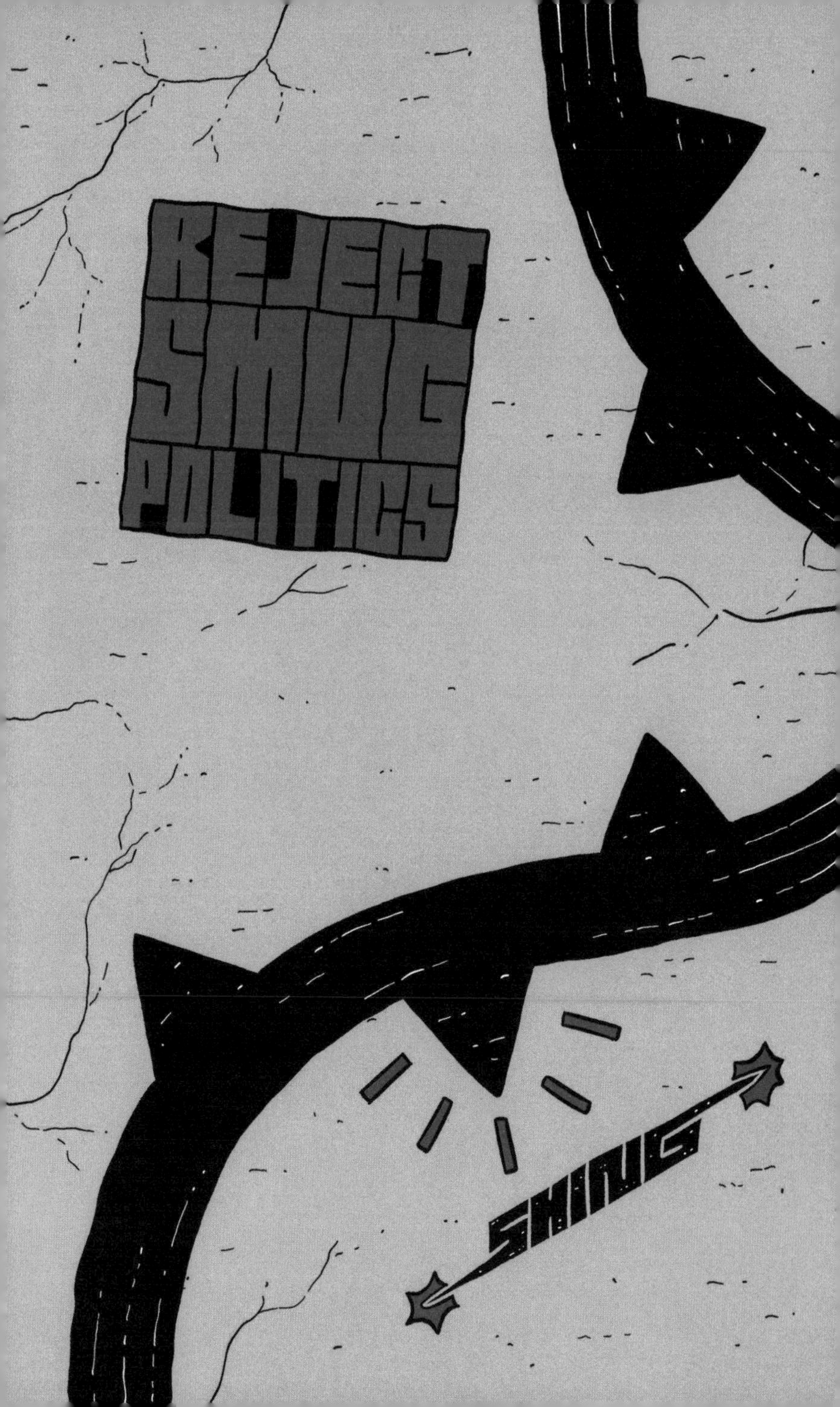
REJECT SMUG POLITICS
SHING

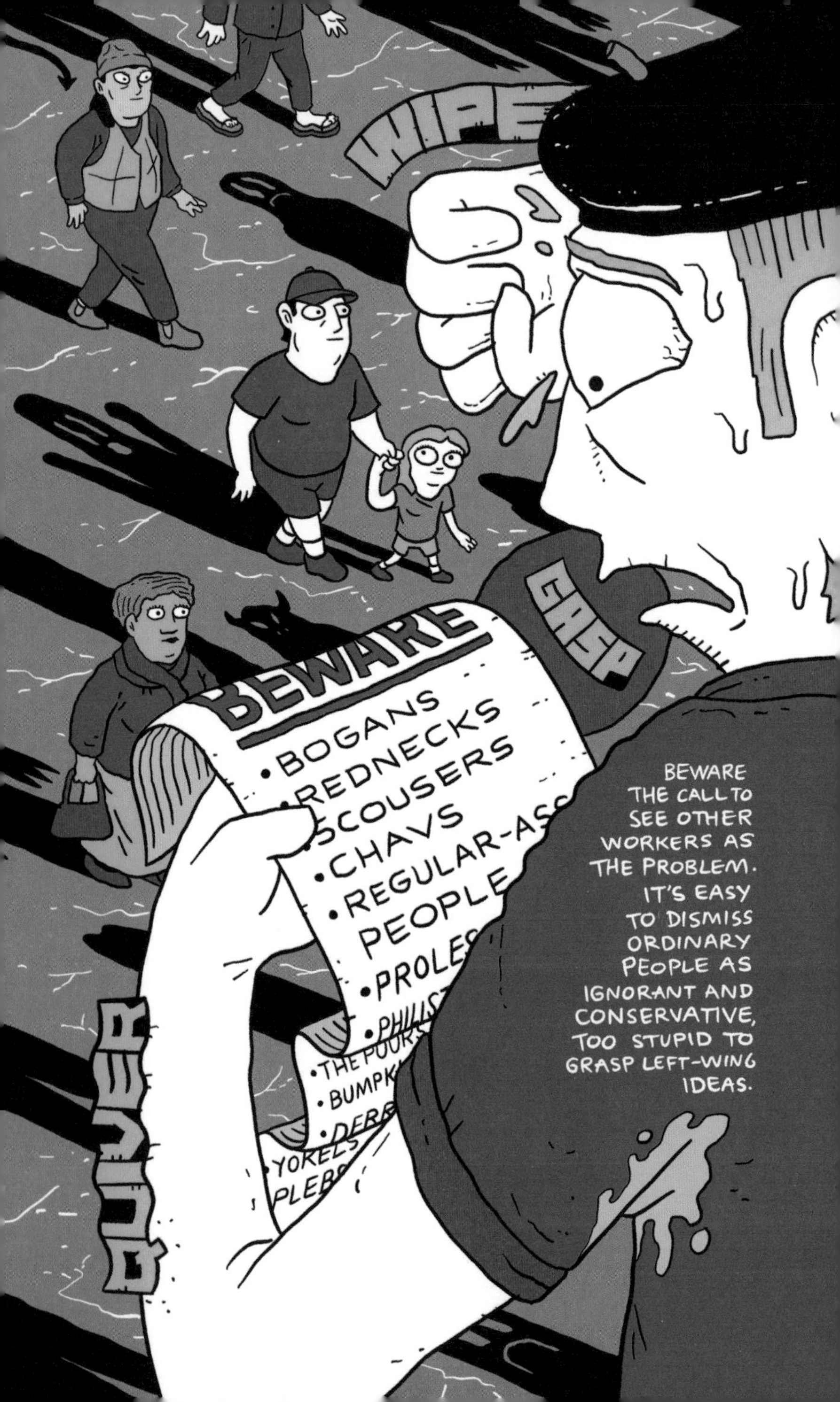

WIPE
GRASP
BEWARE
• BOGANS
• REDNECKS
• SCOUSERS
• CHAVS
• REGULAR-ASS PEOPLE
• PROLES
QUIVER
BEWARE THE CALL TO SEE OTHER WORKERS AS THE PROBLEM. IT'S EASY TO DISMISS ORDINARY PEOPLE AS IGNORANT AND CONSERVATIVE, TOO STUPID TO GRASP LEFT-WING IDEAS.

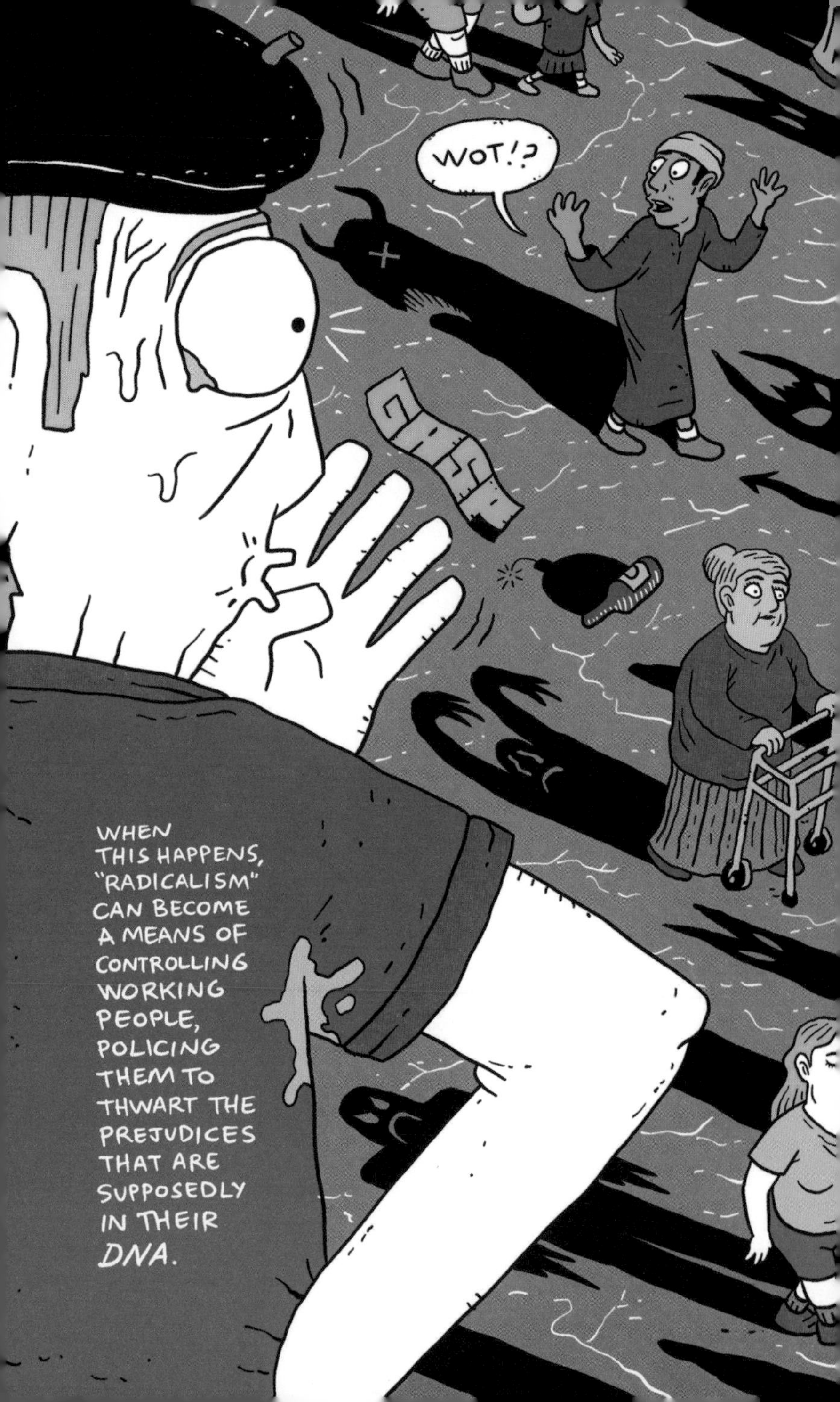
WOT!?
GASP
WHEN THIS HAPPENS, "RADICALISM" CAN BECOME A MEANS OF CONTROLLING WORKING PEOPLE, POLICING THEM TO THWART THE PREJUDICES THAT ARE SUPPOSEDLY IN THEIR *DNA*.

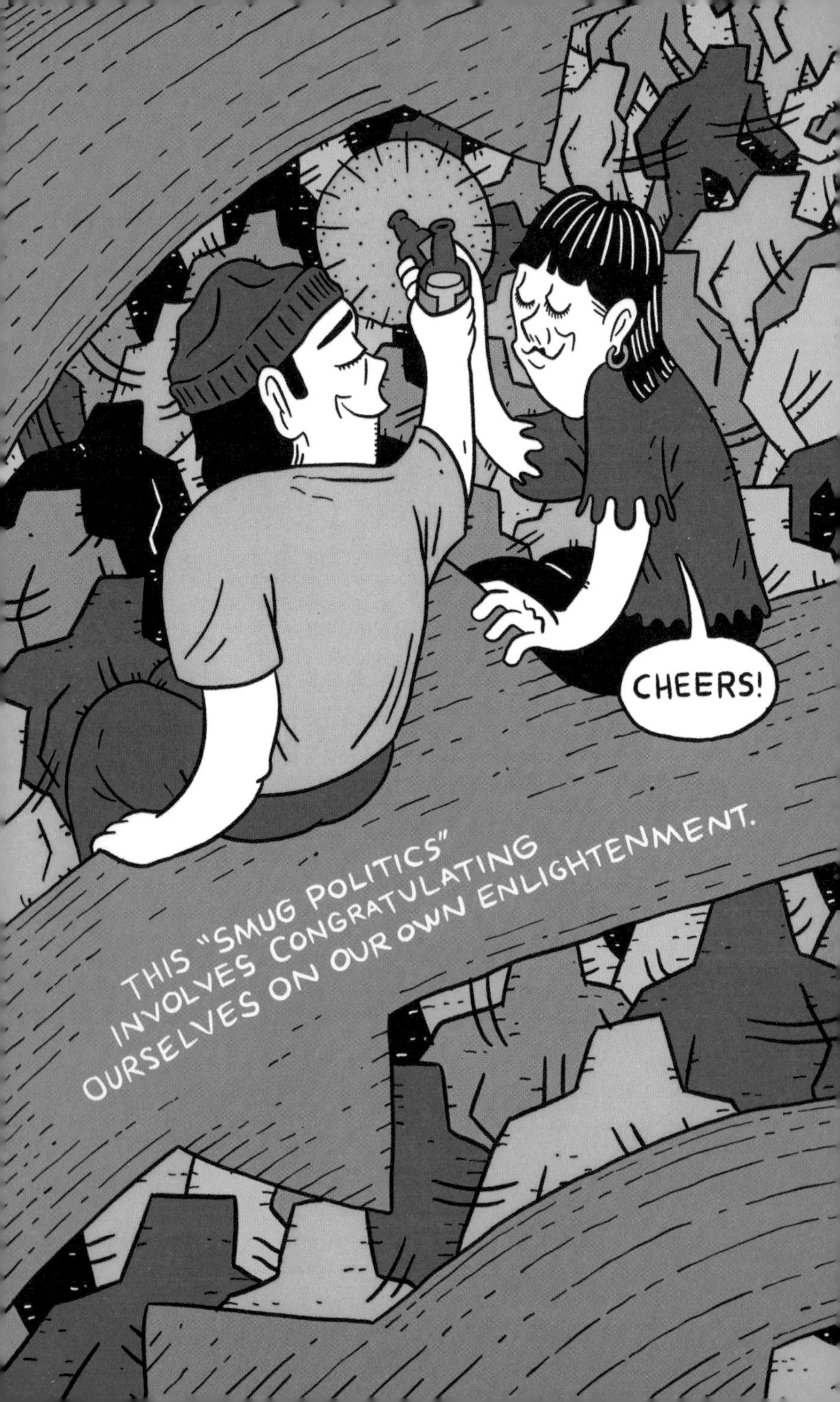
CHEERS!
THIS "SMUG POLITICS" INVOLVES CONGRATULATING OURSELVES ON OUR OWN ENLIGHTENMENT.

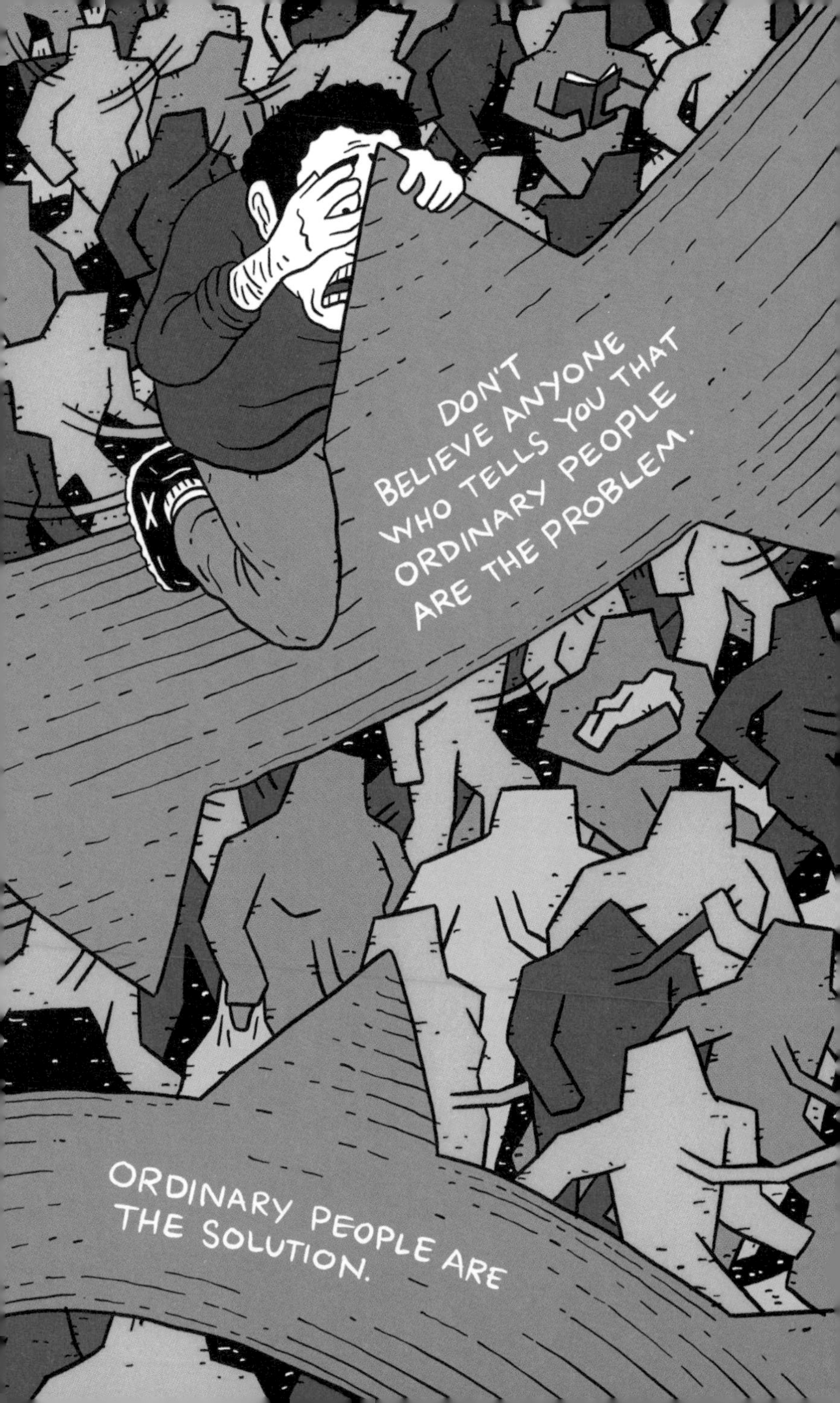

DON'T BELIEVE ANYONE WHO TELLS YOU THAT ORDINARY PEOPLE ARE THE PROBLEM.
ORDINARY PEOPLE ARE THE SOLUTION.

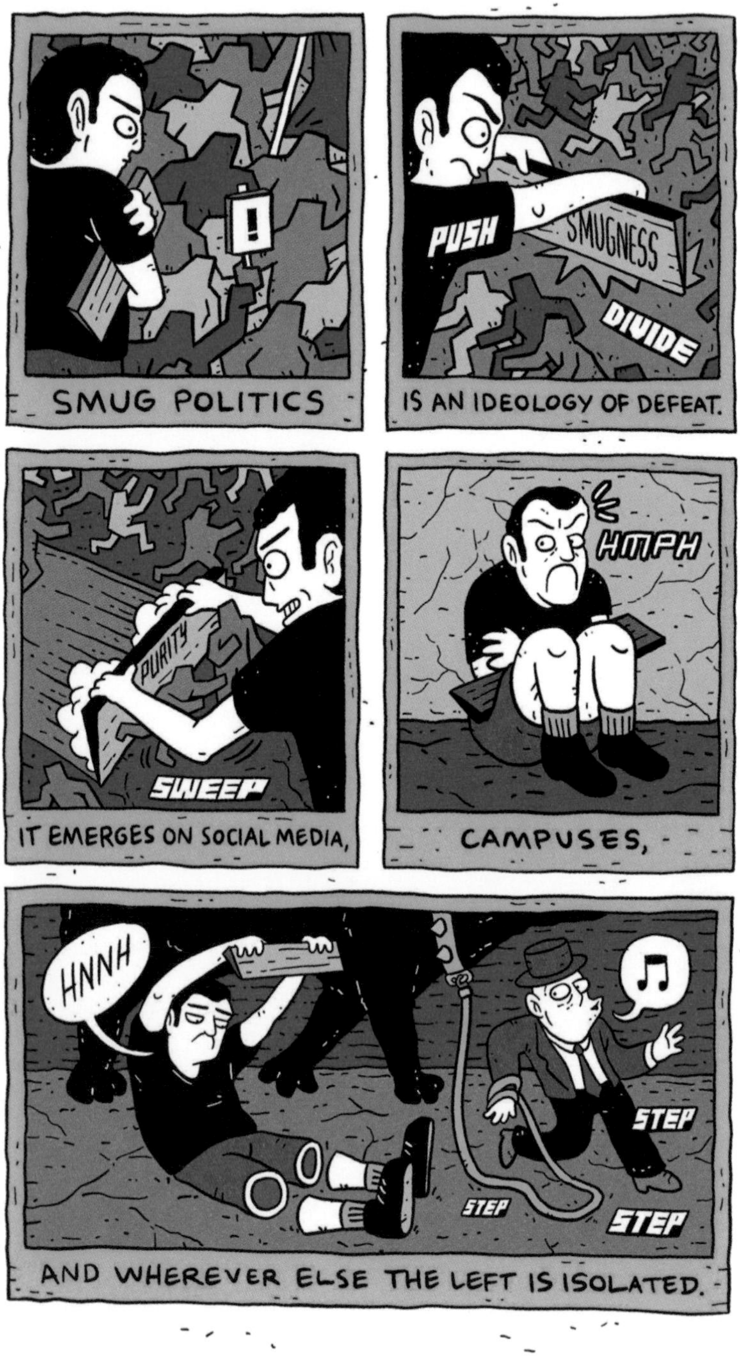
SMUG POLITICS
PUSH
SMUGNESS
DIVIDE
IS AN IDEOLOGY OF DEFEAT.
PURITY
SWEEP
IT EMERGES ON SOCIAL MEDIA,
HMPH
CAMPUSES,
HNNH
STEP
STEP
STEP
AND WHEREVER ELSE THE LEFT IS ISOLATED.

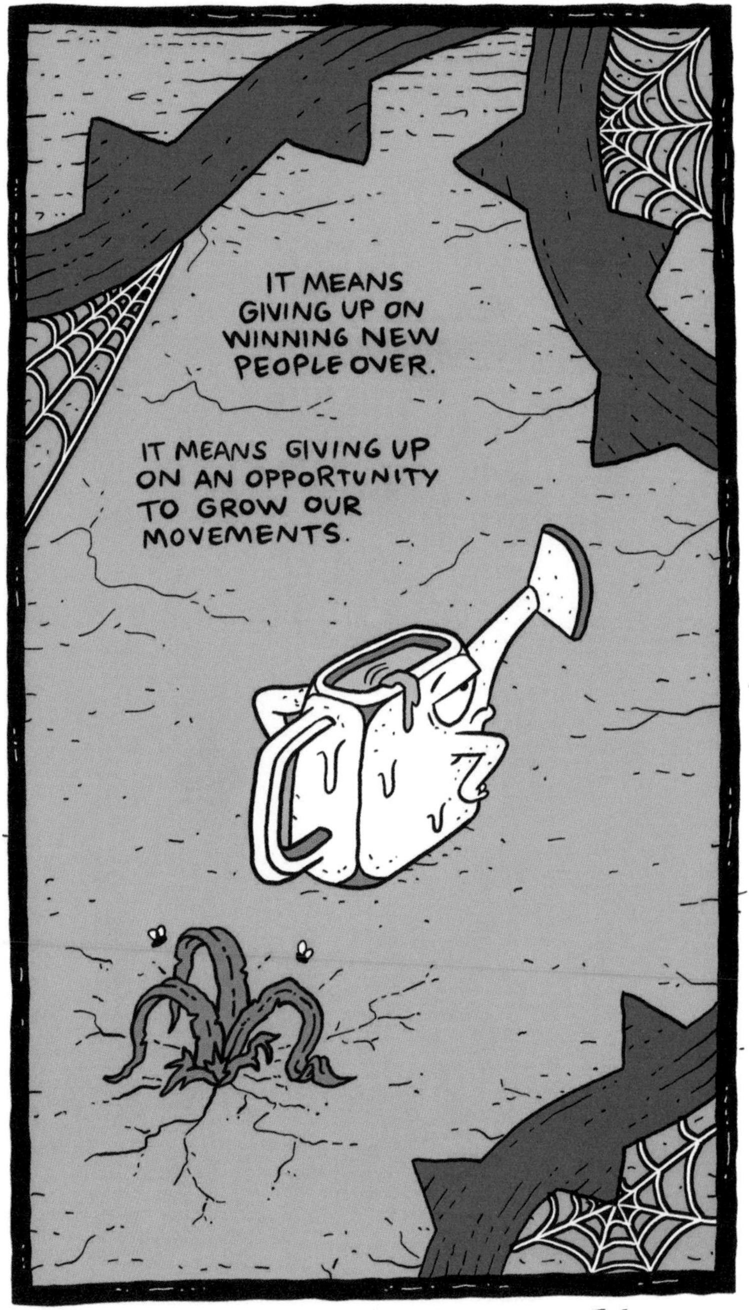
IT MEANS GIVING UP ON WINNING NEW PEOPLE OVER.
IT MEANS GIVING UP ON AN OPPORTUNITY TO GROW OUR MOVEMENTS.

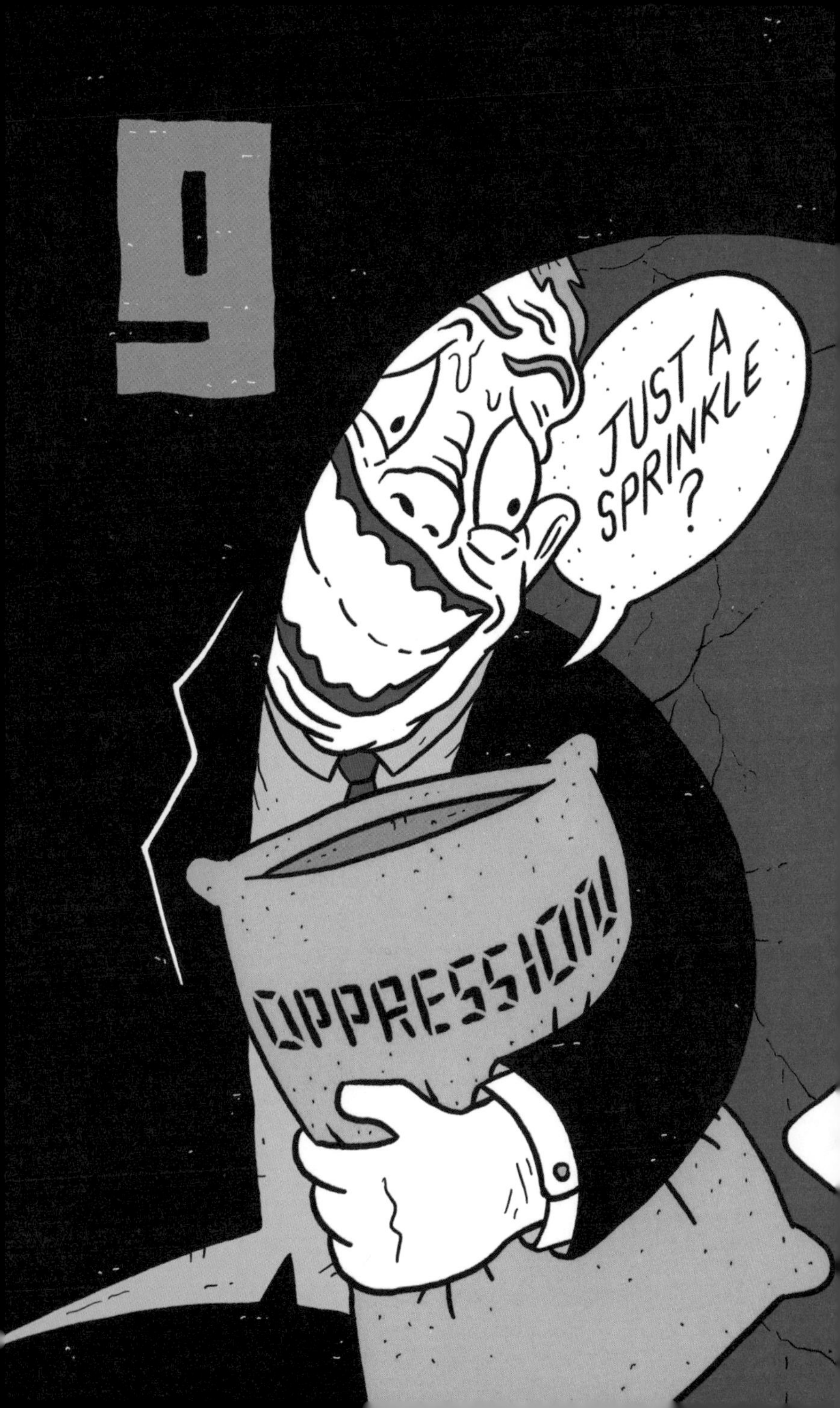
JUST A SPRINKLE ?
OPPRESSION

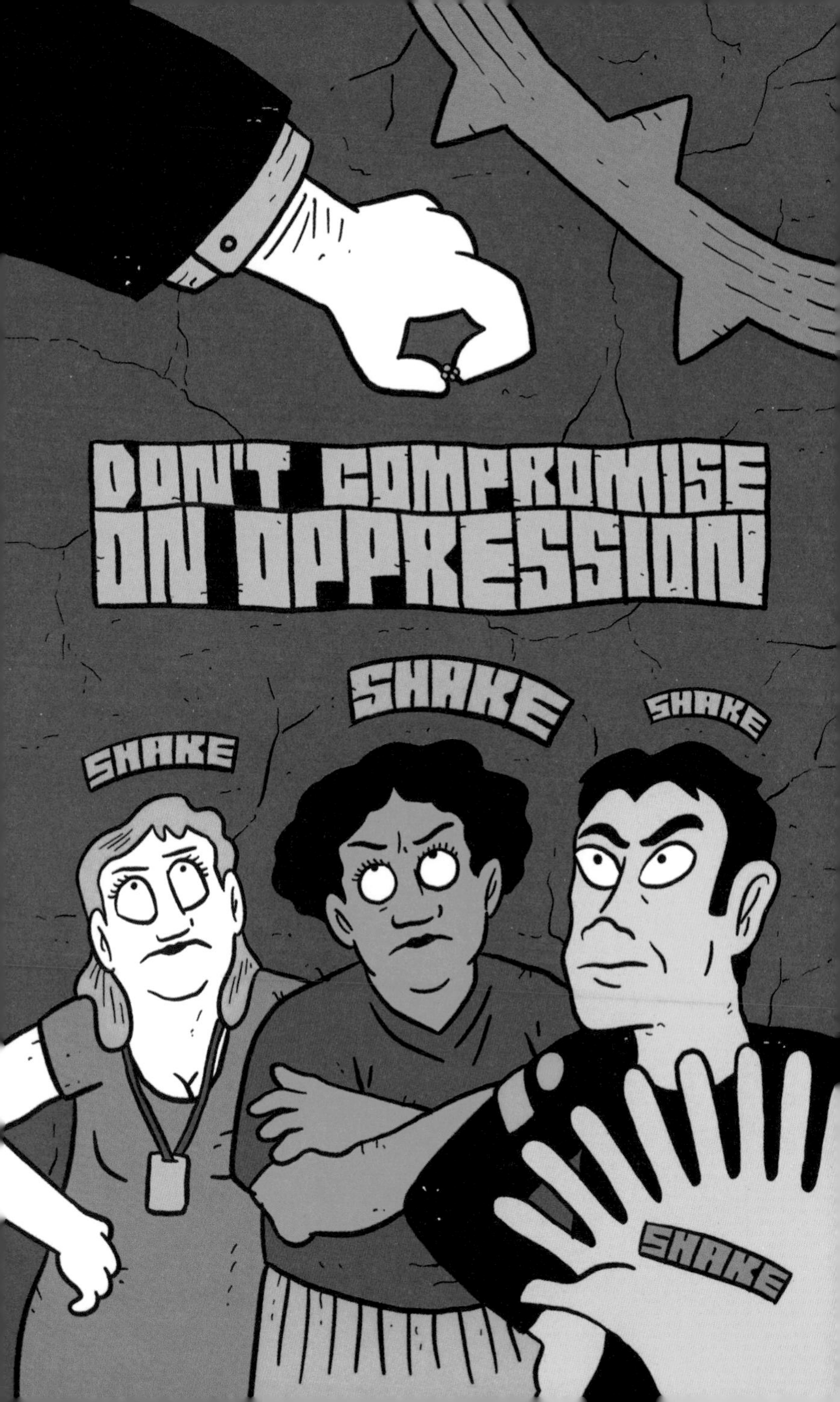
DON'T COMPROMISE ON OPPRESSION
SHAKE
SHAKE
SHAKE
SHAKE

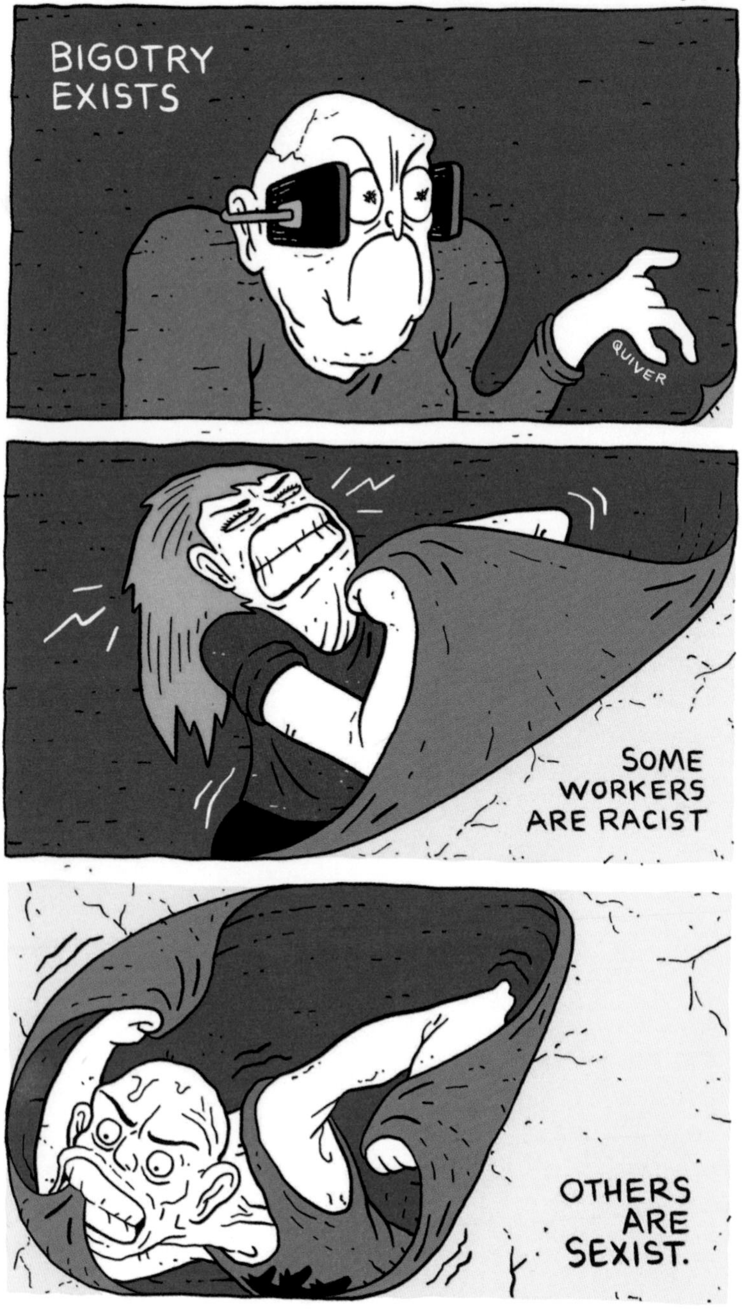

BIGOTRY EXISTS
QUIVER
SOME WORKERS ARE RACIST
OTHERS ARE SEXIST.

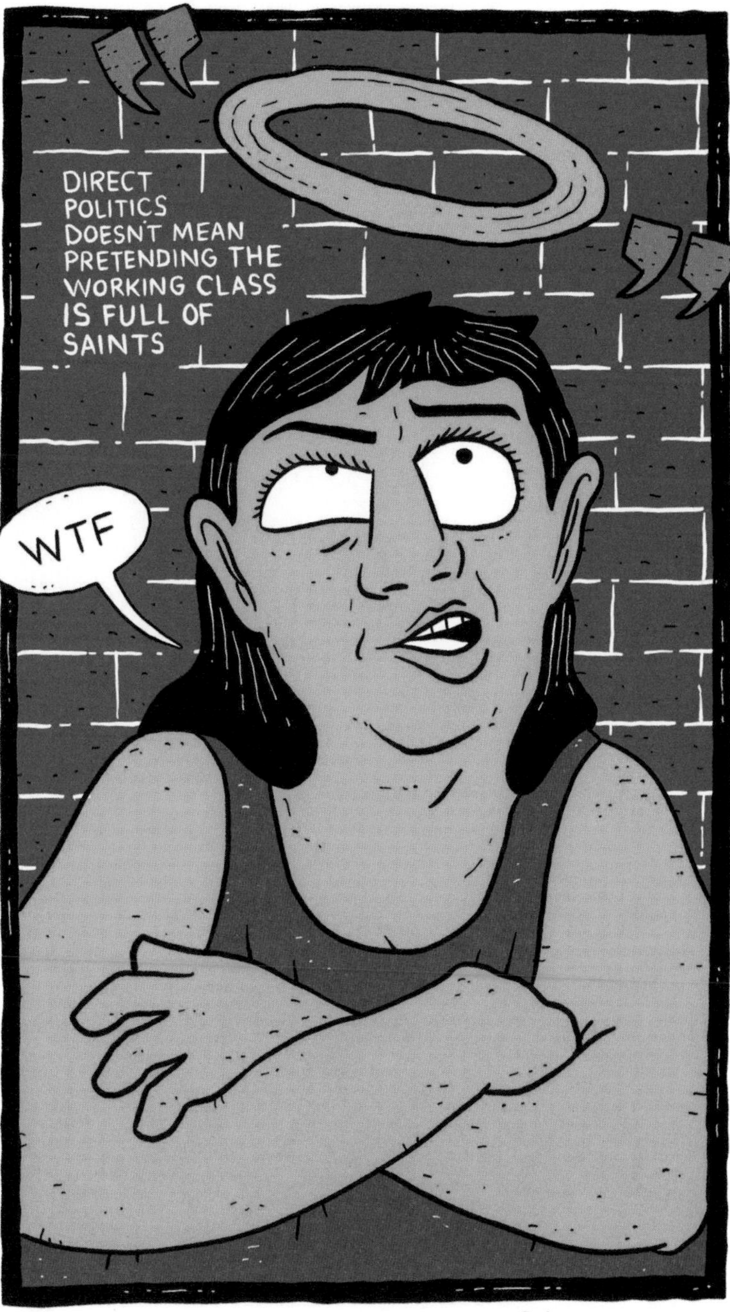
DIRECT POLITICS DOESN'T MEAN PRETENDING THE WORKING CLASS IS FULL OF SAINTS
WTF

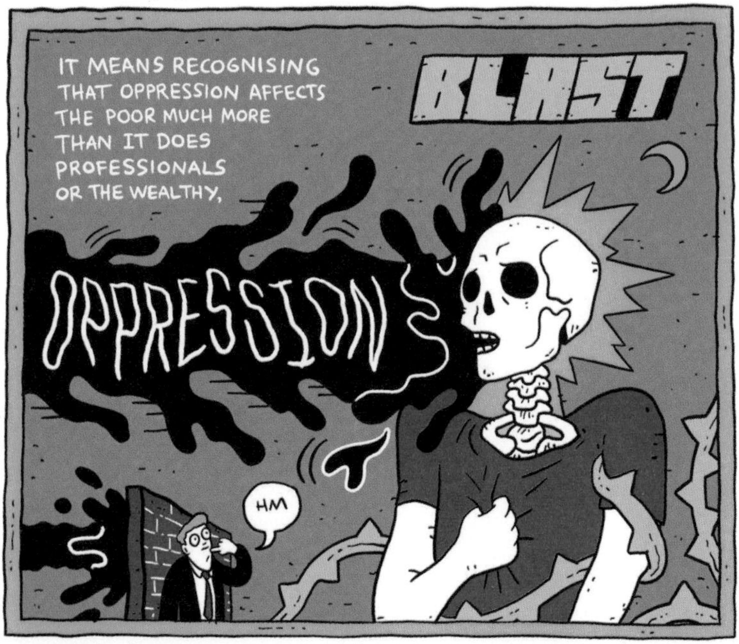
IT MEANS RECOGNISING THAT OPPRESSION AFFECTS THE POOR MUCH MORE THAN IT DOES PROFESSIONALS OR THE WEALTHY,
BLAST
OPPRESSION
HM

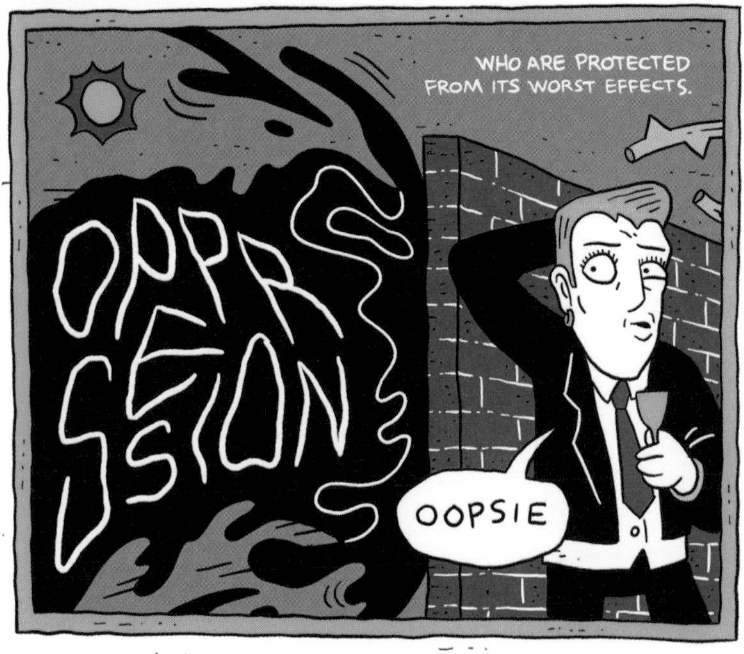
WHO ARE PROTECTED FROM ITS WORST EFFECTS.
OPPRESSION
OOPSIE

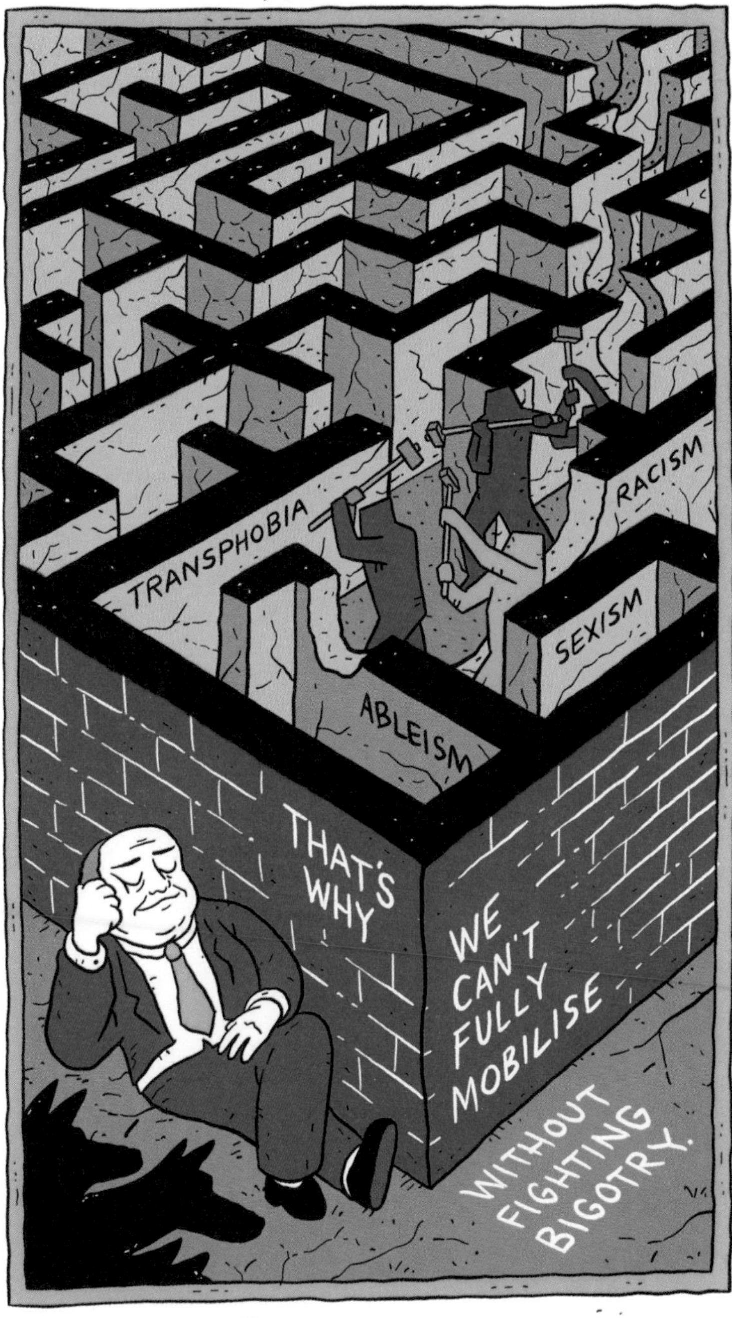
TRANSPHOBIA
RACISM
SEXISM
ABLEISM
THAT'S WHY
WE CAN'T FULLY MOBILISE
WITHOUT FIGHTING BIGOTRY.

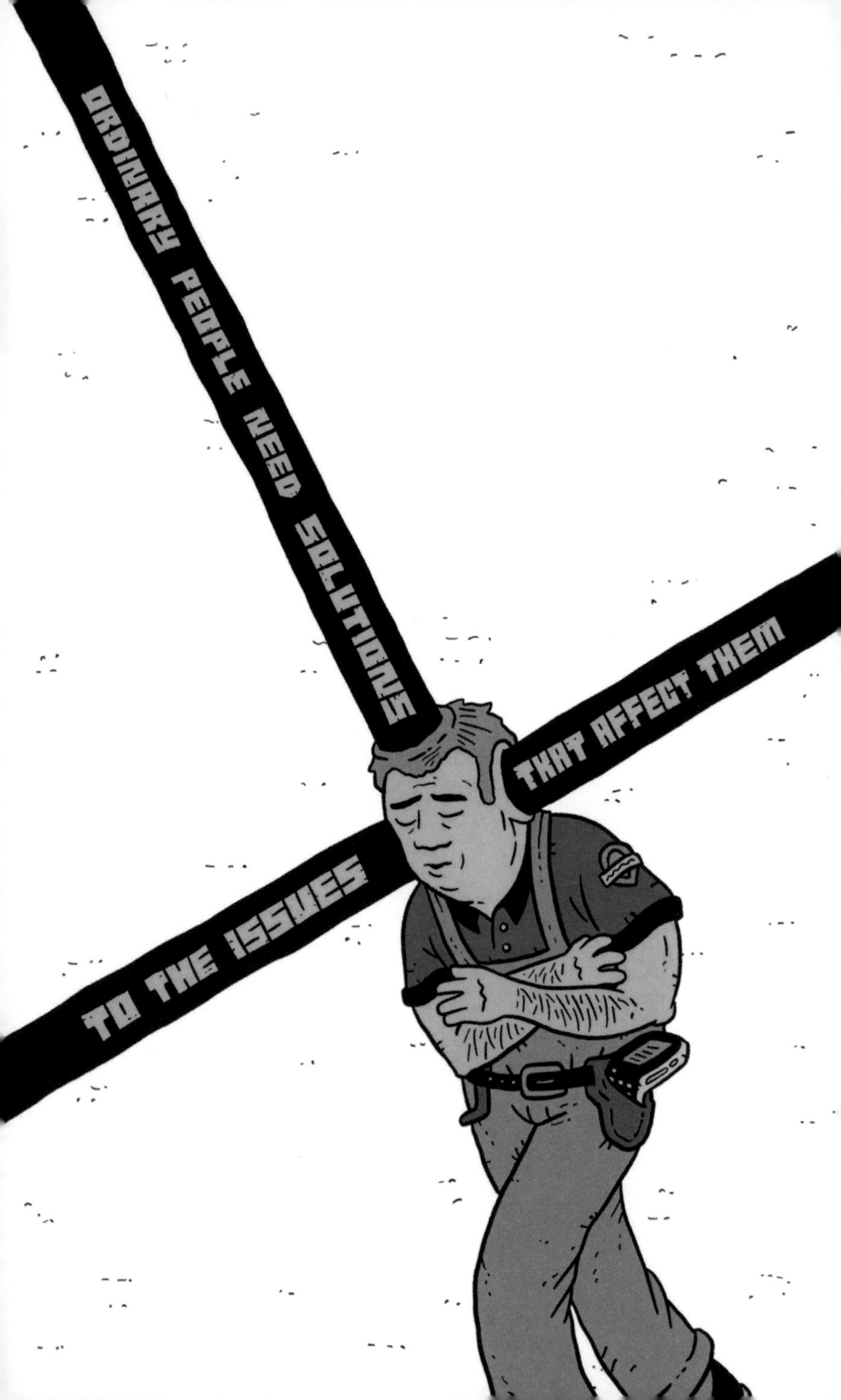
ORDINARY PEOPLE NEED SOLUTIONS
TO THE ISSUES
THAT AFFECT THEM

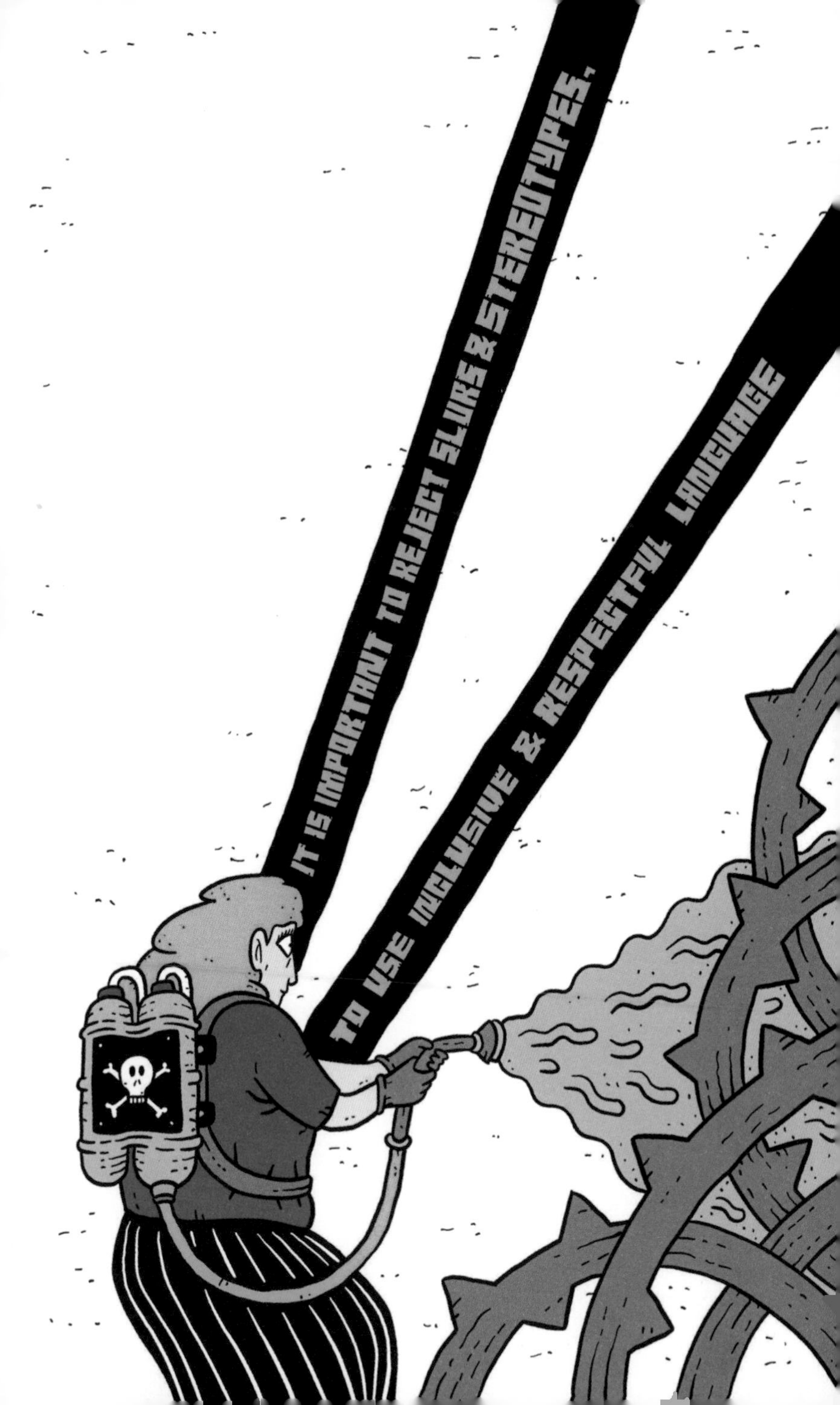
IT IS IMPORTANT TO REJECT SLURS & STEREOTYPES,
TO USE INCLUSIVE & RESPECTFUL LANGUAGE

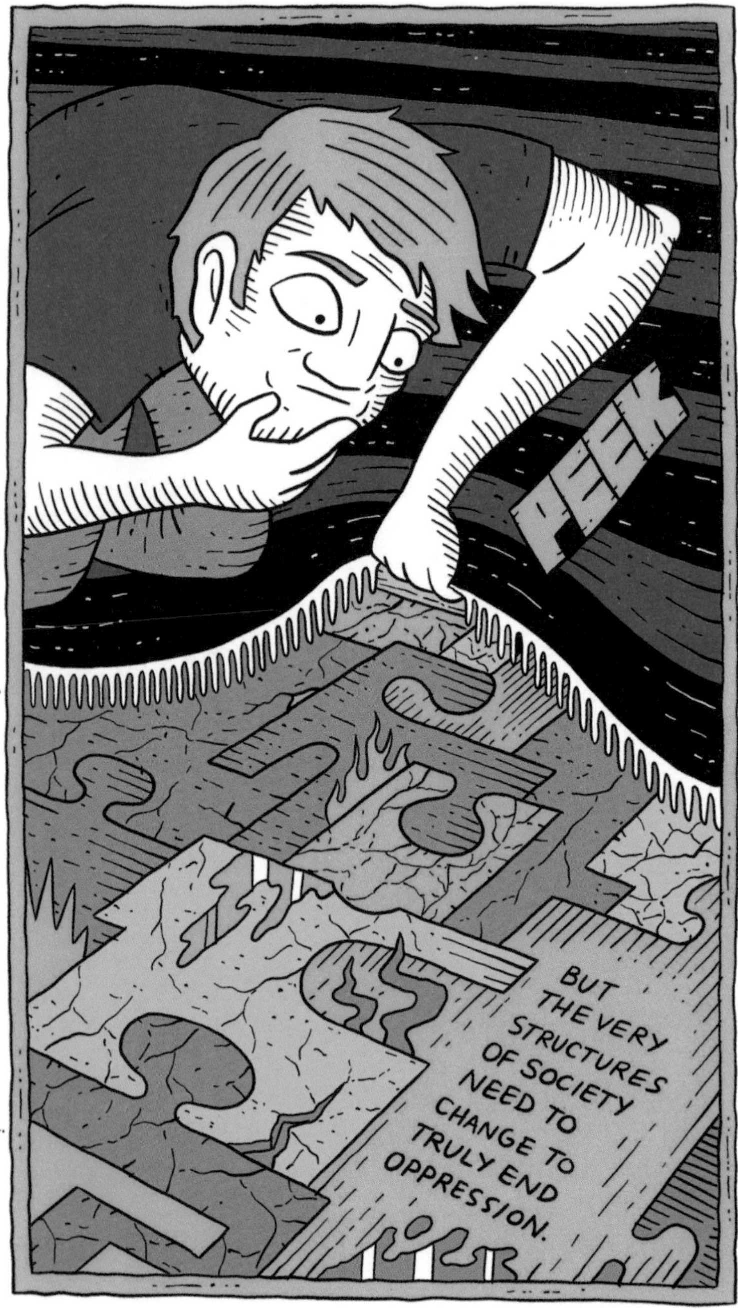
PEEK
BUT THE VERY STRUCTURES OF SOCIETY NEED TO CHANGE TO TRULY END OPPRESSION.

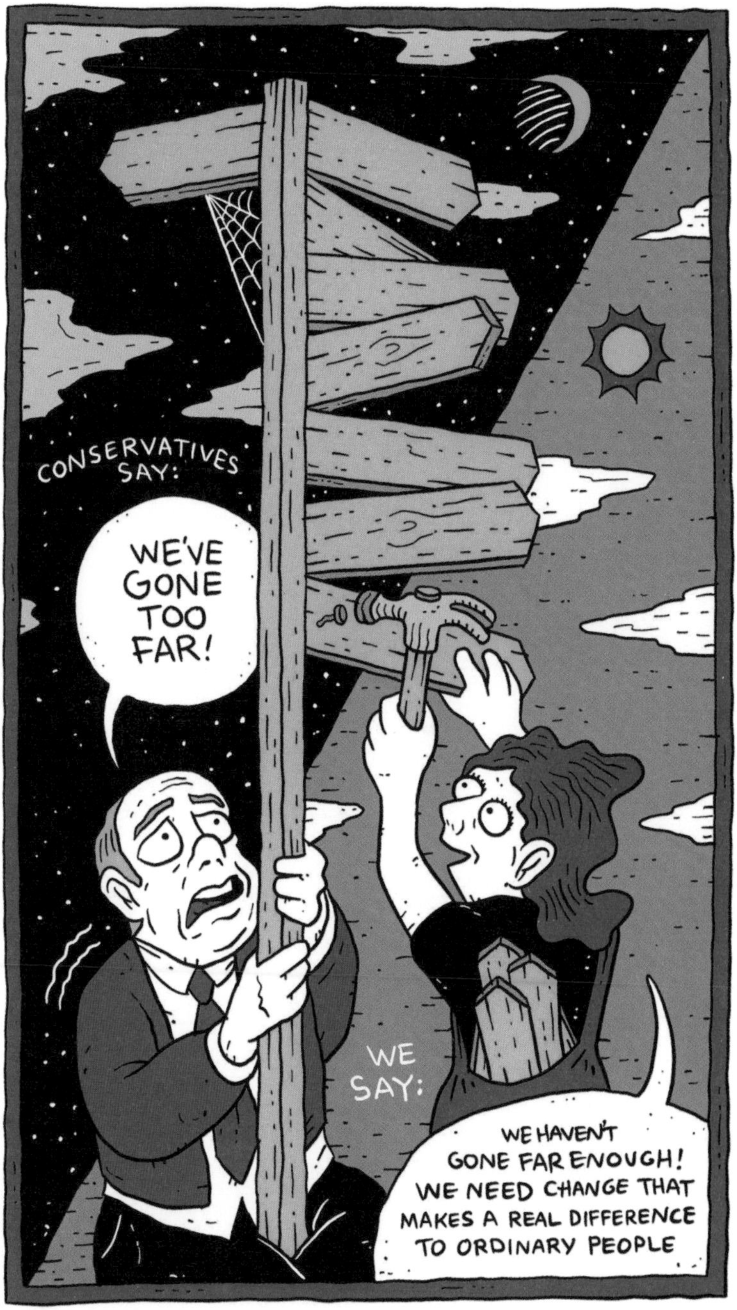

CONSERVATIVES SAY:
WE'VE GONE TOO FAR!
WE SAY:
WE HAVEN'T GONE FAR ENOUGH! WE NEED CHANGE THAT MAKES A REAL DIFFERENCE TO ORDINARY PEOPLE

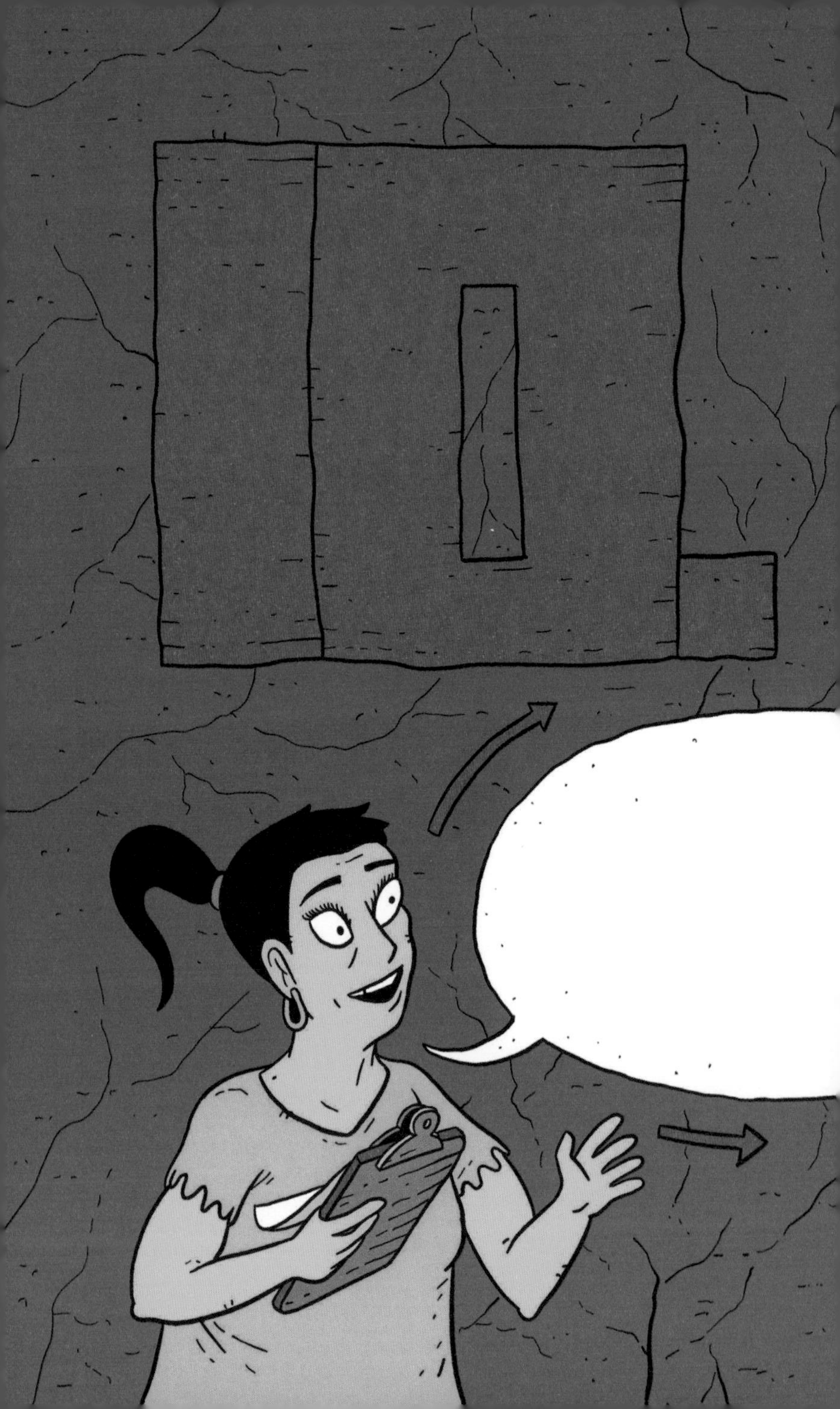

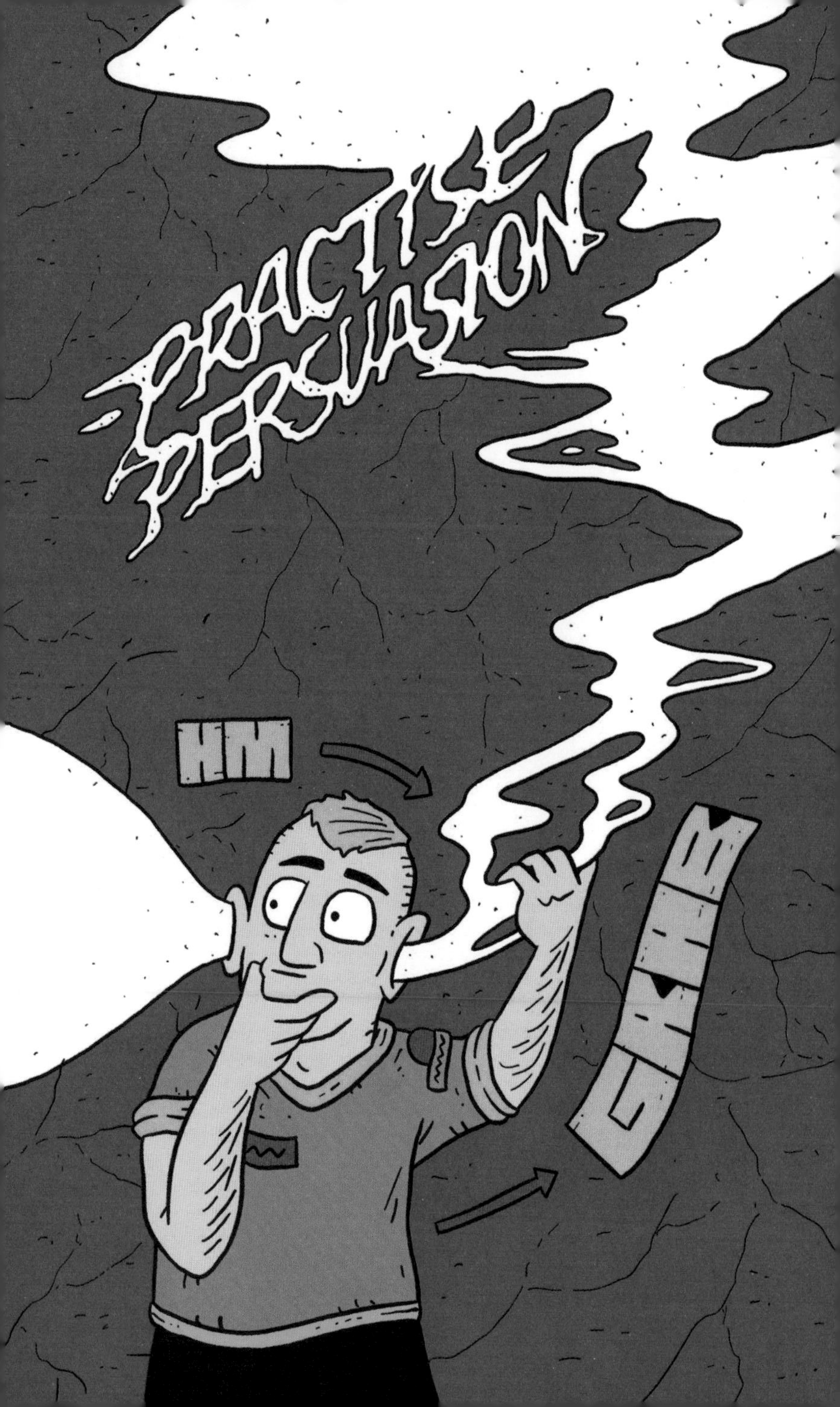
PRACTISE PERSUASION
HM
HMM

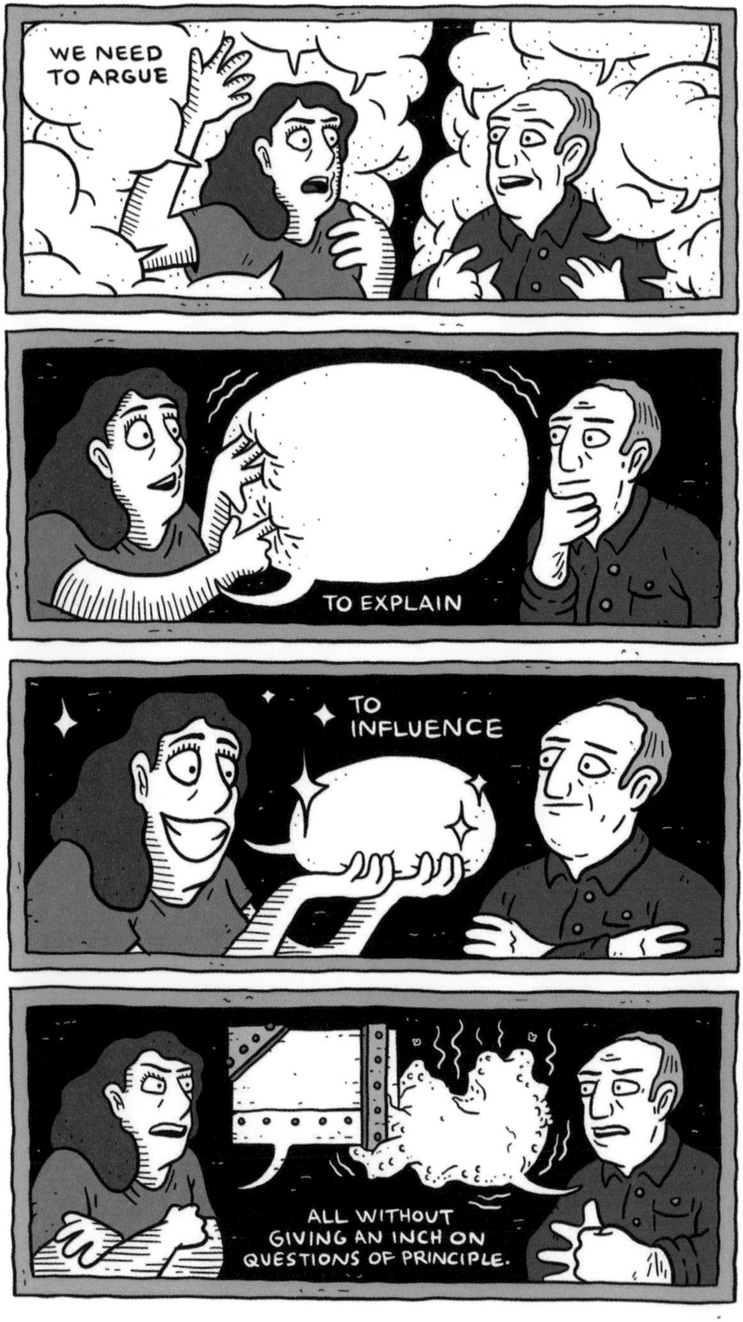
WE NEED TO ARGUE
TO EXPLAIN
TO INFLUENCE
ALL WITHOUT GIVING AN INCH ON QUESTIONS OF PRINCIPLE.

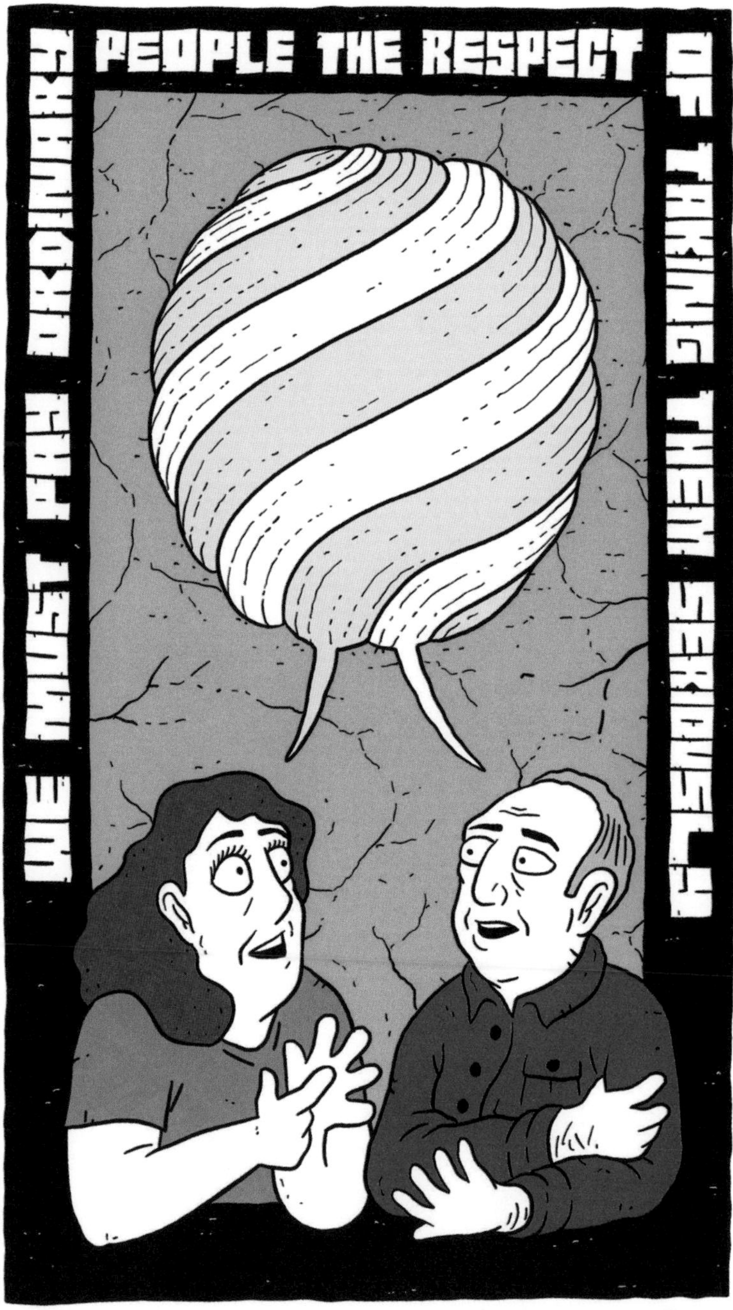
WE MUST PAY ORDINARY
PEOPLE THE RESPECT
OF TAKING THEM SERIOUSLY

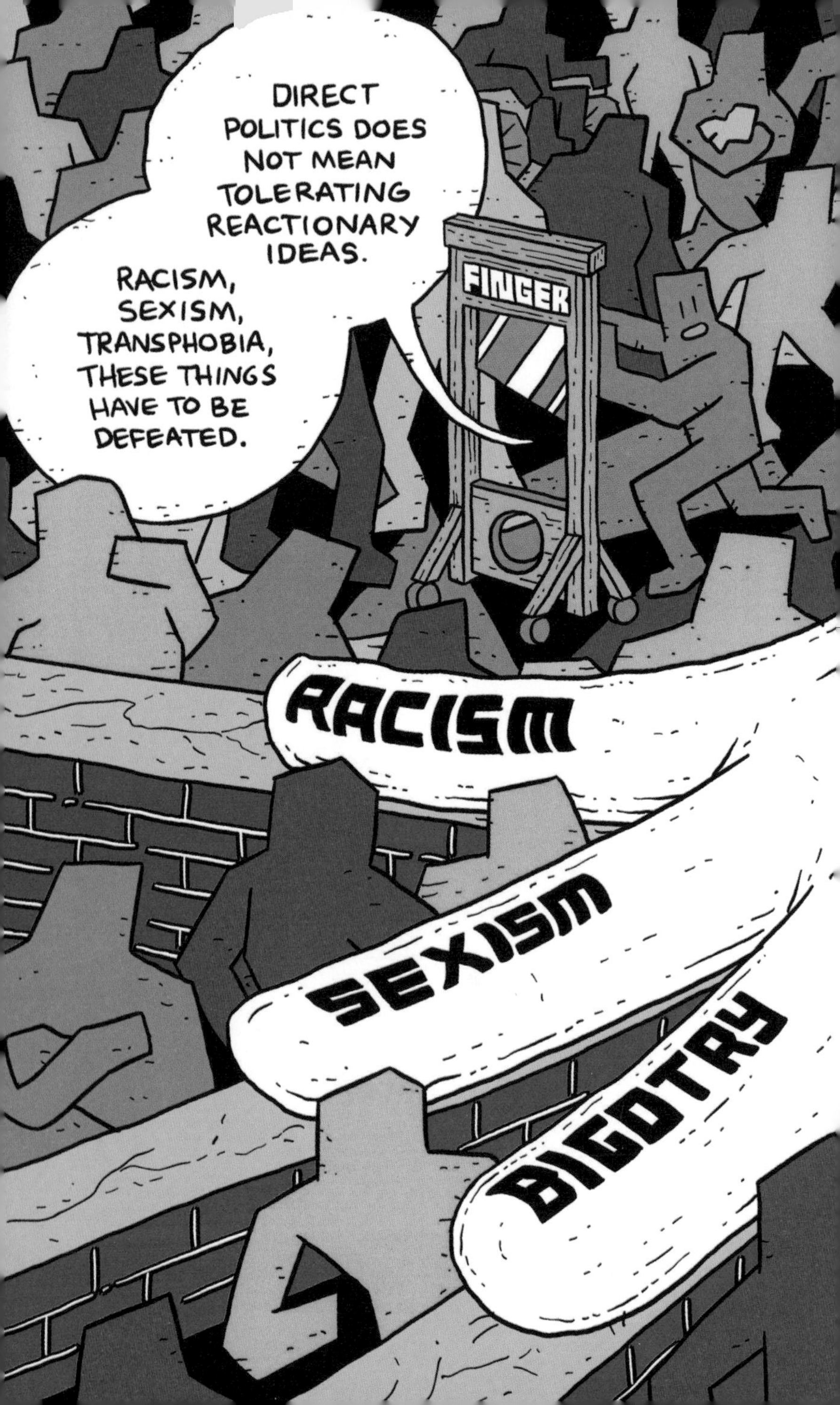
DIRECT POLITICS DOES NOT MEAN TOLERATING REACTIONARY IDEAS.
RACISM, SEXISM, TRANSPHOBIA, THESE THINGS HAVE TO BE DEFEATED.
FINGER
RACISM
SEXISM
BIGOTRY

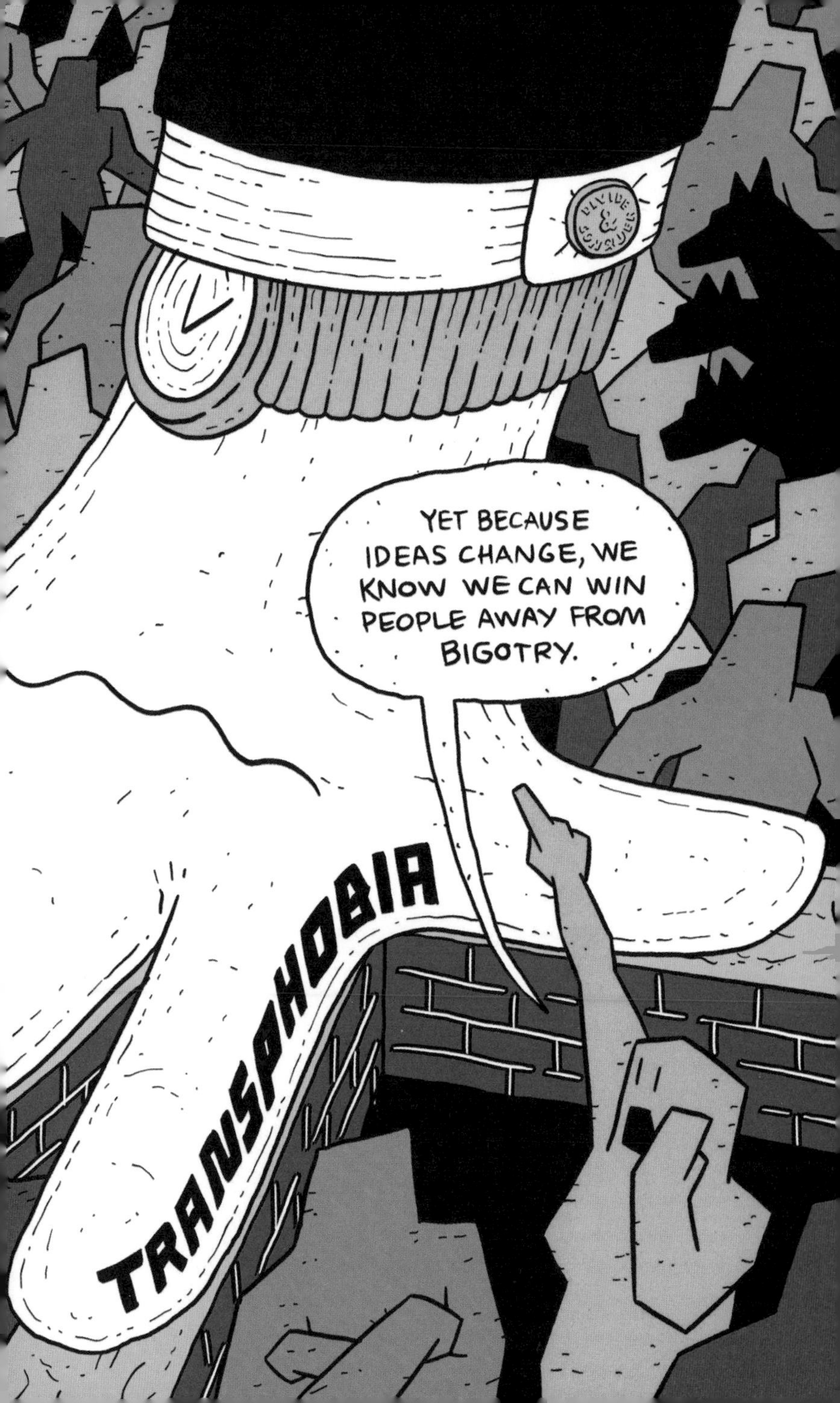
YET BECAUSE IDEAS CHANGE, WE KNOW WE CAN WIN PEOPLE AWAY FROM BIGOTRY.
TRANSPHOBIA

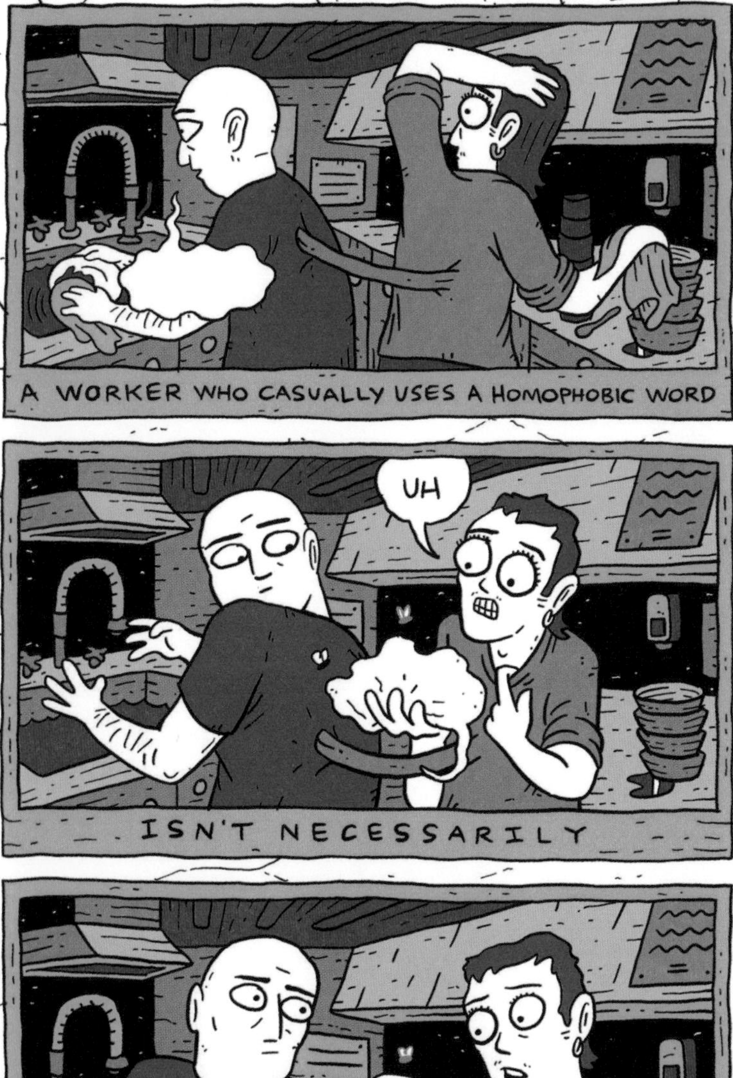
A WORKER WHO CASUALLY USES A HOMOPHOBIC WORD
UH
ISN'T NECESSARILY
A COMMITTED RIGHT-WINGER.

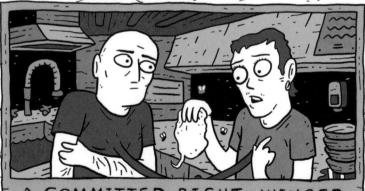

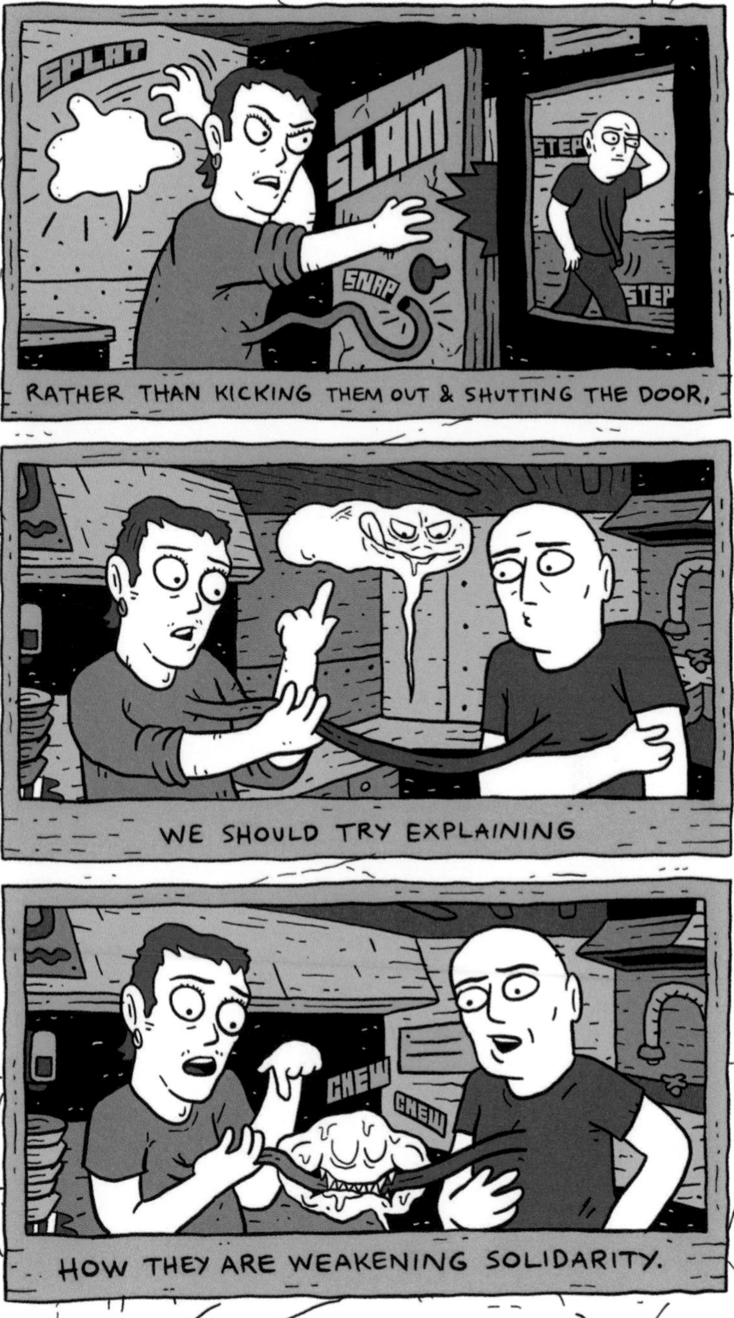
SPLAT
SLAM
SNAP
STEP
STEP
RATHER THAN KICKING THEM OUT & SHUTTING THE DOOR,
WE SHOULD TRY EXPLAINING
CHEW
CHEW
HOW THEY ARE WEAKENING SOLIDARITY.

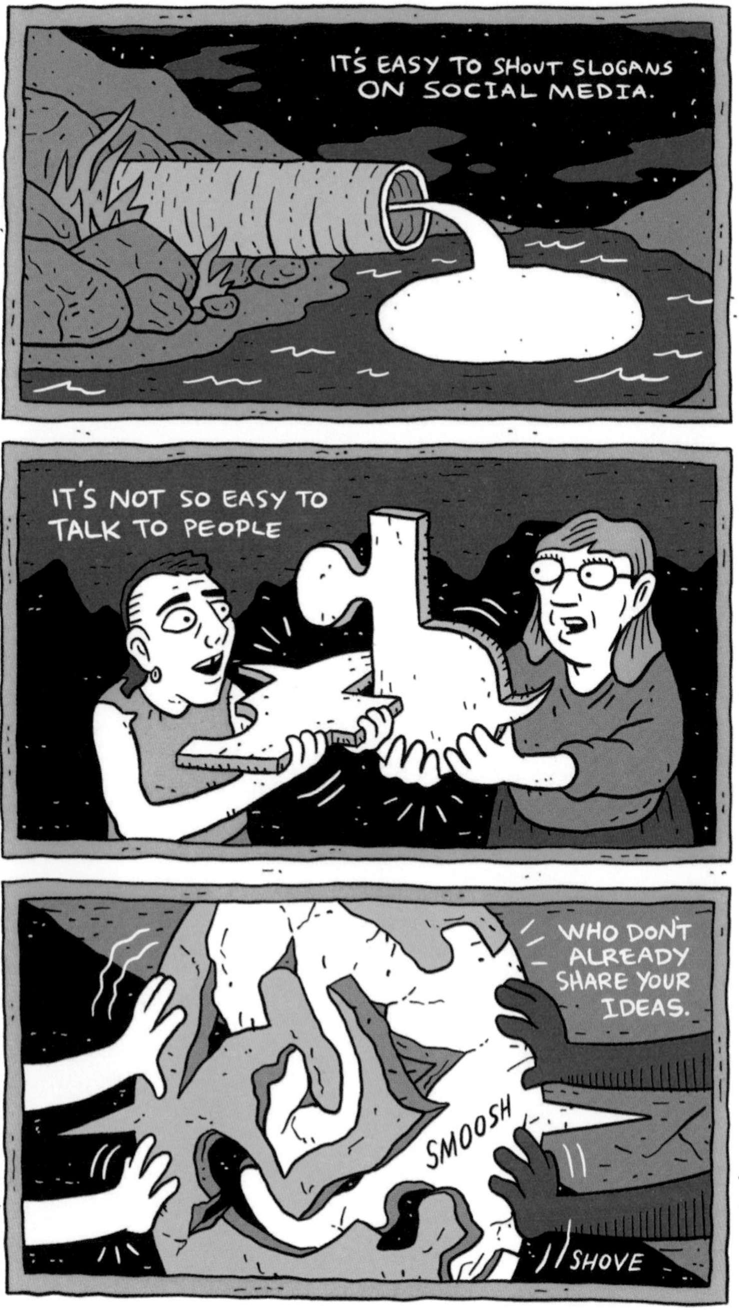

IT'S EASY TO SHOUT SLOGANS ON SOCIAL MEDIA.
IT'S NOT SO EASY TO TALK TO PEOPLE
WHO DON'T ALREADY SHARE YOUR IDEAS.
SMOOSH
SHOVE

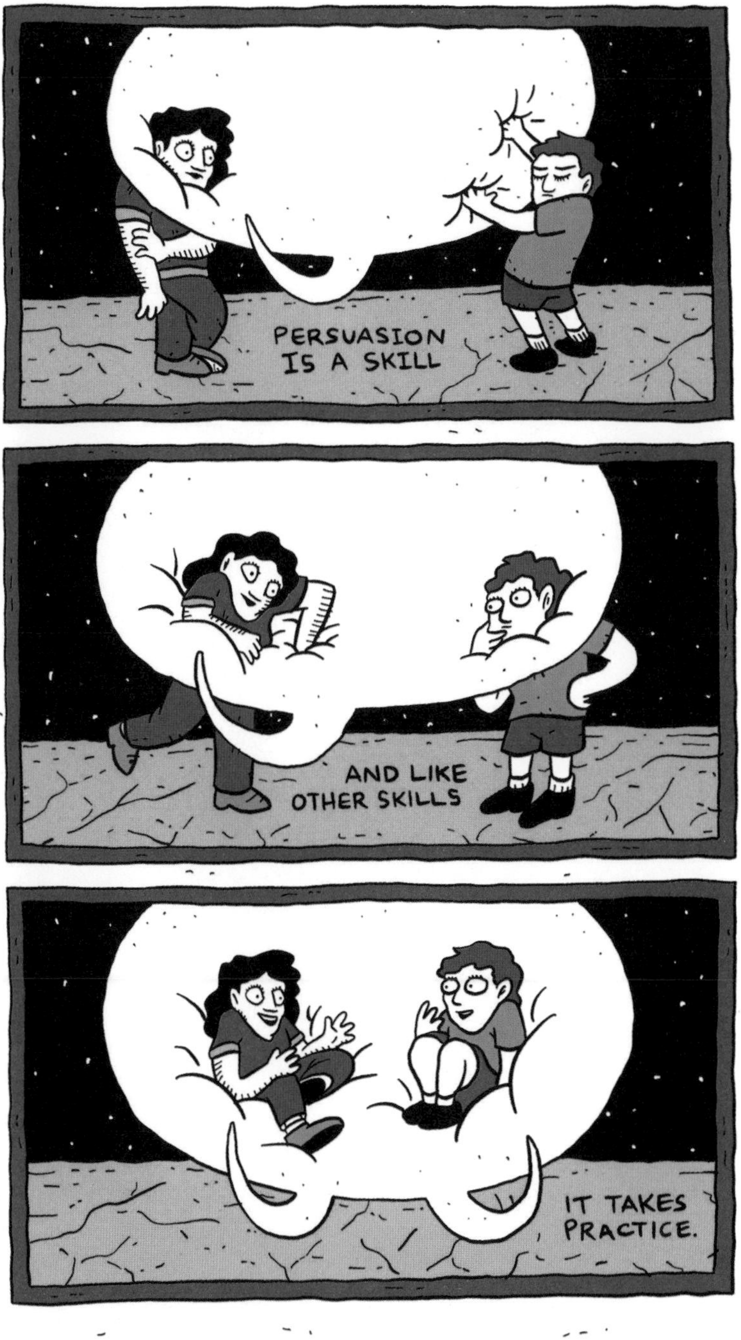
PERSUASION IS A SKILL
AND LIKE OTHER SKILLS
IT TAKES PRACTICE.

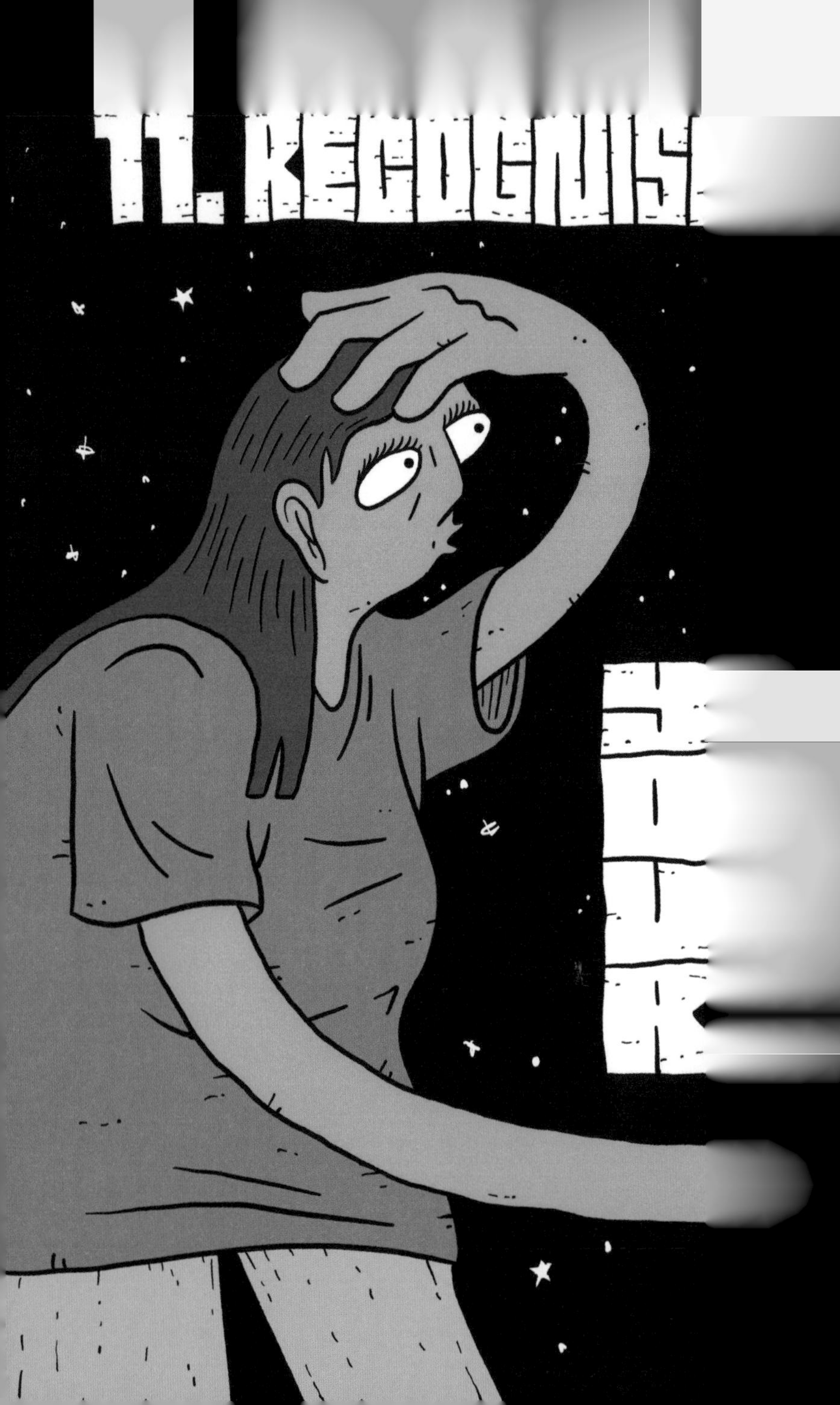
11. RECOGNIS

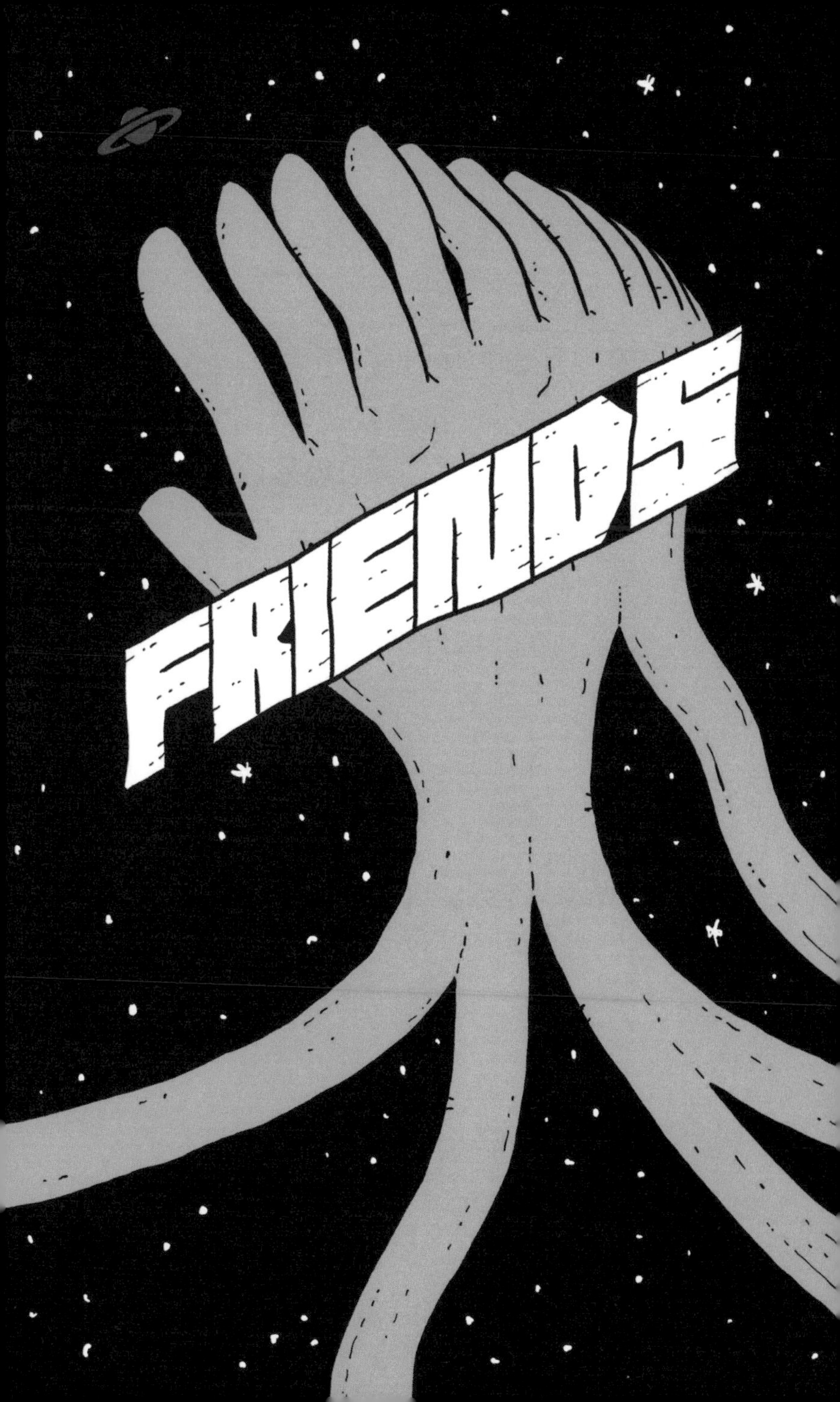
FRIENDS

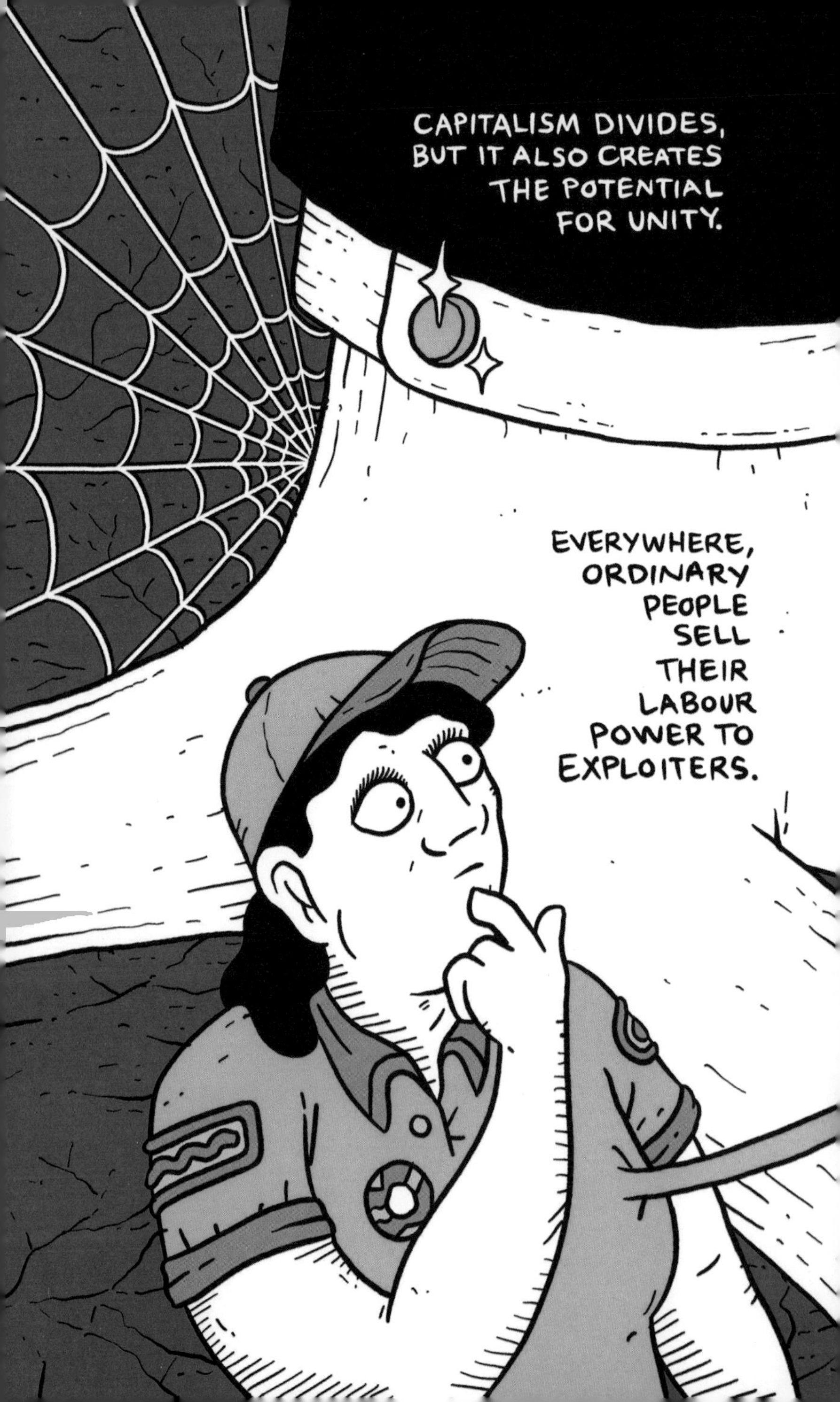
CAPITALISM DIVIDES, BUT IT ALSO CREATES THE POTENTIAL FOR UNITY.
EVERYWHERE, ORDINARY PEOPLE SELL THEIR LABOUR POWER TO EXPLOITERS.

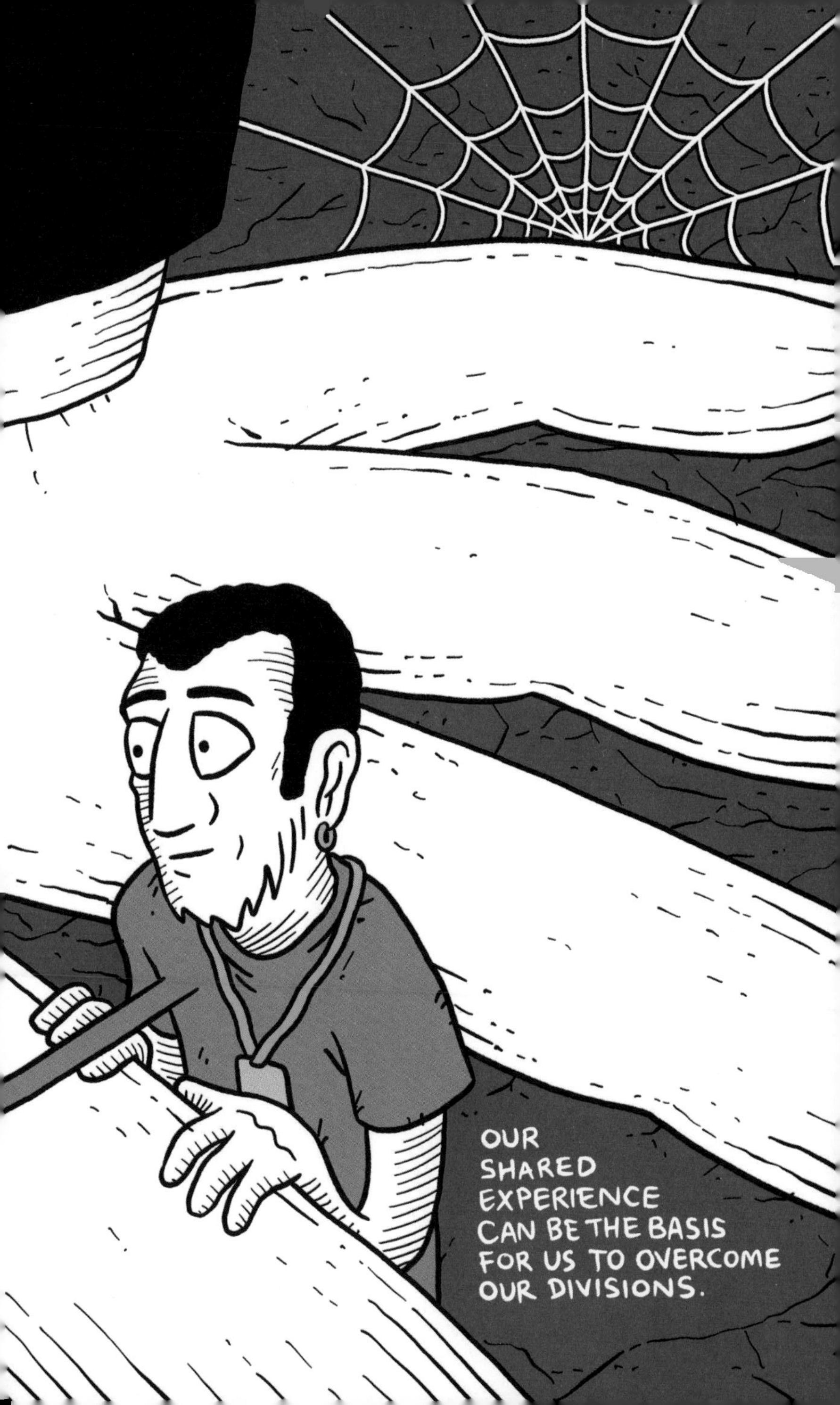
OUR SHARED EXPERIENCE CAN BE THE BASIS FOR US TO OVERCOME OUR DIVISIONS.

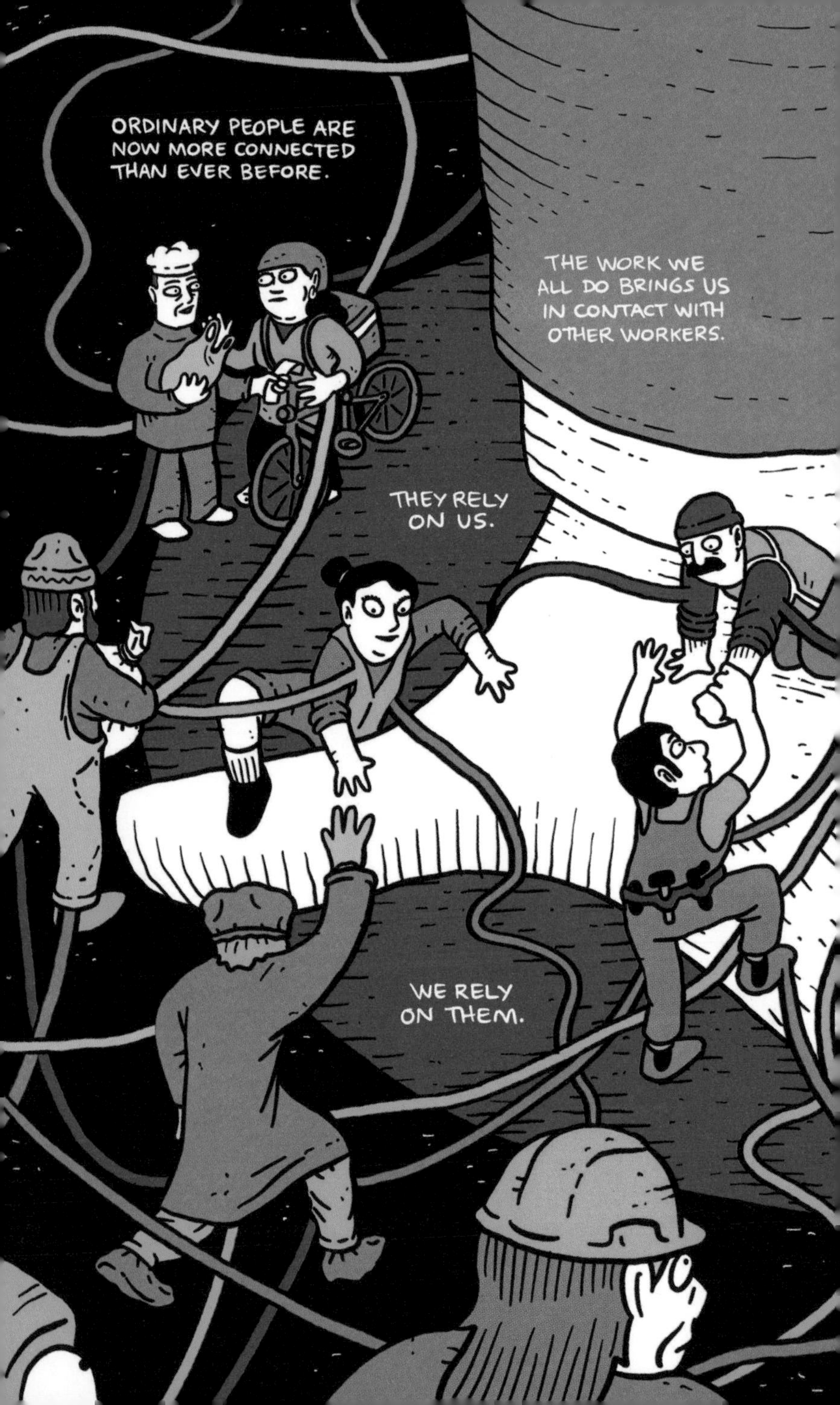
ORDINARY PEOPLE ARE NOW MORE CONNECTED THAN EVER BEFORE.
THE WORK WE ALL DO BRINGS US IN CONTACT WITH OTHER WORKERS.
THEY RELY ON US.
WE RELY ON THEM.

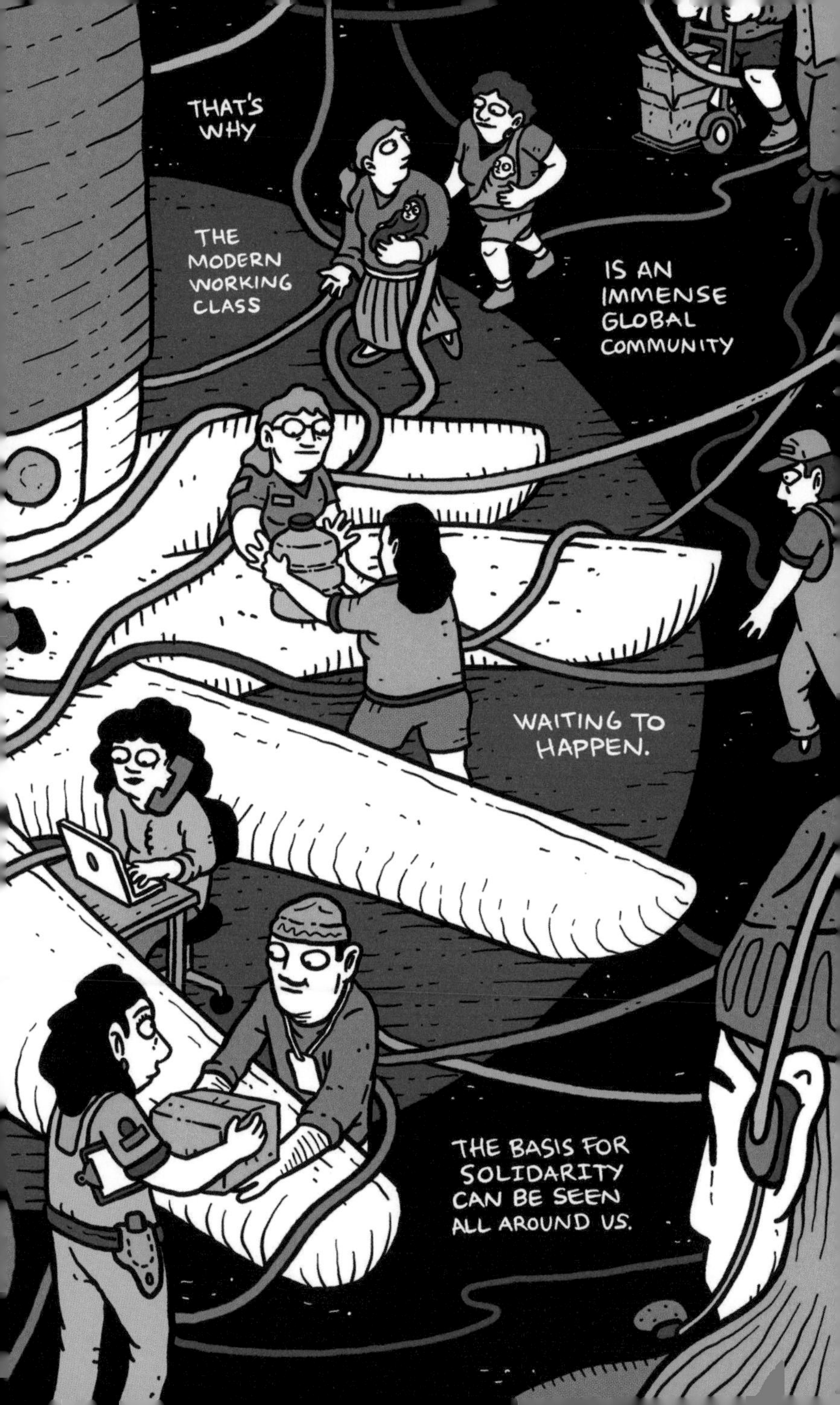
THAT'S WHY
THE MODERN WORKING CLASS
IS AN IMMENSE GLOBAL COMMUNITY
WAITING TO HAPPEN.
THE BASIS FOR SOLIDARITY CAN BE SEEN ALL AROUND US.

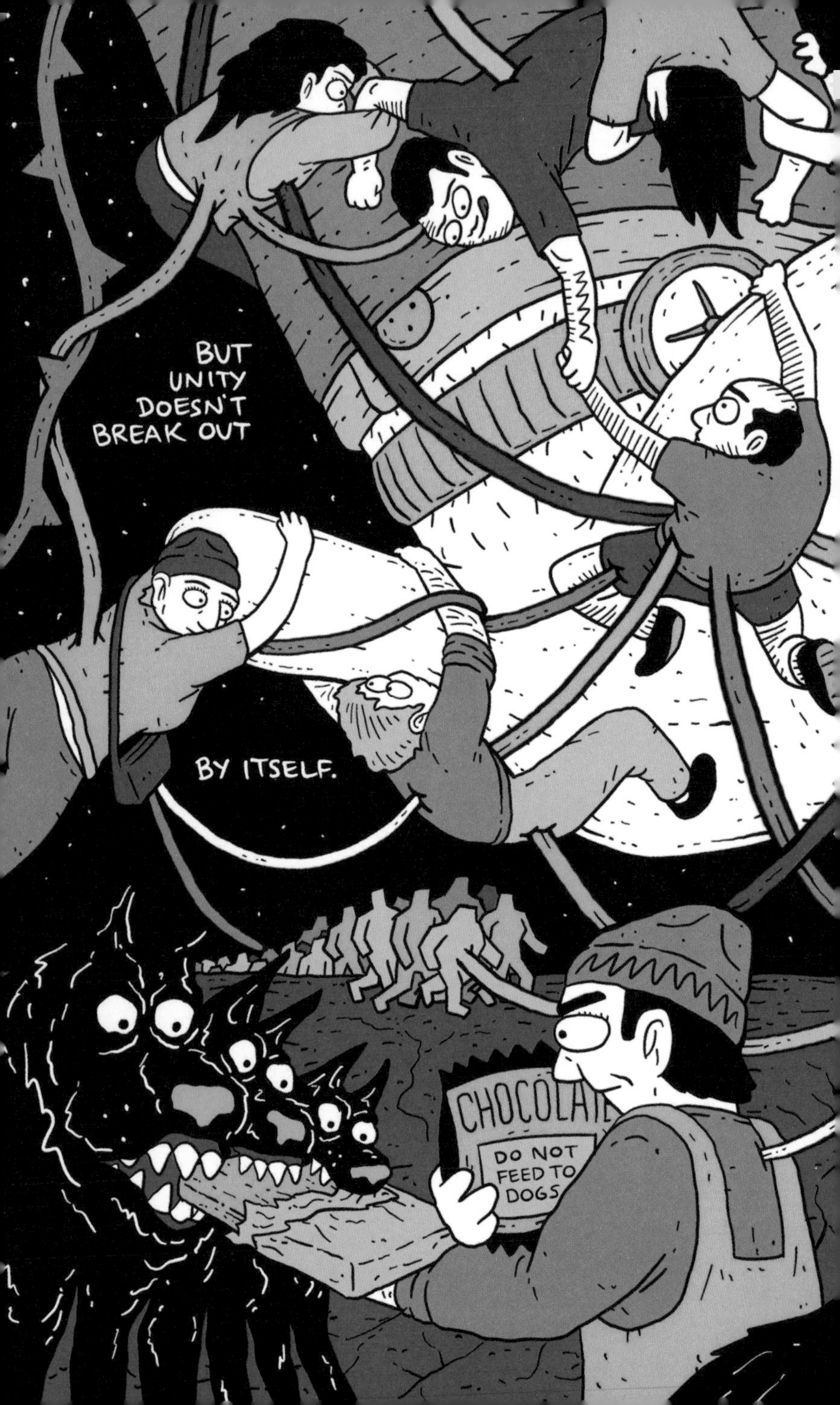
BUT UNITY DOESN'T BREAK OUT
BY ITSELF.
CHOCOLATE
DO NOT FEED TO DOGS

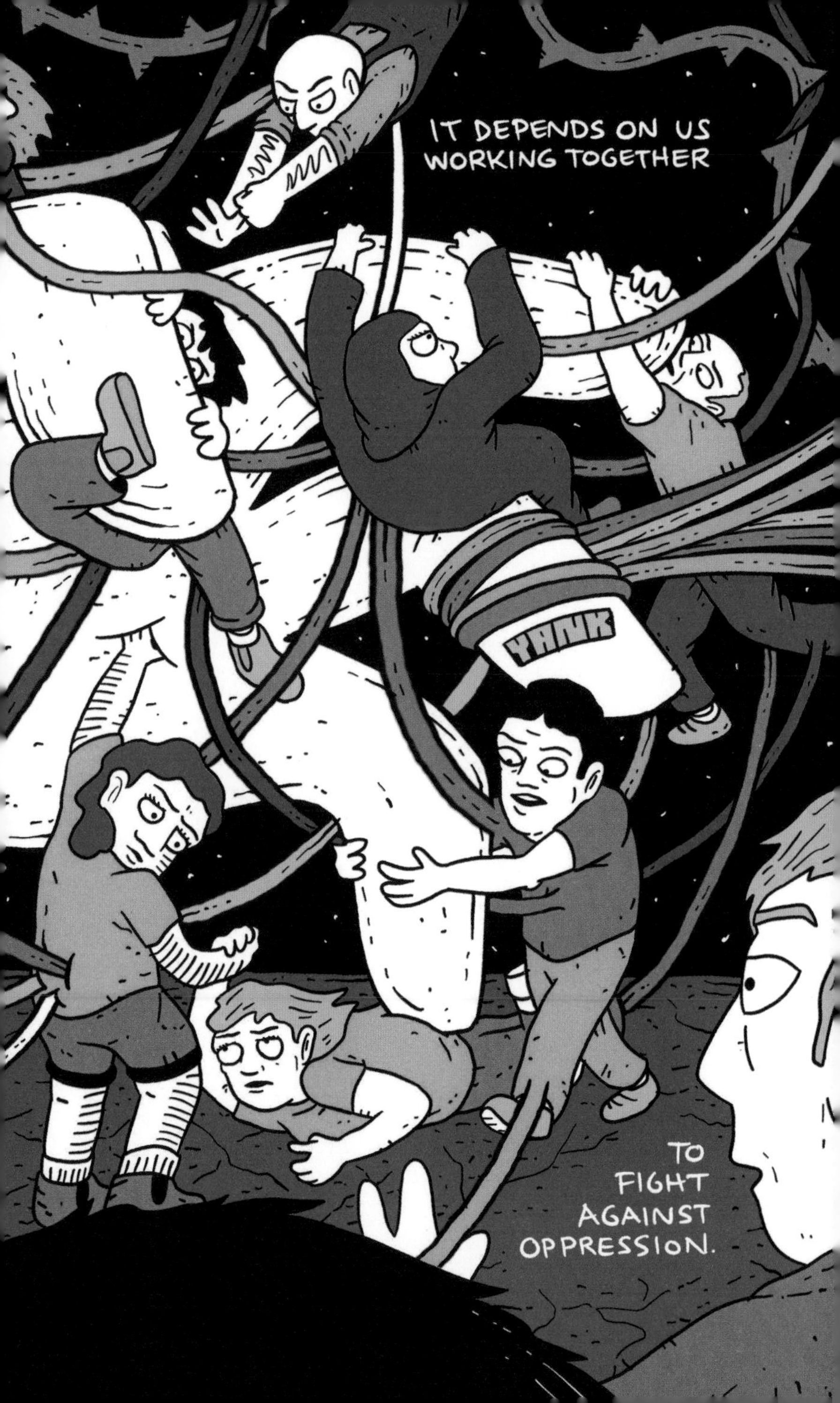
IT DEPENDS ON US WORKING TOGETHER
YANK
TO FIGHT AGAINST OPPRESSION.

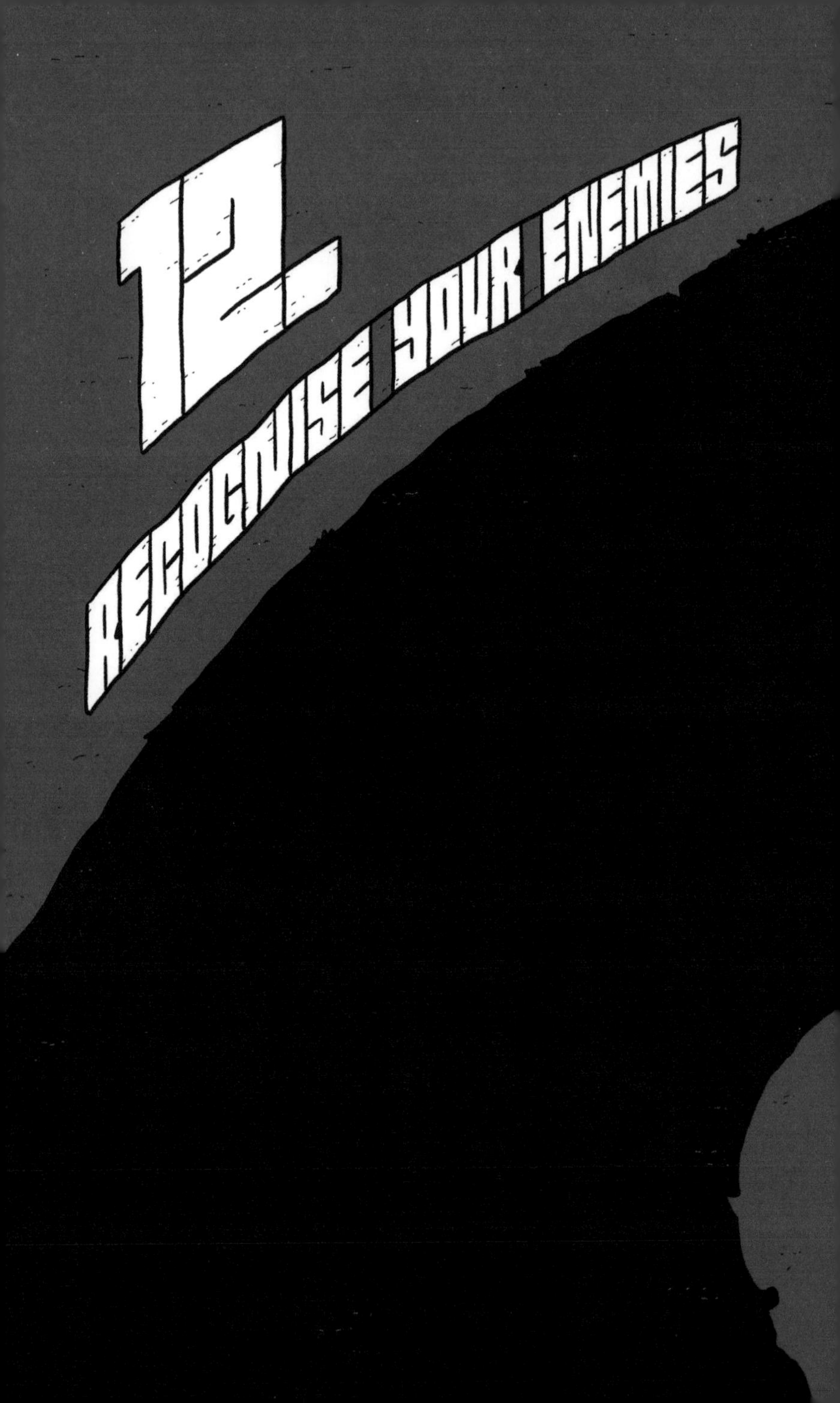
12
RECOGNISE YOUR ENEMIES

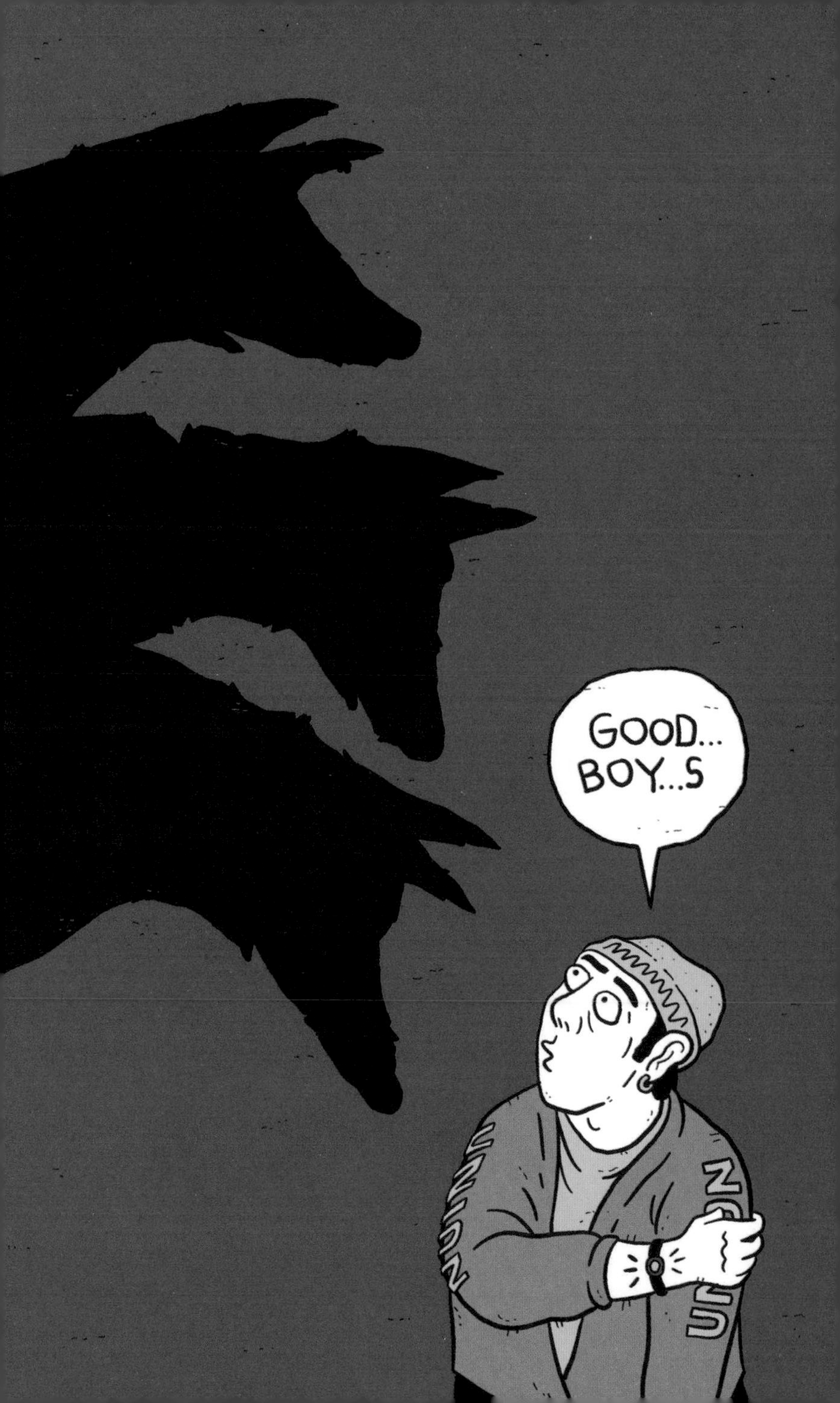
GOOD...
BOY...S

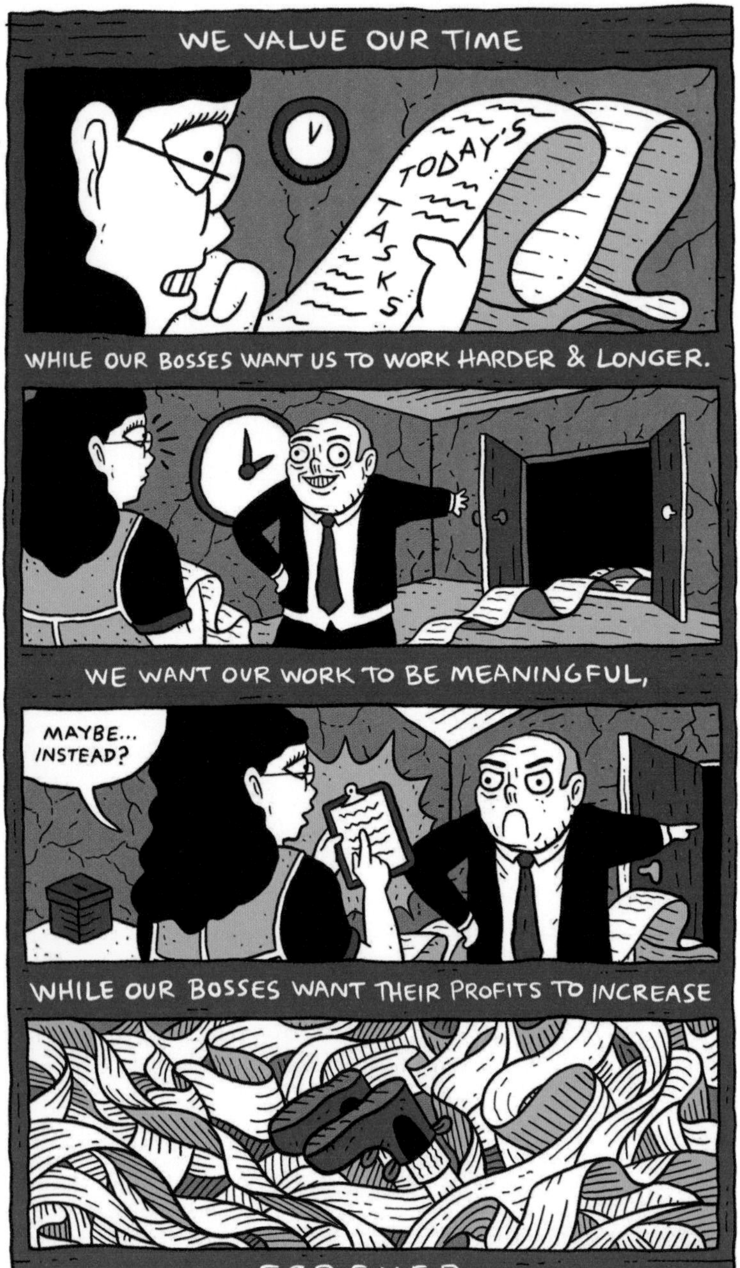
WE VALUE OUR TIME
TODAY'S TASKS
WHILE OUR BOSSES WANT US TO WORK HARDER & LONGER.
WE WANT OUR WORK TO BE MEANINGFUL,
MAYBE... INSTEAD?
WHILE OUR BOSSES WANT THEIR PROFITS TO INCREASE
FOREVER.

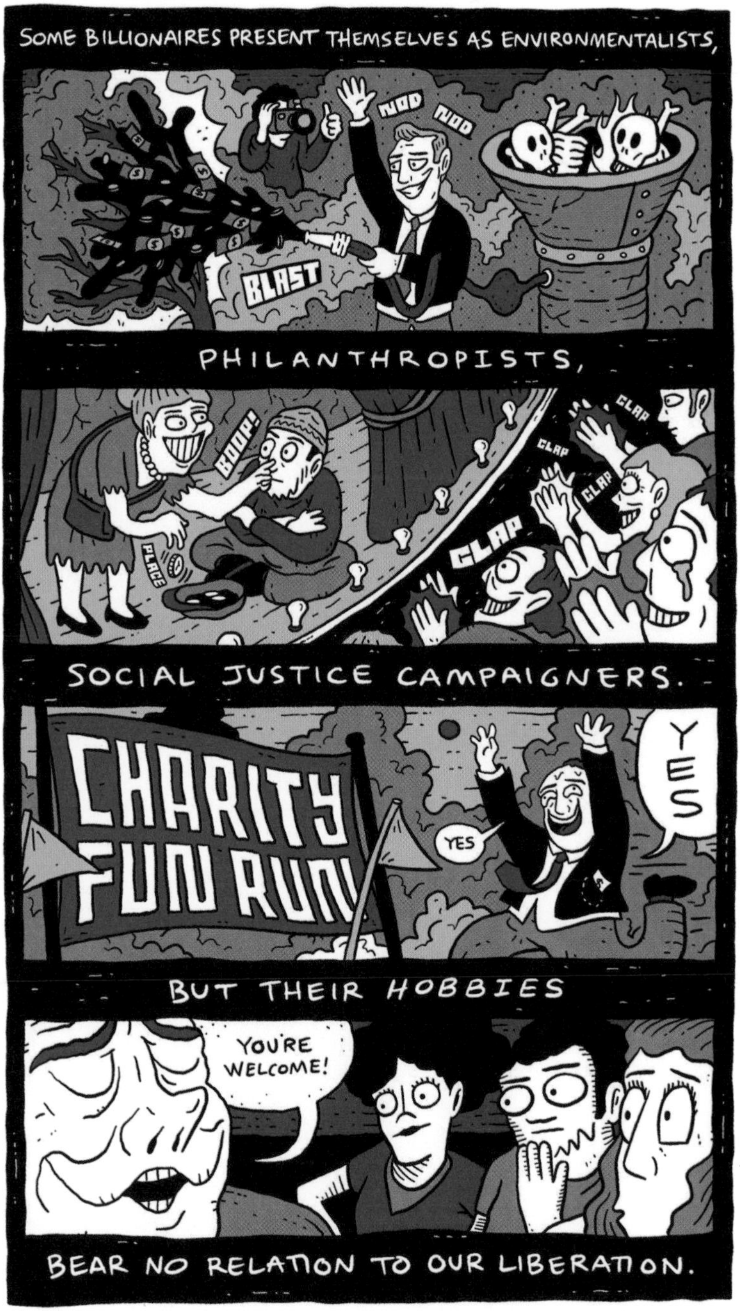

SOME BILLIONAIRES PRESENT THEMSELVES AS ENVIRONMENTALISTS,
NOD
NOD
BLAST
PHILANTHROPISTS,
BOOP!
PLACE
CLAP
CLAP
CLAP
CLAP
CLAP
SOCIAL JUSTICE CAMPAIGNERS.
CHARITY FUN RUN
YES
YES
BUT THEIR HOBBIES
YOU'RE WELCOME!
BEAR NO RELATION TO OUR LIBERATION.

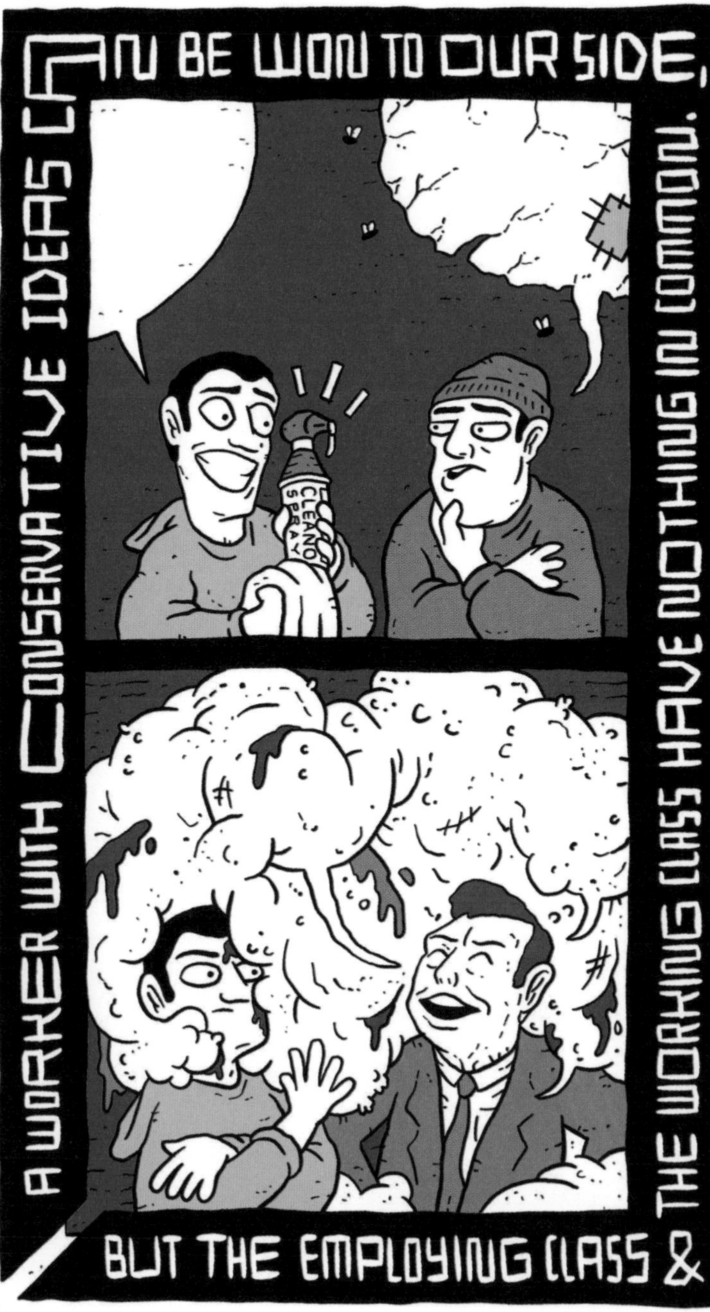
A WORKER WITH CONSERVATIVE IDEAS CAN BE WON TO OUR SIDE,
BUT THE EMPLOYING CLASS & THE WORKING CLASS HAVE NOTHING IN COMMON.
CLEANO SPRAY

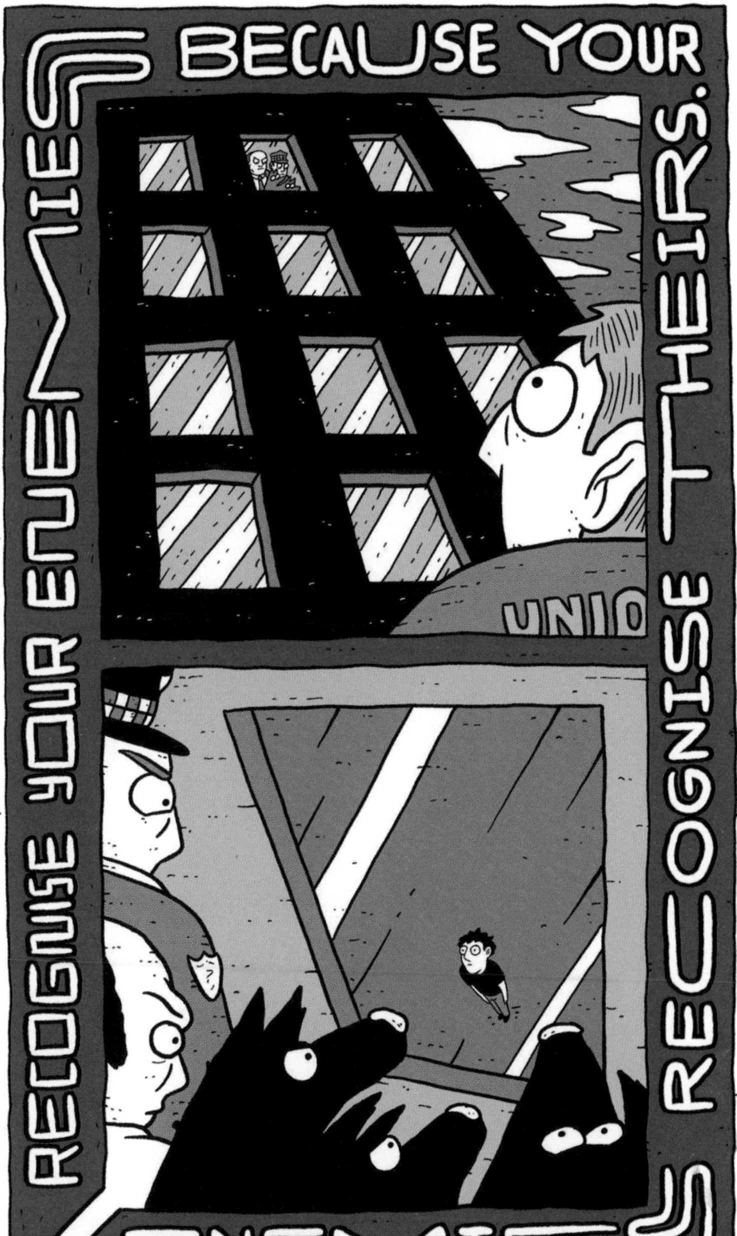

RECOGNISE YOUR ENEMIES
BECAUSE YOUR
ENEMIES
RECOGNISE THEIRS.
UNIO

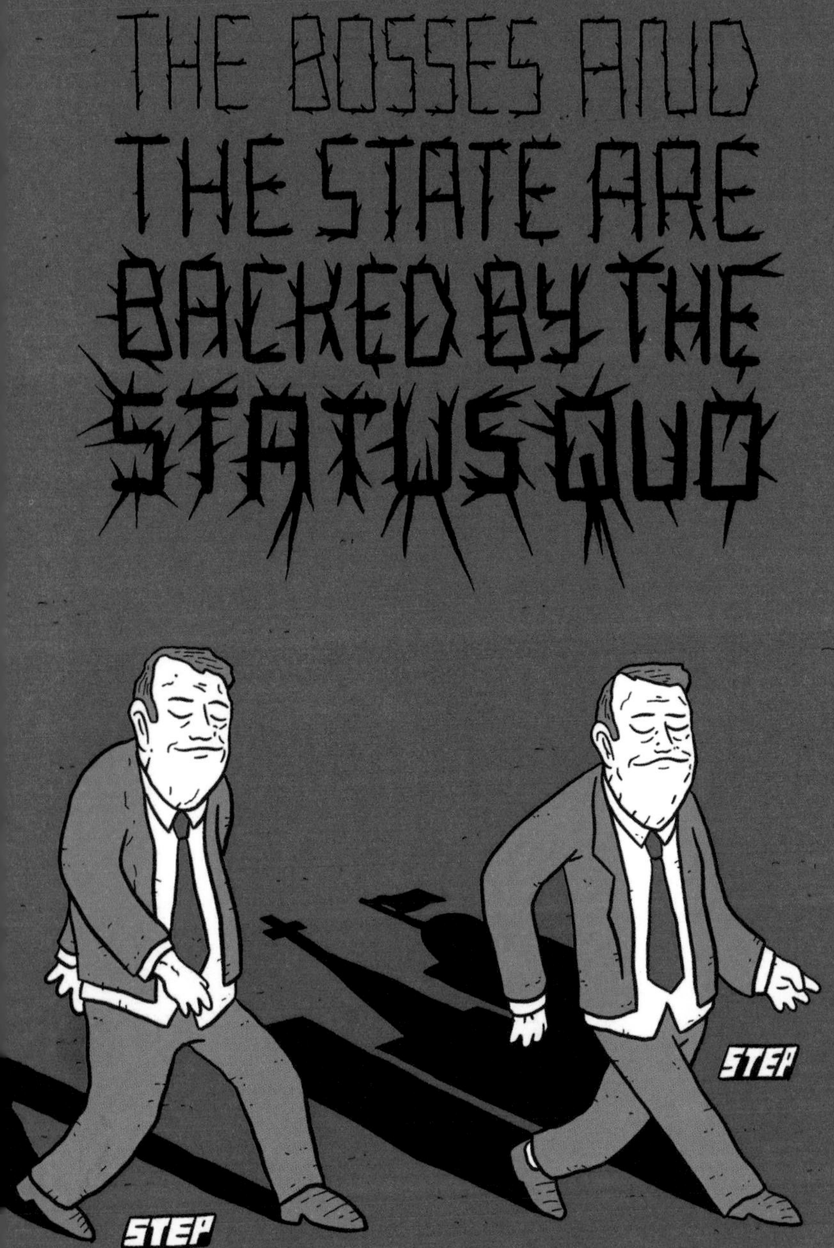
THE BOSSES AND
THE STATE ARE
BACKED BY THE
STATUS QUO
STEP
STEP

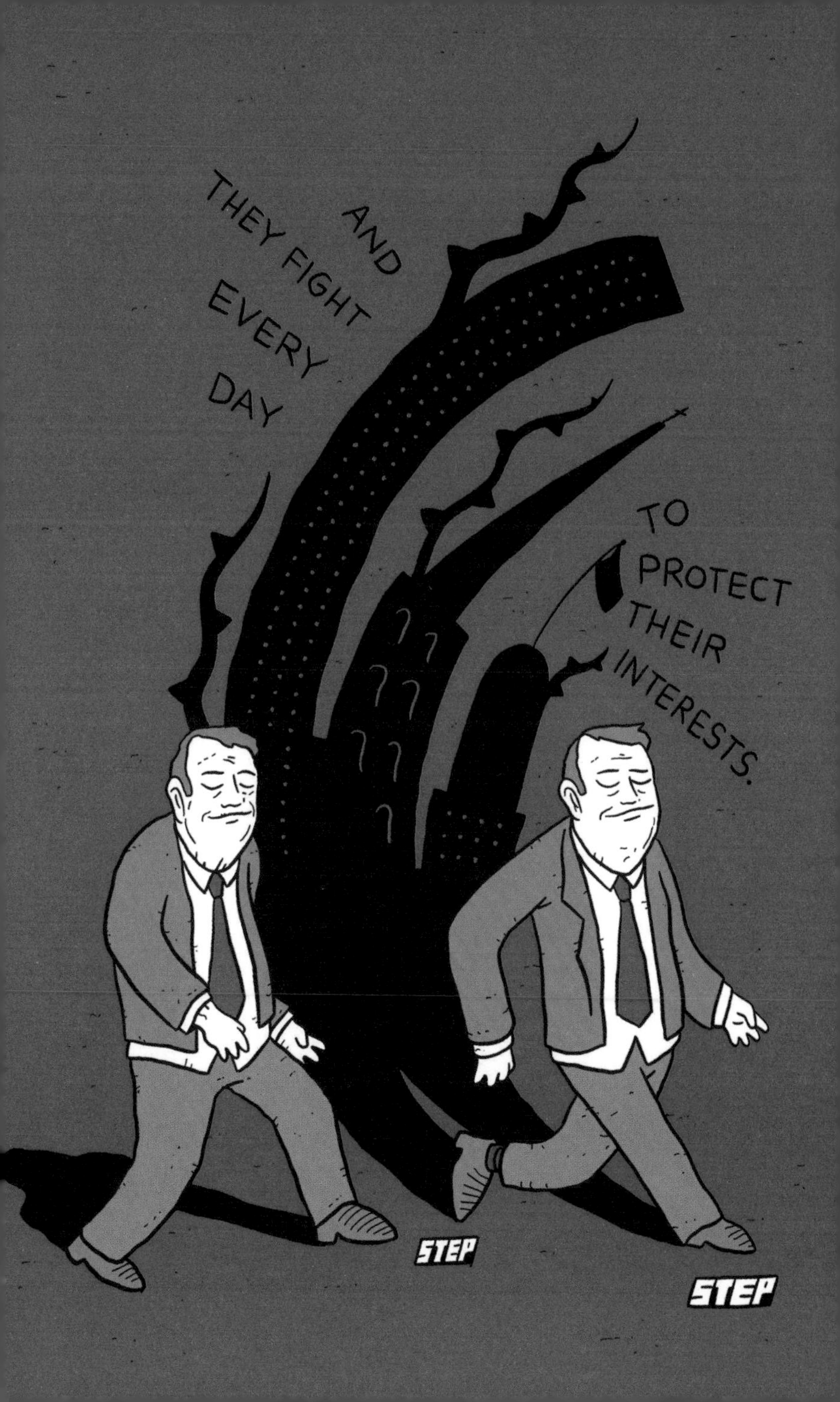
AND
THEY FIGHT
EVERY
DAY
TO
PROTECT
THEIR
INTERESTS.
STEP
STEP

OUR POWER LIES IN *STRIFE*
IN SOLIDARITY & COLLECTIVE ACTION

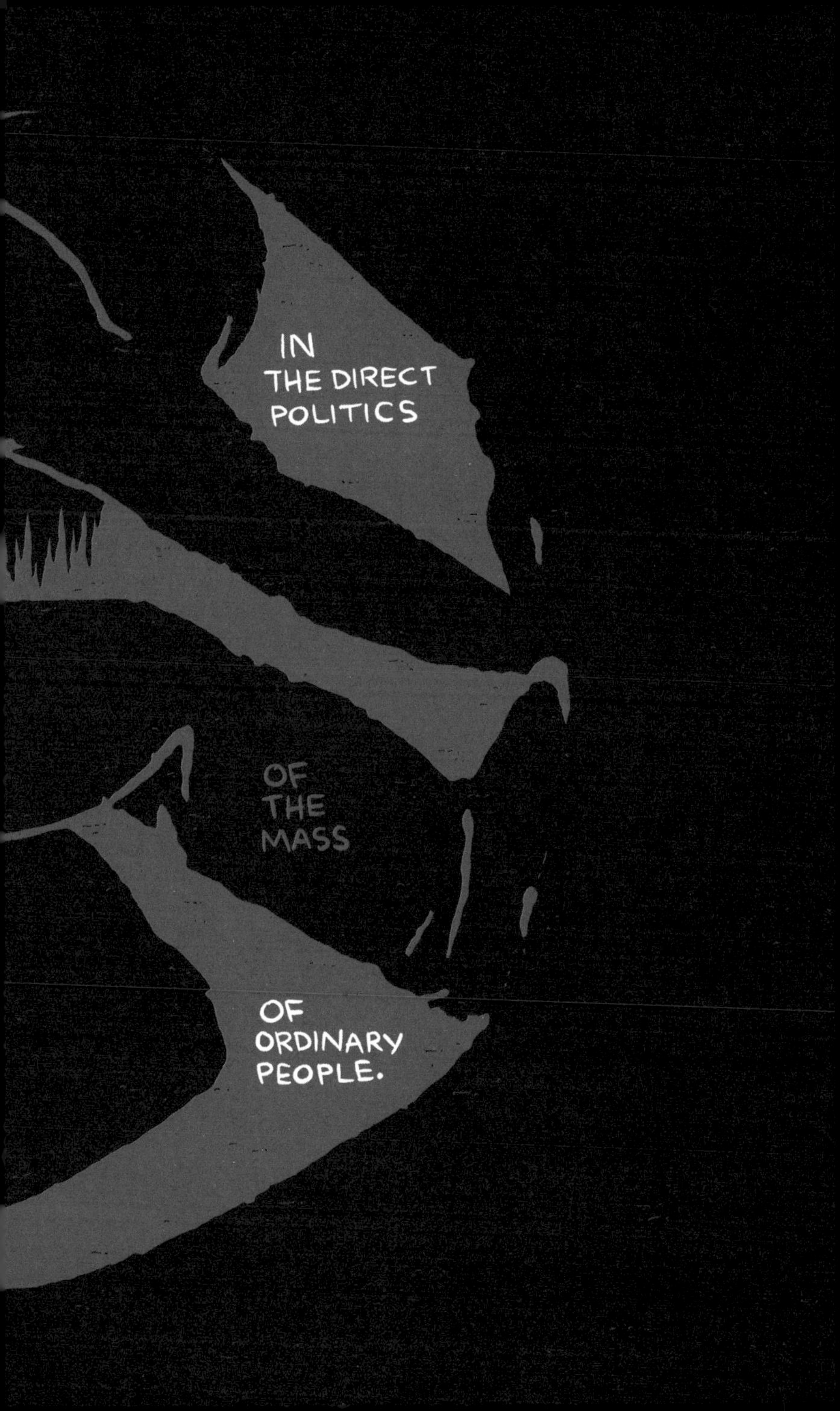
IN THE DIRECT POLITICS
OF THE MASS
OF ORDINARY PEOPLE.

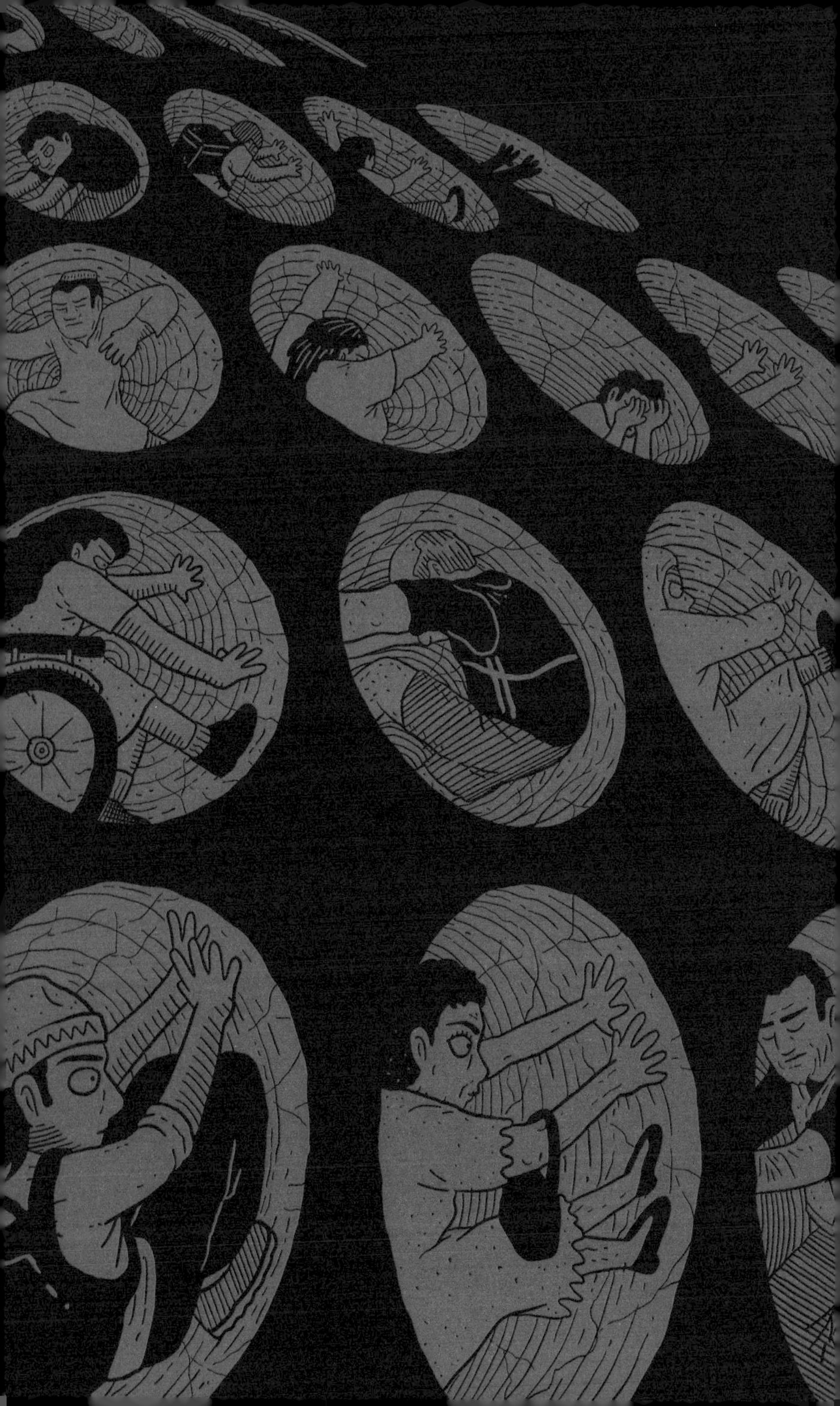

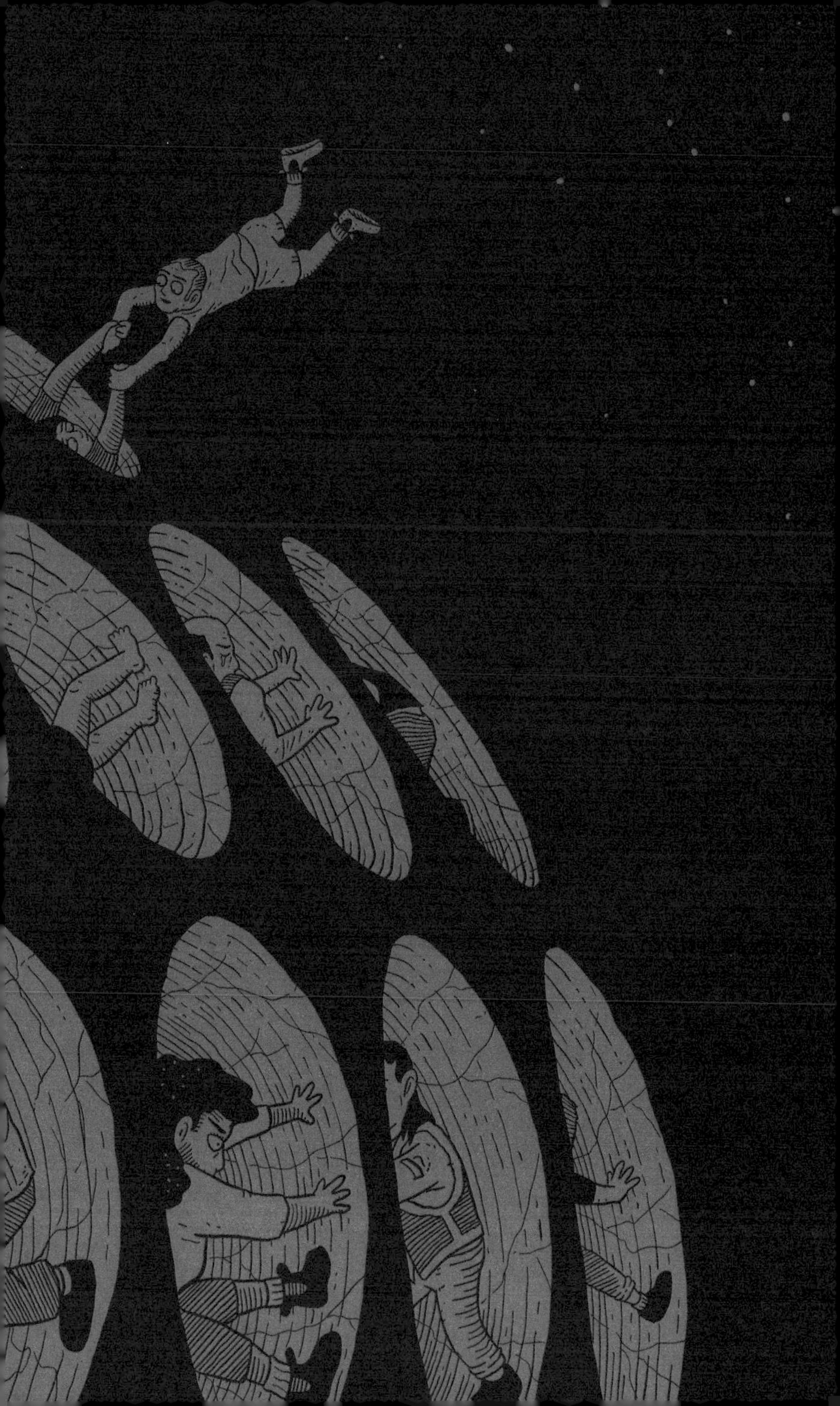

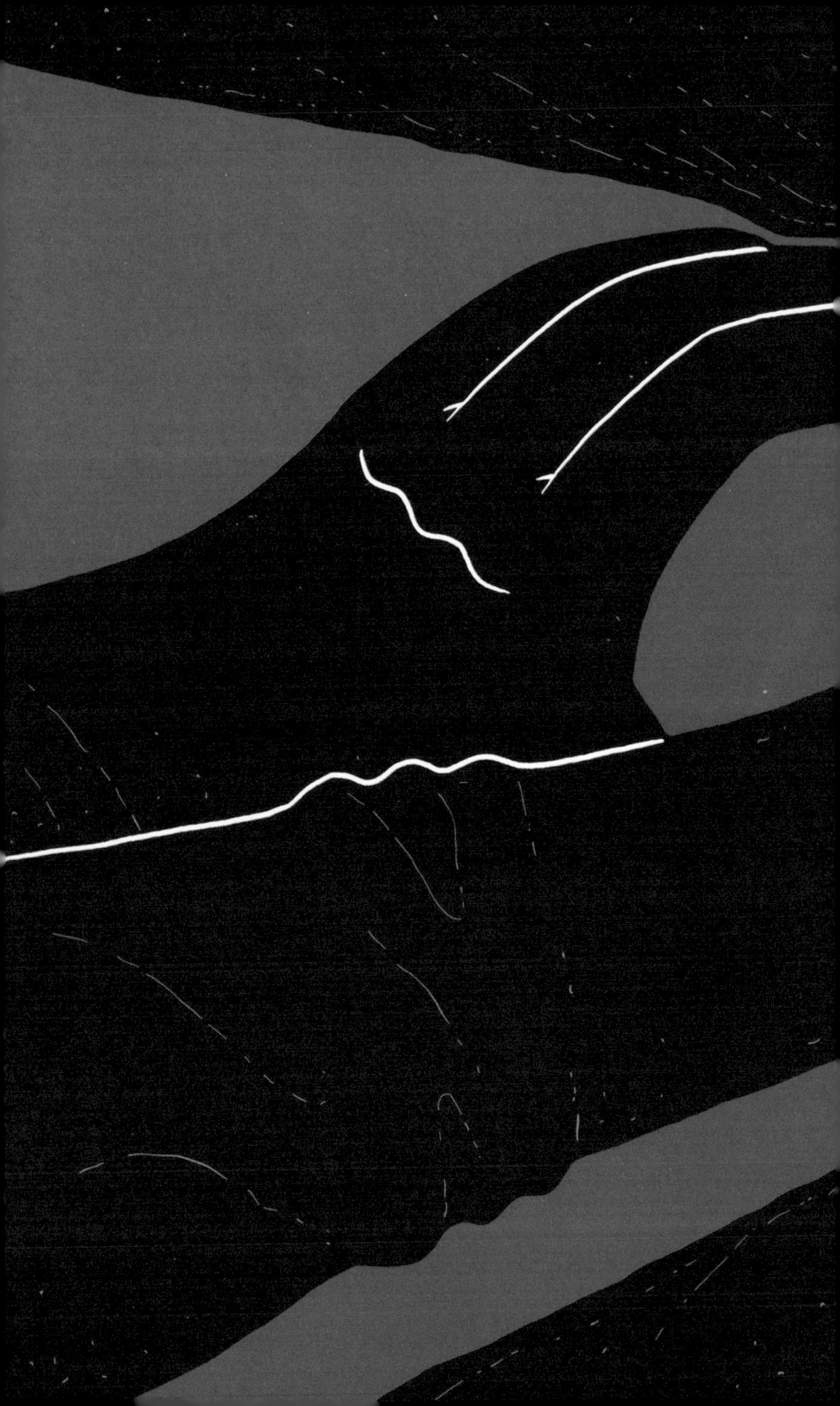

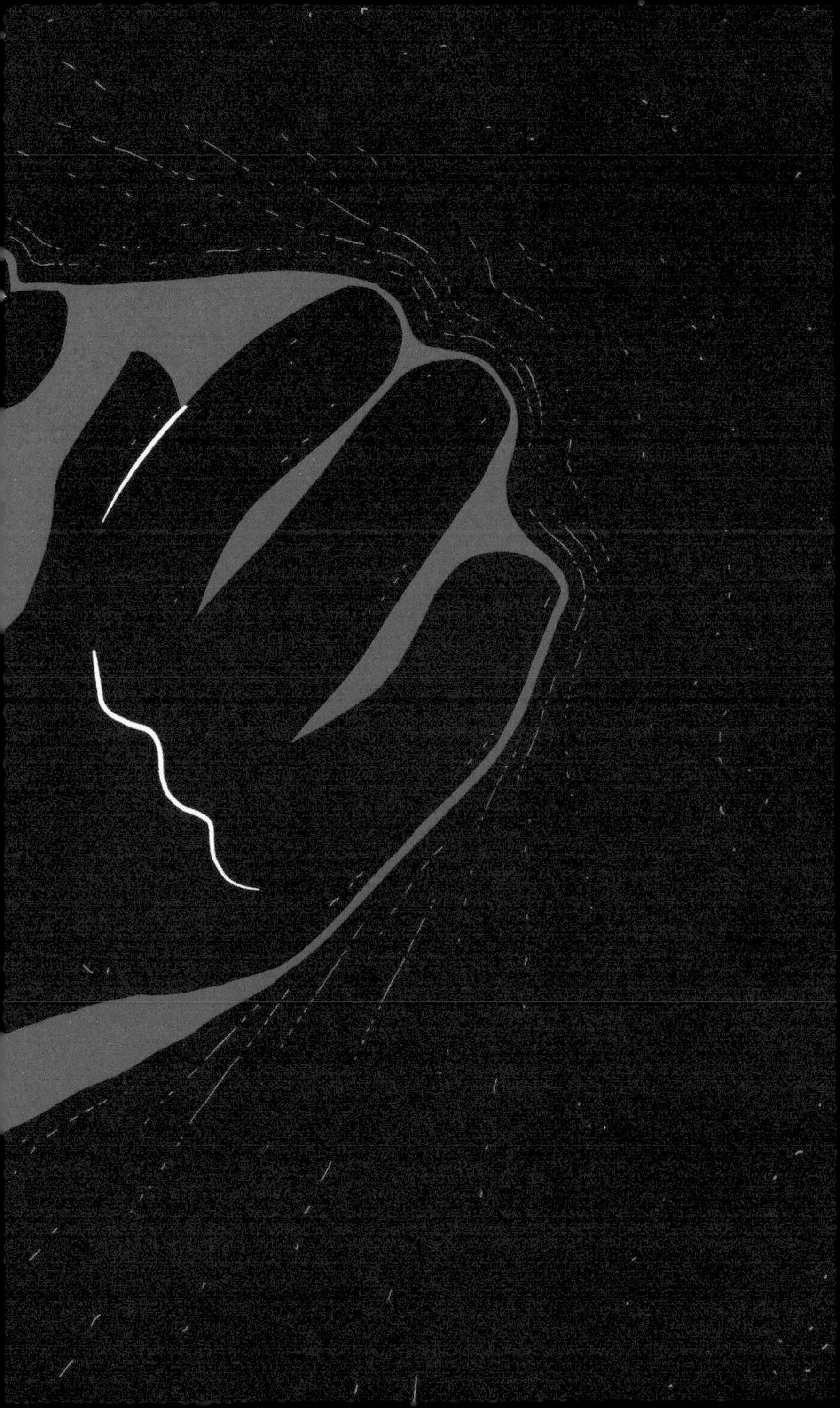

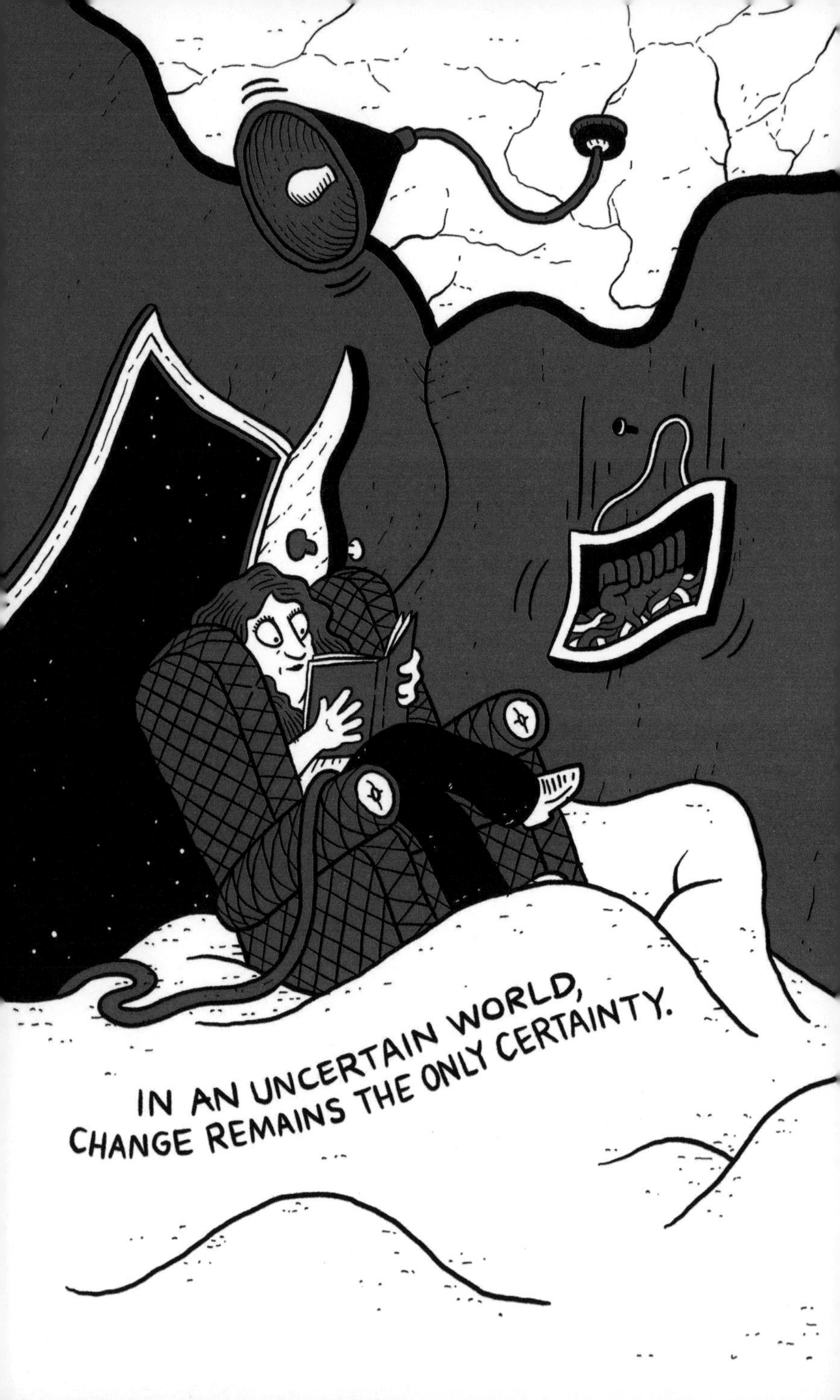
IN AN UNCERTAIN WORLD,
CHANGE REMAINS THE ONLY CERTAINTY.

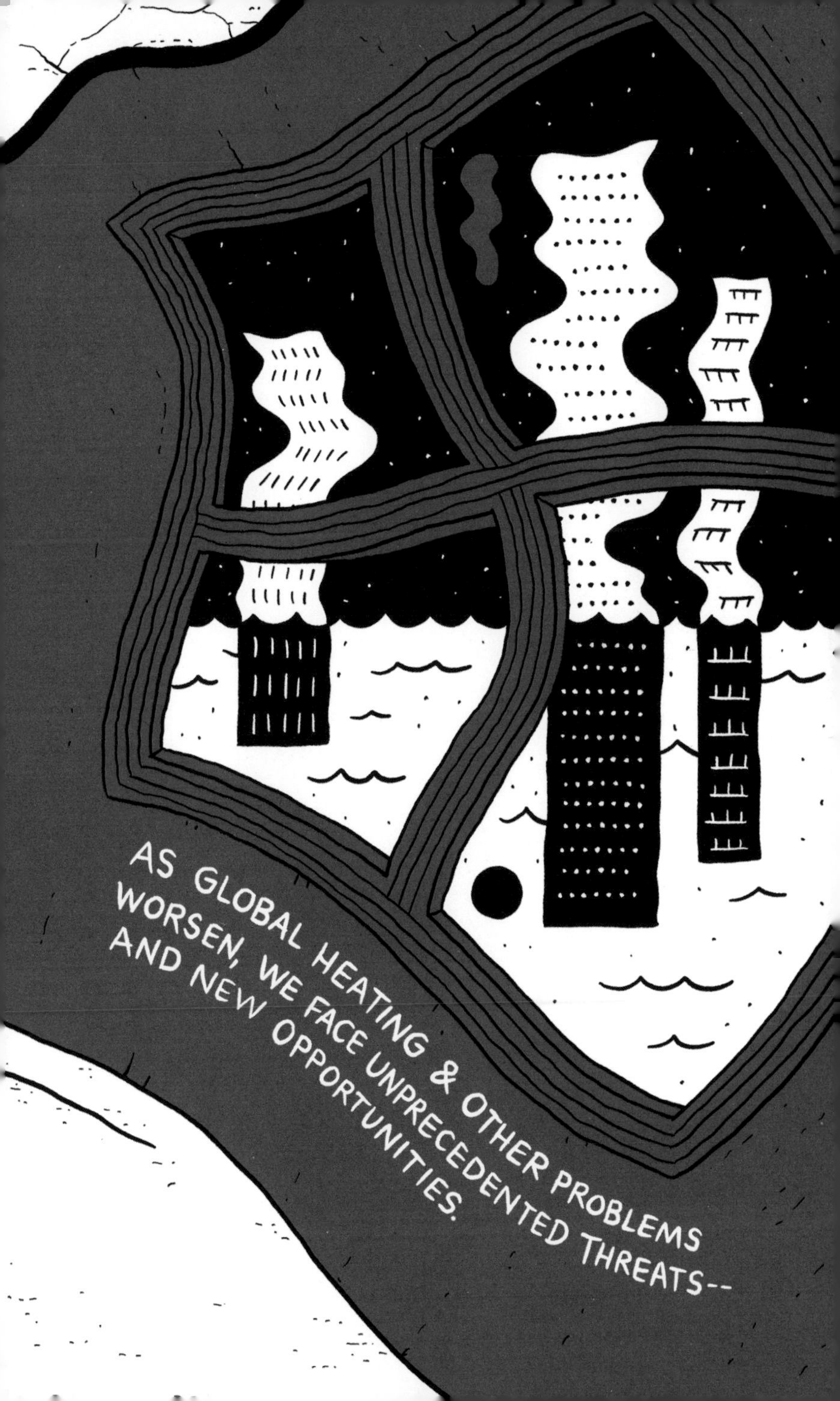
AS GLOBAL HEATING & OTHER PROBLEMS WORSEN, WE FACE UNPRECEDENTED THREATS-- AND NEW OPPORTUNITIES.

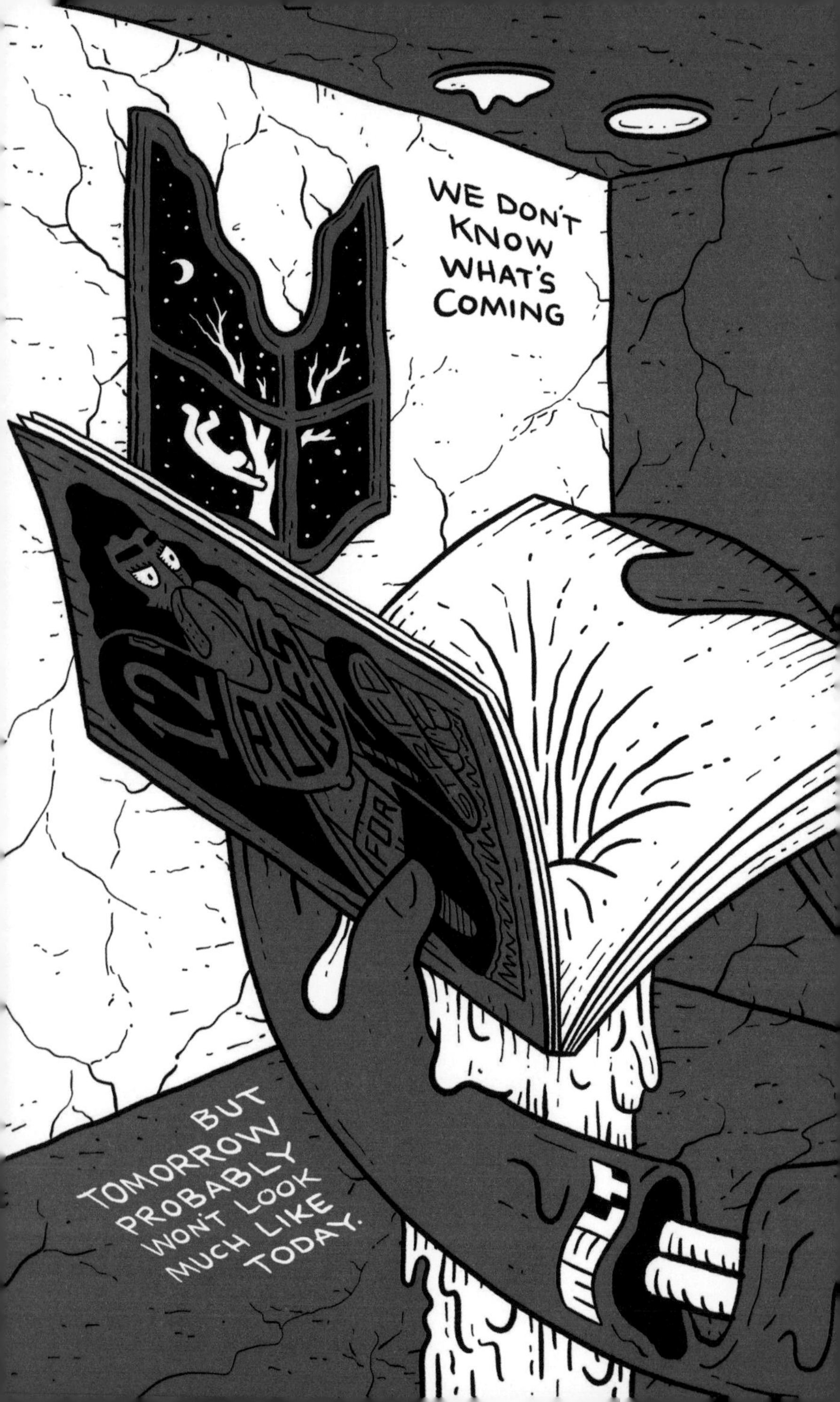
WE DON'T KNOW WHAT'S COMING
BUT TOMORROW PROBABLY WON'T LOOK MUCH LIKE TODAY.
MELT

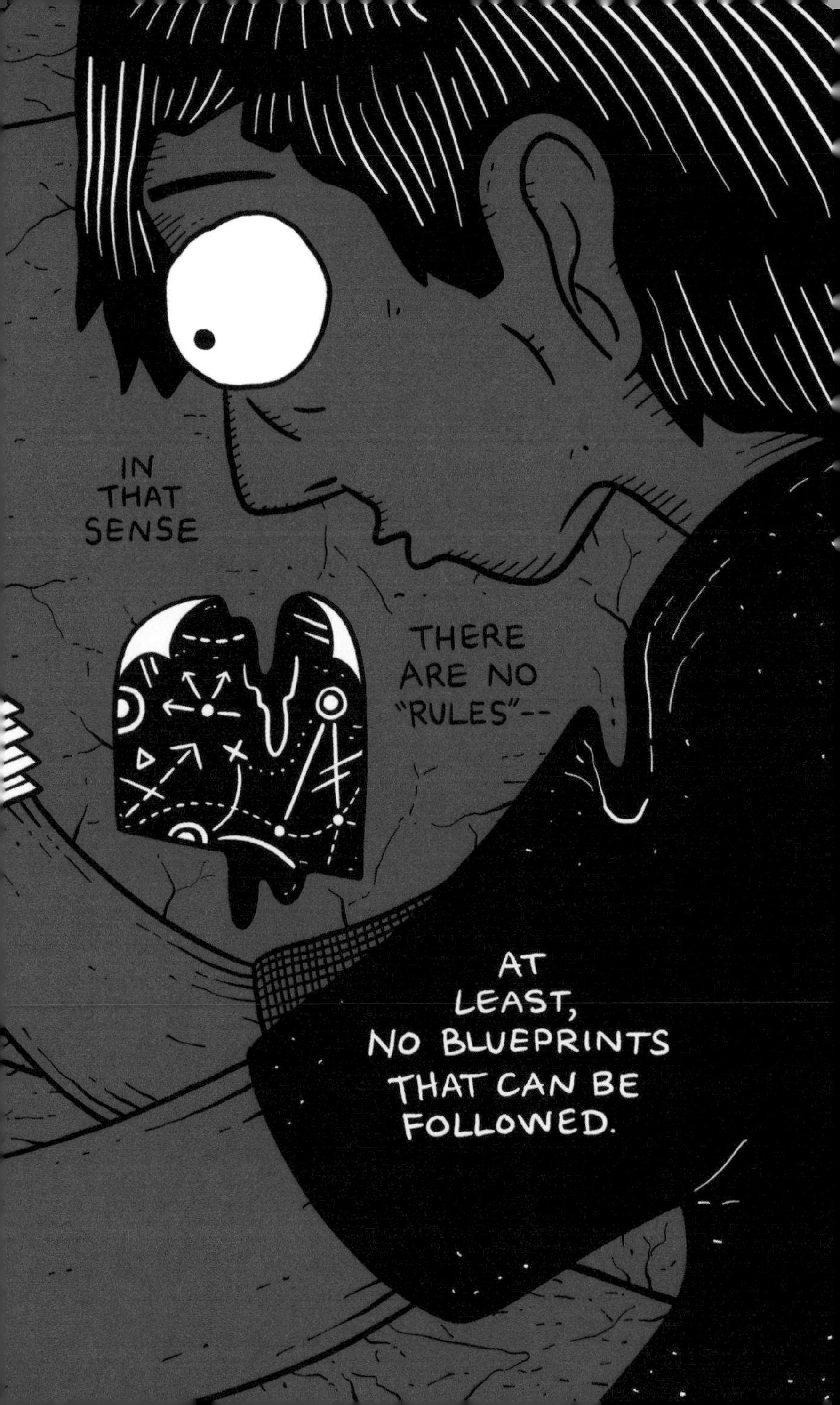
IN THAT SENSE
THERE ARE NO "RULES"--
AT LEAST, NO BLUEPRINTS THAT CAN BE FOLLOWED.

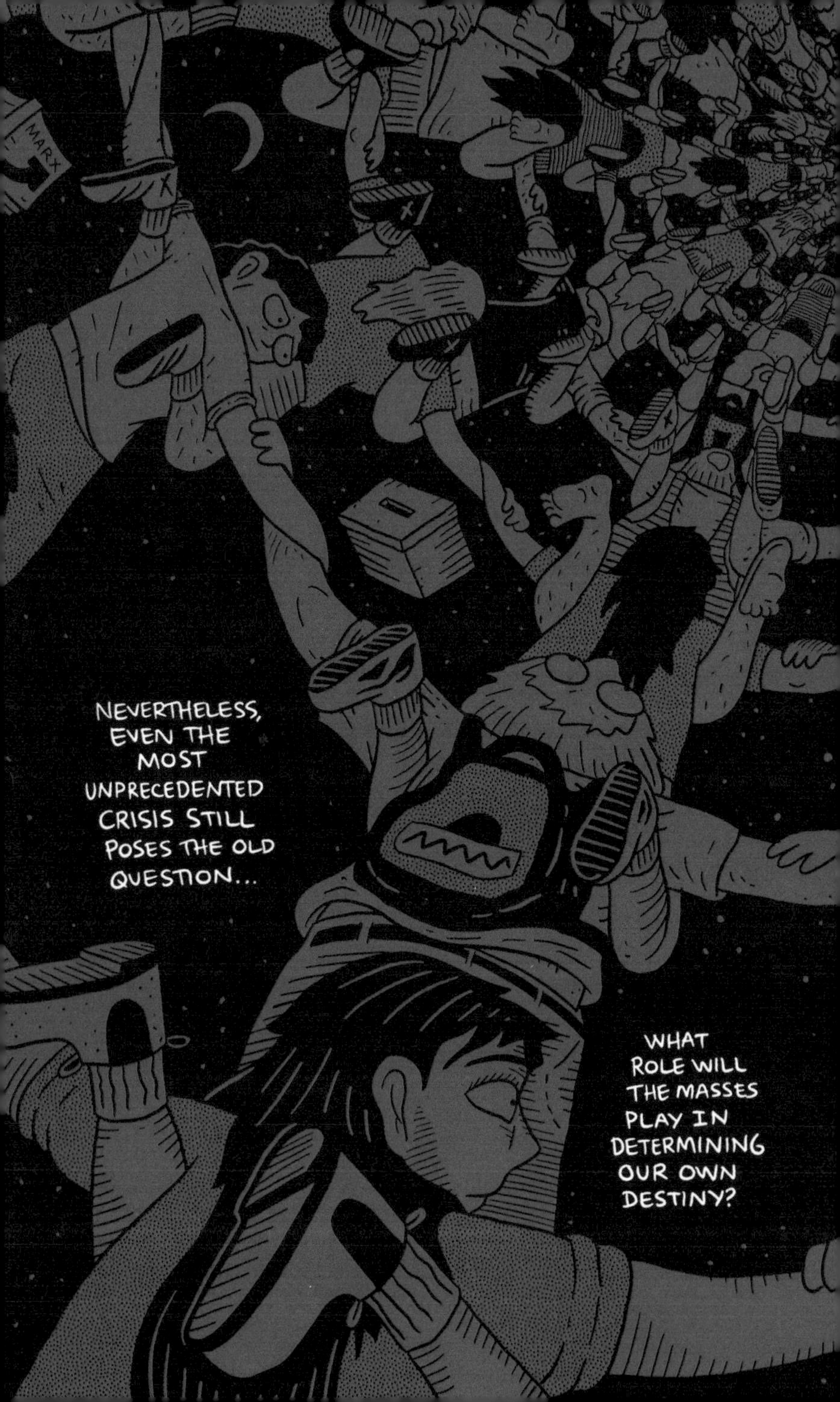
MARX
NEVERTHELESS, EVEN THE MOST UNPRECEDENTED CRISIS STILL POSES THE OLD QUESTION...
WHAT ROLE WILL THE MASSES PLAY IN DETERMINING OUR OWN DESTINY?

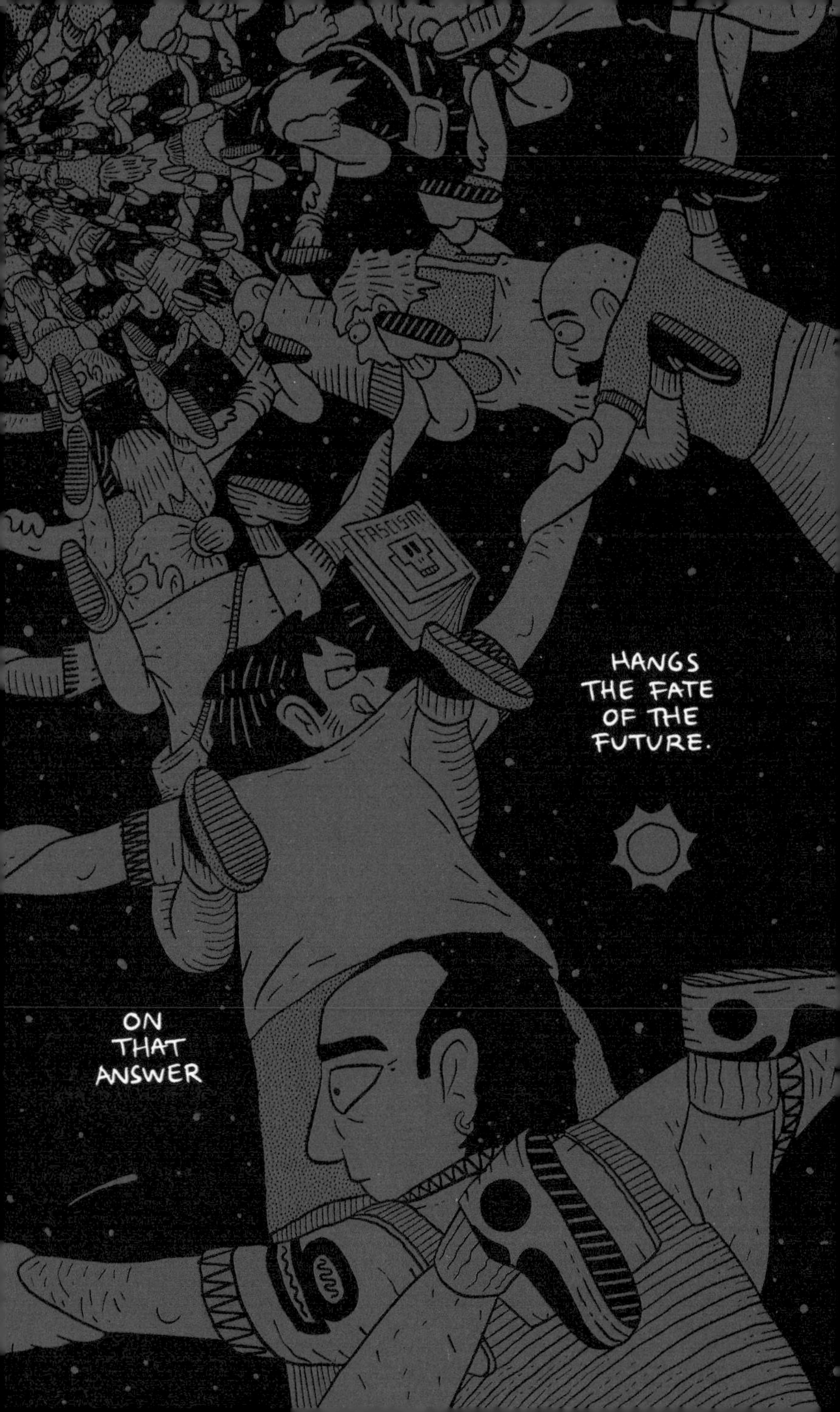
FASCISM
ON THAT ANSWER
HANGS THE FATE OF THE FUTURE.

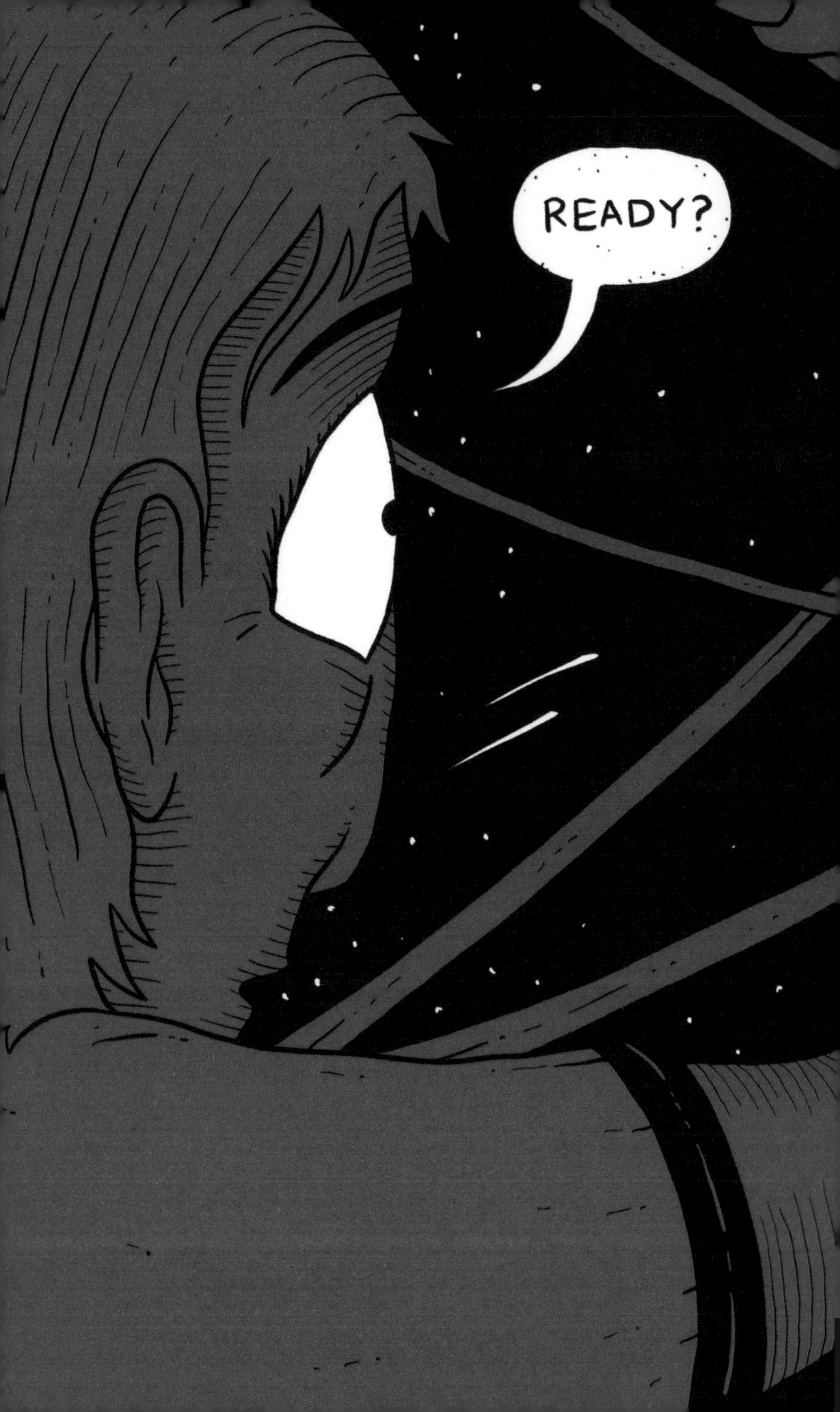
READY?

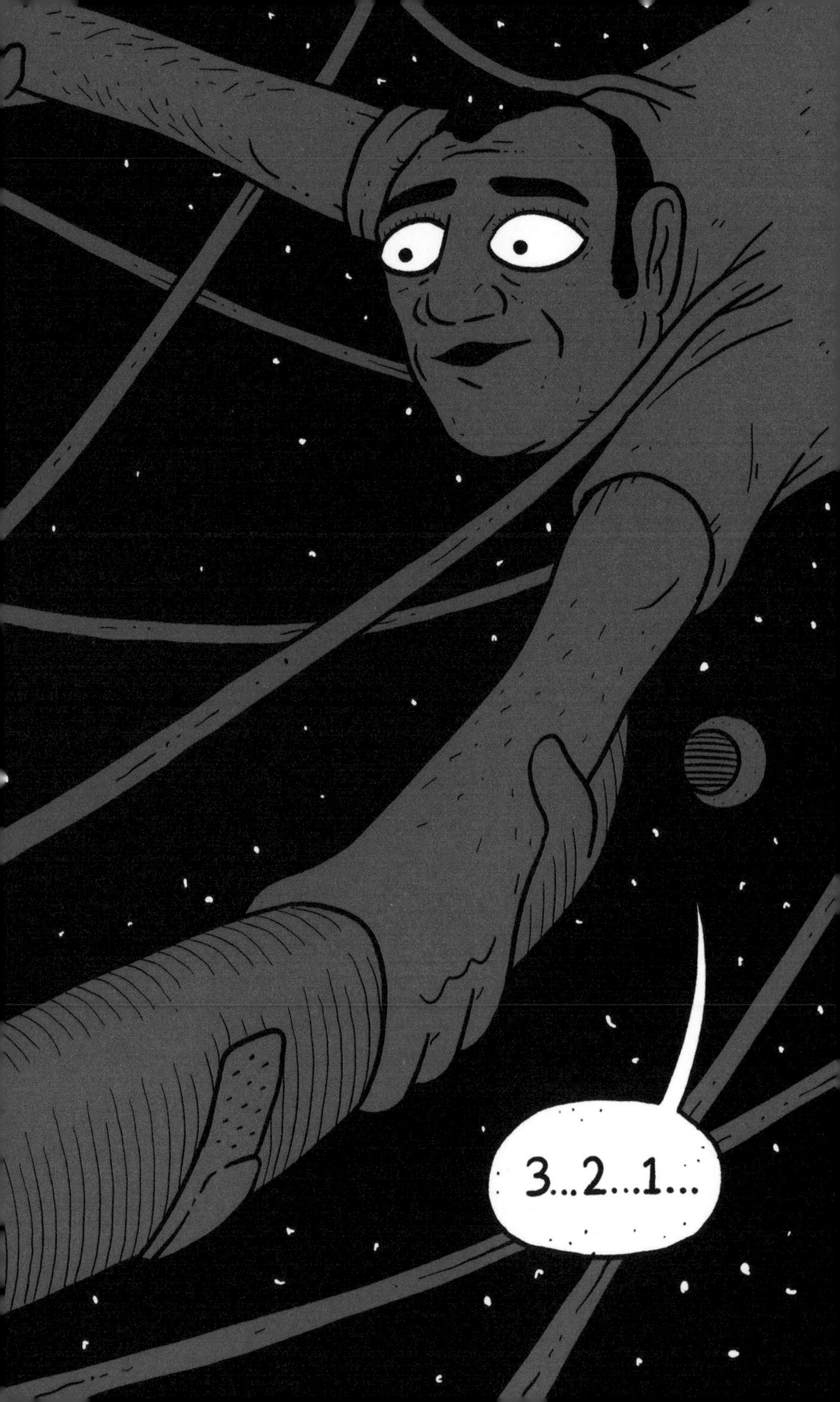
3...2...1...

WE ACKNOWLEDGE THAT INDIGENOUS SOVEREIGNTY
WAS NEVER CEDED AND WE EXTEND OUR SOLIDARITY
IN THE ONGOING STRUGGLE FOR JUSTICE.

THANKS TO STEPHANIE HONOR CONVERY AND TO SEAN.
THANKS ALSO TO THE CENTRE FOR STORIES IN WESTERN
AUSTRALIA -- IN PARTICULAR, CAROLINE, JOHN, BADEN,
AND CHRISTOPHER. AND THE STAFF AT SCRIBE -- OUR
EDITOR DAVID GOLDING, MICK PILKINGTON, LAURA
THOMAS, TACE KELLY, CHRIS BLACK, MARINA SANO,
EMILY COOK, AND FREELANCE PROOFREADER
RONNIE SCOTT.

IN CHAPTER 12, THE TWO PAGES STARTING WITH
"OUR POWER LIES IN STRIFE" WERE INSPIRED BY THE
LINOCUT "STRIFE" (1930) BY HERBERT MCCLINTOCK.

SCRIBE PUBLICATIONS
18-20 EDWARD ST, BRUNSWICK, VICTORIA 3056, AUSTRALIA
2 JOHN ST, CLERKENWELL, LONDON, WC1N 2ES, UNITED KINGDOM
3754 PLEASANT AVE, SUITE 100, MINNEAPOLIS,
MINNESOTA 55409, USA

PUBLISHED BY SCRIBE 2024

PRINTED AND BOUND IN CHINA BY R.R. DONNELLEY

SCRIBE IS COMMITTED TO THE SUSTAINABLE USE OF NATURAL RESOURCES AND THE USE OF PAPER PRODUCTS MADE RESPONSIBLY FROM THESE RESOURCES.

SCRIBE ACKNOWLEDGES AUSTRALIA'S FIRST NATIONS PEOPLES AS THE TRADITIONAL OWNERS AND CUSTODIANS OF THIS COUNTRY, AND WE PAY OUR RESPECTS TO THEIR ELDERS, PAST AND PRESENT.

978 1 761380 60 0 (AUSTRALIAN EDITION)
978 1 957363 73 8 (U.S. EDITION)
978 1 761385 53 7 (EBOOK)

CATALOGUE RECORDS FOR THIS BOOK ARE AVAILABLE FROM THE NATIONAL LIBRARY OF AUSTRALIA.

THIS PROJECT HAS BEEN ASSISTED BY THE AUSTRALIAN GOVERNMENT THROUGH CREATIVE AUSTRALIA, ITS PRINCIPAL ARTS INVESTMENT AND ADVISORY BODY.

Australian Government

Creative Australia

IT ALSO RECEIVED SUPPORT FROM THE HEAD OF SCHOOL INVESTMENT FUND AT THE SCHOOL OF CULTURE AND COMMUNICATION AT THE UNIVERSITY OF MELBOURNE.

SCRIBEPUBLICATIONS.COM.AU
SCRIBEPUBLICATIONS.CO.UK
SCRIBEPUBLICATIONS.COM

FURTHER READING

A FEW SUGGESTIONS TO EXPLORE
FURTHER THE IDEAS IN THIS BOOK.

IAN ALLINSON, *WORKERS CAN WIN:
A GUIDE TO ORGANISING AT WORK*
(PLUTO, 2022)
A HANDBOOK ON ORGANISING AT WORK 'TO CHANGE
THINGS RELATED TO YOUR JOB AND TO CHANGE
EVERYTHING ELSE'

JASON BAUMANN (ED.) *THE STONEWALL READER*
(PENGUIN CLASSICS, 2019)
ORIGINAL DOCUMENTS SHOWING THE EXTRAORDINARY
IMPACT OF THE STONEWALL RIOTS.

MEREDITH & VERITY BURGMANN, *GREEN BANS,
RED UNION: ENVIRONMENTAL ACTIVISM AND
THE NEW SOUTH WALES BUILDERS LABOURERS'
FEDERATION* (UNSW, 1998)
THE FULL STORY OF THE PINK BANS
AND MUCH, MUCH MORE.

KOSHKA DUFF (ED.) *ABOLISHING THE POLICE*
(DOG SECTION, 2021)
ESSAYS ON STATE VIOLENCE AND THE
ALTERNATIVES TO IT.

DAN GEORGAKAS & MARVIN SURKIN,
*DETROIT: I DO MIND DYING: A STUDY IN URBAN
REVOLUTION* (3RD EDITION, HAYMARKET, 2012)
AN INSPIRATIONAL ACCOUNT OF DIRECT
POLITICS IN THE SIXTIES.

CHRIS HARMAN, *A PEOPLE'S HISTORY
OF THE WORLD* (VERSO, 2017)
INTERNATIONAL HISTORY FROM THE BOTTOM UP.

MIKKI KENDALL & A. D'AMICO, *AMAZONS,
ABOLITIONISTS, AND ACTIVISTS*
(TEN SPEED, 2019)
A COMIC BOOK TRACING THE STRUGGLE
FOR WOMEN'S RIGHTS THE WORLD OVER.

NAOMI KLEIN, *THIS CHANGES EVERYTHING:*
CAPITALISM VS THE CLIMATE
(SIMON AND SCHUSTER, 2014)
KLEIN MAKES THE RADICAL CASE FOR CLIMATE ACTION
IN AN ENGAGING, ACCESSIBLE WAY.

JANE McALEVEY, *A COLLECTIVE BARGAIN:*
UNIONS, ORGANIZING, AND THE FIGHT FOR
DEMOCRACY (ECCO, 2020),
AN ACCESSIBLE ARGUMENT (FROM A U.S. PERSPECTIVE)
ABOUT REBUILDING THE UNION MOVEMENT.

LAURA MILES, *TRANSGENDER RESISTANCE: SOCIALISM*
AND THE FIGHT FOR TRANS LIBERATION
(BOOKMARKS, 2020)
A DIRECT-POLITICS TAKE ON CONTEMPORARY TRANS ACTIVISM.

DAVID SMITH AND PHIL EVANS, *MARX'S CAPITAL*
ILLUSTRATED (HAYMARKET, 2014)
A PUNCHY, GRAPHIC INTRODUCTION TO
MARXIST THINKING.

JEFF SPARROW, *TRIGGER WARNINGS: POLITICAL*
CORRECTNESS AND THE RISE OF THE RIGHT
(SCRIBE, 2018)
A LONGER ACCOUNT OF DIRECT, DELEGATED,
AND SMUG POLITICS.

JEFF SPARROW, *CRIMES AGAINST NATURE:*
CAPITALISM AND GLOBAL HEATING
(SCRIBE, 2021)
DIRECT POLITICS AND THE CLIMATE CRISIS.

OLÚFẸ́MI O. TÁÍWÒ, *ELITE CAPTURE: HOW THE*
POWERFUL TOOK OVER IDENTITY POLITICS
(AND EVERYTHING ELSE) (HAYMARKET, 2022),
AN AMERICAN PHILOSOPHER ON THE APPROPRIATION
OF RADICAL RHETORIC.

KEEANGA-YAMAHTTA TAYLOR, *FROM*
#BLACKLIVESMATTER TO BLACK LIBERATION
(HAYMARKET, 2016)
TAYLOR TRACKS DIFFERENT FORCES INVOLVED IN
THE AMERICAN ANTI-RACIST STRUGGLE.

SAM WALLMAN, *OUR MEMBERS BE UNLIMITED:*
A COMIC ABOUT WORKERS AND THEIR UNIONS
(SCRIBE, 2022)
WHY SOLIDARITY MATTERS,
IN THE PAST AND TODAY.

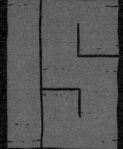
"MEANING -FUL ACTION IS

UP

WHATEVER INCREASES

INHALE

THE CONFIDENCE,

NOD

SEPARATE TOGETHE!

THE AUTONOMY,

THE INITIATIVE,

STEP

THE PARTICIPATION,

THE SOLIDARITY,

PLACE

THE EQUALITARIAN TENDENCIES

GRIP

& THE SELF-ACTIVITY OF THE MASSES

& WHATEVER ASSISTS

FAN CLEAR

IN THEIR DEMYSTIFICATION.

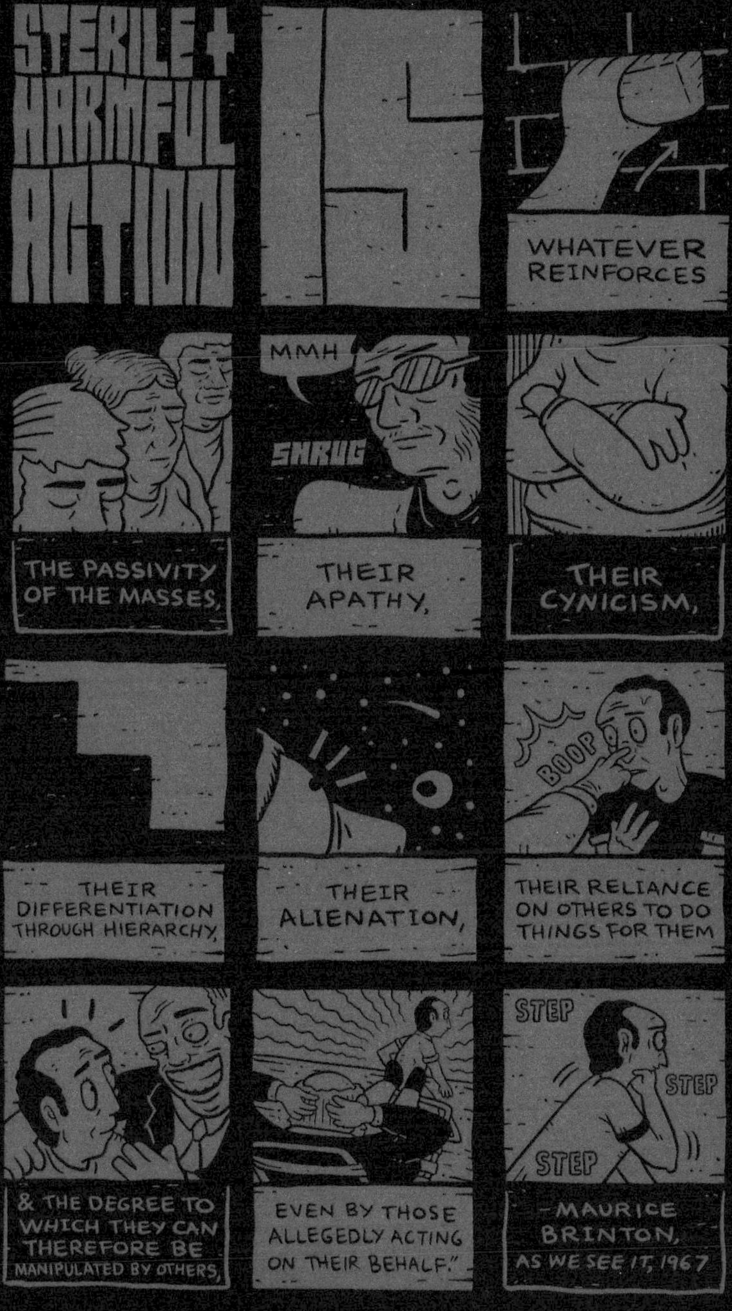
STERILE + HARMFUL ACTION
IS
WHATEVER REINFORCES
MMH
SHRUG
THE PASSIVITY OF THE MASSES,
THEIR APATHY,
THEIR CYNICISM,
THEIR DIFFERENTIATION THROUGH HIERARCHY,
THEIR ALIENATION,
BOOP
THEIR RELIANCE ON OTHERS TO DO THINGS FOR THEM
& THE DEGREE TO WHICH THEY CAN THEREFORE BE MANIPULATED BY OTHERS,
EVEN BY THOSE ALLEGEDLY ACTING ON THEIR BEHALF."
STEP
STEP
STEP
—MAURICE BRINTON,
AS WE SEE IT, 1967

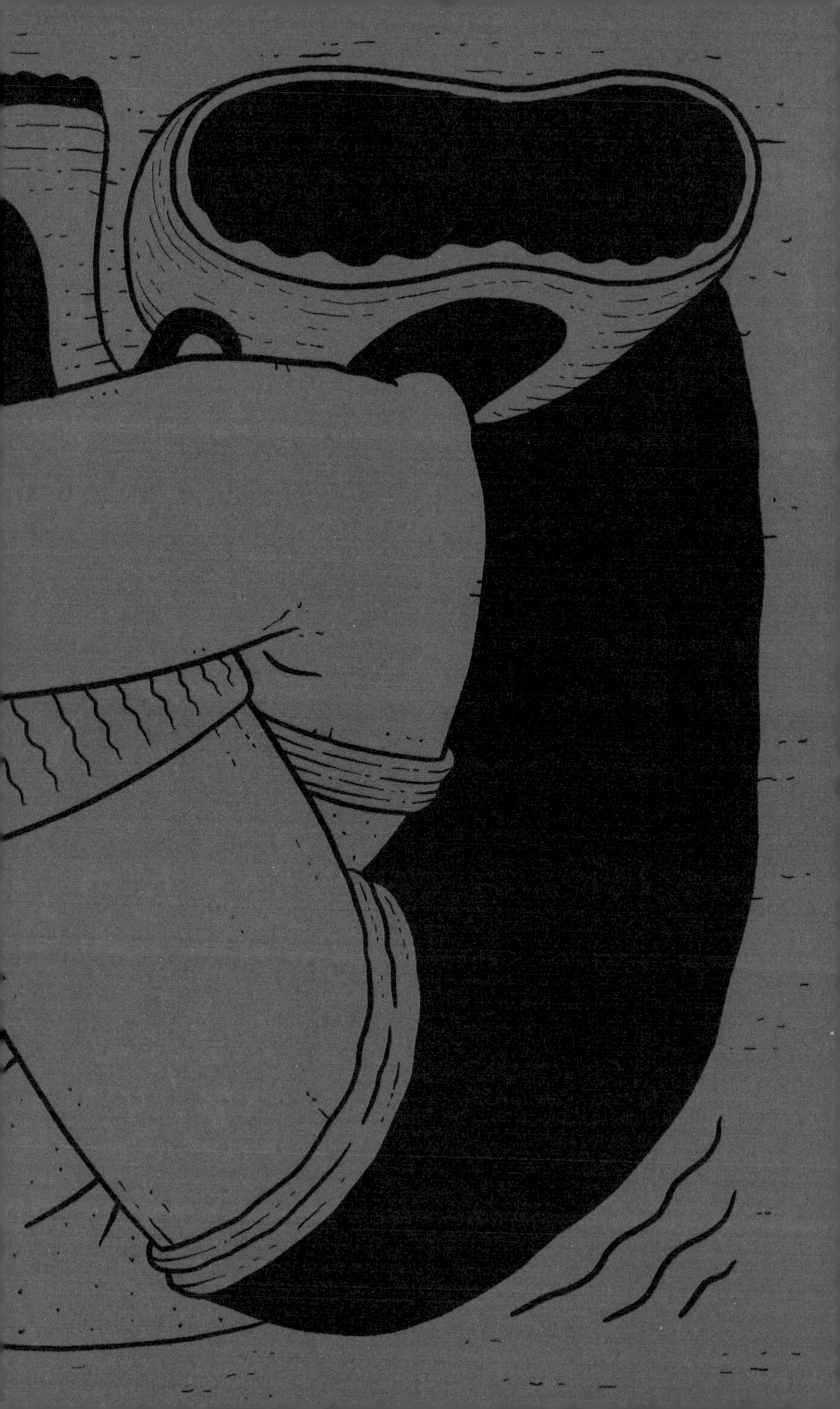